A DIRECTOR PREPARES

STANLEY L. GLENN
UNIVERSITY OF CALIFORNIA, SANTA BARBARA

DICKENSON PUBLISHING COMPANY, INC.
ENCINO, CALIFORNIA, AND BELMONT, CALIFORNIA

Grateful acknowledgement is made to the following for permission to reproduce copyrighted material:

Atheneum Publishers, Inc.: From *Curtains* by Kenneth Tynan. Copyright © 1961 by Kenneth Tynan. Reprinted by permission of Atheneum Publishers.

Calder & Boyars, Ltd.: From *Notes and Counter-Notes* by Eugene Ionesco, translated by Donald Watson, 1962. Reprinted with permission.

Samuel French, Inc.: From *The Adding Machine* by Elmer L. Rice. Copyright 1922, 1929 by Elmer L. Rice. Copyright 1923 by Doubleday Page & Company. Copyright 1949 (in renewal) by Elmer L. Rice. Copyright 1950 (in renewal) by Elmer Rice. Copyright 1956 (in renewal) by Elmer Rice. Reprinted with permission.

Grove Press, Inc.: From *The Visit* by Friedrich Durrenmatt, translated by Patrick Bowles. Reprinted by permission of Grove Press, Inc. Copyright © 1956 by Peter Schifferli Verlag AG. 'Die Arche,' Zurich, Switzerland. English version copyright © by Jonathan Cape Limited, London, England. From *Notes and Counter-Notes* by Eugene Ionesco, translated by Donald Watson. Reprinted by permission of Grove Press, Inc. Copyright © 1964 by Grove Press, Inc.

Edward Gordon Craig Estate: From *Edward Gordon Craig Designs for the Theatre* edited by Janet Leeper, Penguin Books, Ltd., 1948. Reprinted by permission of the publisher and the Administrators of the Edward Gordon Craig, C.H., Estate.

The Macmillan Company: From *A Macbeth Production* by John Masefield. Copyright 1946 by John Masefield. Reprinted with permission.

Macmillan & Co., Ltd.: From *Shakespearean Tragedy* by A. C. Bradley, 1951, by permission of St. Martin's Press and Macmillan London and Basingstoke.

The Society of Authors: From *A Macbeth Production* by John Masefield. Copyright 1946 by John Masefield and reprinted with permission of The Society of Authors as the literary representative of the Estate of John Masefield.

ISBN-0-8221-0096-7
Library of Congress Catalog Card Number: 72-93648

Printed in the United States of America

Printing (last digit): 9 8 7 6 5 4 3 2 1

This book is dedicated to my wife, Eadie, and to directors' "widows" everywhere

Contents

Preface

It was probably inevitable that some day someone would exploit Stanislavski's acting book title and apply it to a treatise on directing. I believe that my decision to do so was not a frivolous attempt to capitalize on the popularity of *An Actor Prepares.* The emphasis of this text clearly is on the director's work before the first rehearsal. Most works dealing with a director's functions have tended to stress the mechanics of directing, or the techniques that govern the manipulation of stage movement and images. Such books are very important for the guidance of the novice director, and although some of them do, in fact, inform him of the necessity of directorial analysis and research, they appear to minimize the value of such preliminary work by subordinating preparation to the technique of directing.

The contention of this book is that the director's obvious work at rehearsals is but the tip of the iceberg in relation to his total effort to ready a play for its audience. It is a very important tip to be sure, but it cannot emerge without thought and research to support it. Too many young directors are encouraged to work out the expressive details of a production in a vacuum, with the result that effect rather than meaning is achieved. This book attempts to reverse the emphasis so that the director's means of expression becomes a natural outgrowth of his analytical explorations. If this were the only book on directing, it might justifiably be criticized for its heavier concentration on preparation. But because it is not, it should be viewed as an effort to balance the scales in the literature of directing theory.

Because a book such as this requires numerous examples from play texts to amplify its ideas, it seemed prudent to use one major play for this purpose. The chief advantage of this decision is that the reader, by being familiar with *Macbeth,* will be better able to follow the progression suggested by the text, and will have a clearer understanding of the examples than if scores of unfamiliar plays had been used. *Macbeth* was chosen because it lends itself so well and so completely to most of the demands of directing. Its structure and characterization are rich, complex, and rewarding; it enables us to appreciate the contribution of a play's language to its texture and thought; it challenges the director's imagination in terms of stage business and design; it lends itself well to the application of directorial research.

The disadvantages of emphasizing a single play include the limitations of any one play's genre and style as well as its potential staging methods. To cope with these problems, I have referred to other plays when necessary to illustrate principles for which *Macbeth* appeared to be unsuitable. For the most part, however, *Macbeth* does work, and the reader is advised to familiarize himself with it and to keep a copy at hand as a sort of co-text.

I would like to express my gratitude to those who contributed so graciously and generously in helping me with this book. They include my colleagues in the Department of Drama at the University of California, Santa Barbara: Professors Theodore Hatlen, Brian Johnston, Robert Morgan, and Georgij Paro; Professors Ralph Freud and William Melnitz of UCLA; Professor Stuart Hyde of San Francisco State College; the staffs of such institutions as the Royal Shakespeare Company and the Shakespeare Birthplace Trust, both in Stratford, England; and the library staff at the University of California at Santa Barbara. I would like also to mention the secretarial staff of my department, Mrs. Colleen Ellis, Miss Pat Peters, and Mrs. Martha Swing, for their help and encouragement. Finally, my very special thanks to Professor Homer Swander of the Department of English at the University of California, Santa Barbara, from whom I have learned so much and been so inspired that he might well be considered the coauthor of this book.

University of California   S. G.
Santa Barbara

The Function of the Director

TIME: *The present*

LOCALE: A theatre

The director is about to begin a play rehearsal when a woman about 25 years old addresses him.

WOMAN: Excuse me, Mr. Smith. May I make a request before you begin?

DIRECTOR: Yes.

WOMAN: My name is Mrs. Jones. I belong to a new theatre group and we're going to put on *The Importance of Being Earnest* as our first production. I've been asked to direct it. (*Pause.*)

DIRECTOR: That's nice. It's a delightful play, Mrs. Jones.

WOMAN: Yes. Well. (*Modestly*) You see I've never directed a play before, and I wondered if you would mind my sitting in on two or three of your rehearsals—to—to get the hang of it. . . .

DIRECTOR: Two or three?

WOMAN: Yes. Would you mind? I won't disturb you.

DIRECTOR: No, no, not at all. In fact, if you have any questions, I will be glad to answer them afterward. . . .

WOMAN: No, no. I know how busy you are. I'll just watch, if you don't mind?

DIRECTOR: Not at all.

Although this dialogue may appear to be an absurd extreme concerning the training of a director, it is typical of the ignorance, even among regular theatregoers, about the contemporary director's function. When asked what they believe the director does with a play, most people will respond, "Why, he tells the actors where to go." This will often be true of the director's function in more ways than one, but some very successful directors avoid telling the actors when or how to move on the stage. Neither does it occur to the uninformed that the director is more than a traffic officer—that behind each stage direction are numerous and complex justifications. Audience comments in the lobby or in restaurants following a play will often include references to the direction as being "beautiful" or "pedestrian"; ordinarily this comment will be based only on whether the viewer liked or disliked the performance. For some, the fact that a play was well-acted means that it must have been well-directed. For others, a series of sensational effects in lighting or in the setting will evoke the remark, "Terrific direction!"

Several reasons besides ignorance account for the confusion about a director's function. With a painting, we know that the artist is directly responsible for all that we observe: color, form, size, shape, subject. But when we see a play, we observe actors in a set created and lighted by a designer and listen to words written by a playwright. Everyone in the theatre except the playwright is an interpretative artist, but although the setting and the actors can be observed directly, the director's contribution is much less apparent. He does not appear, and it is difficult to discern exactly what his contribution has been. The director is most often compared to the music conductor. Both are interpretative artists whose creativity is channeled through other interpretative artists. But during a performance the audience is able to perceive the conductor in direct control of the orchestra, while the play director sits helplessly in the back row of the house, or paces nervously backstage. It is interesting to note, too, that the director, unlike the orchestra conductor, does not join the curtain call. Little wonder, then, that the layman is not easily able to determine what a director does.

In one way, however, the director is responsible for *everything* an audience sees or hears in the theatre. This does not mean that he invents everything the audience experiences during a performance. It does mean that he has *permitted* everything that happens to happen. He may have had very little to do with stimulating his designers and actors, but if he merely has said "yes" to suggestions that provide clarity and insight into the playwright's intention and "no" to irrelevant suggestions, he will be performing the most fundamental task of the director. On the surface this may appear to be trivial and unexciting, but in reality the capacity to approve or disapprove is based on the director's thorough awareness of what a play is about and his recognition of the ingredients that will successfully express its meaning to an audience. This explains why our novice directress is being so naive to expect that her brief observations will prepare her for directing a play. It takes more than this to learn when to say "yes" or "no"; it takes more than this to learn the director's job of controlling and unifying a play.

Essentially the director's role is fairly universal in today's international theatre, even though methods of direction vary considerably, and in some instances the role may be watered down to the status of nonruling royalty. That an individual assumes the total responsibility of interpreting the writings of others for the theatre with the cooperation of actors, designers, and technicians is relatively new in the history of the theatre. Basically, the theatre requires only four things: a manuscript, actors, an acting place, and an audience. Some will deny the necessity of a manuscript, and they are correct. But because western drama for 300 years has been predominantly literary, the manuscript has become an integral part of the theatre. Throughout most of the history of the theatre, a director in today's sense of the word was unnecessary. The reasons for his origin and emergence as a pivot of dramatic production will perhaps best explain his function.

The Evolution of the Modern Director

Drama, from the time that it assumed a literary form, has been an interpretative art. Unlike painting or sculpture, in which the art object is created solely by the artist and presented directly to the viewer, a play must be expressed by agents other than its originator. Today those agents are represented in a variety of areas of theatrical art, but the theatre can exist without any of them except the actor. The difference between direct artistic expression and interpretative art may be demonstrated by the following formula:

Painting: Artist $\longrightarrow$ art object $\longrightarrow$ viewer

Drama: Playwright $\rightarrow$ manuscript $\rightarrow$ actor in an acting place $\rightarrow$ audience

Essentially, then, the responsibility for accurately interpreting a play to the audience is the actor's, but historically, the performer has often been guided and controlled in his interpretation by other forces. During the tragic festivals of fifth-century Greece, for example, the playwright himself might take the role of protagonist, or instruct the actors how to conform to the intentions of his manuscript. We know that Shakespeare was an actor and a member of the company that produced his plays. We can assume from what we know about the conditions of the Elizabethan theatre and from speeches such as Hamlet's advice to the players that the actor was often guided by others in converting the written word to appropriate sound and gestures. During the seventeenth-century literary renaissance in France, the playwright's function as a guide to individual performers is suggested by Molière's satirical one-act play *L'Impromptu de Versailles*. In this comedy, Molière depicts himself conducting a rehearsal, during which he attempts to persuade the actors to sacrifice their selfish interests and exhibitionistic tendencies for the more important purpose of appropriately interpreting his text.

We cannot be certain what other controls were consistently exerted during these "golden" periods of theatre. We do not know, for example, whether composition or ensemble acting were given much attention, or whether a single individual was entirely responsible for coordinating set pieces, properties, and costumes for each play. Nor can we be certain that coordinating these details to be relevant to the idea of the play was considered very important. We do know, however, that each era had strong basic traditions and theatrical conventions that automatically dictated certain details of production. In the fully realized Greek theatre it is believed that the orchestra and the scene building were used as the setting for *all* plays and that basic costumes were conventionalized for tragedy and comedy. The writer structured his plays with these conventions in mind, and knew that his cast would include a chorus and three actors who wore masks.

The Elizabethan dramatist writing for the public theatre also wrote for a traditional, unchanging stage. Plays were written to be played on a platform with an open stage, inner and upper areas, and permanent doors for entrances and exists. The French neoclassic tradition used a proscenium stage, and all plays adhered rigidly to the unities and to classical decorum. The plays of the classical and renaissance periods, then, might achieve their unity in presentation through two factors: the recognized importance and domination of the playwright, and the consistency and regularity of theatrical means and modes of expression.

After the eighteenth century, however, developments in western theatre were becoming so complicated that it was increasingly difficult to find adequate means of fulfilling the essential purpose of the literary theatre — to express with utmost integrity the intentions of the playwright. Indeed one major reason for the creation of the modern director is to fulfill this all-too-frequently forgotten purpose. Described in terms of the actor, the stage, and the writer, the following is a brief resumé of the theatrical tendencies that, while developing new conventions and shifting emphases, created a disorder of which the serious playwright became the major casualty.

If the Greek, Elizabethan, and French neoclassic theatres were the theatres of the playwright, the western drama of subsequent periods became the theatre of the actor and of stage spectacle. It would be erroneous to suggest that the eighteenth and nineteenth centuries produced no important playwrights, or that in the previous Greek, Elizabethan, and French theatres the actor and the stage spectacle were unimportant. The difference is that the drama of the later period became subordinate to the star and the spectacle, and because of shifting conventions and emphases, previous tendencies to unite actor, stage, and writer diminished.

From the eighteenth century, it became more and more prevalent for the audience to go to the theatre to see actors rather than plays, and the stars relied heavily on established vehicles—usually those of Shakespeare's plays that offered the meatiest roles—or commissioned plays that would demonstrate their virtuosity. Now nothing is wrong with the kind of pleasure that results. Comparing this year's *Hamlet* with last year's and the several before that has been a pleasant British custom for 300 years. But emphasis on the star often has obscured the sense of a play. The actor might draw attention away from intended meaning through his emphasis on effect. It was not uncommon to cut portions of the play in which the star did not appear, or portions that afforded him little opportunity to "emote." During the nineteenth century, the only part of Massinger's *A New Way to Pay Old Debts* that was staged was the mad scene of Sir Giles Overreach. Often, especially when a star was touring, inferior actors were used in supporting roles. They were relegated to the weaker or less prominent parts of the stage so that the star might enjoy undisturbed focus in the center. The star system denied the kind of ensemble playing and meaningful positioning of all performers that is essential for the best expression of the values of the play. Instead, all elements of the theatre became subordinate to the virtuosity of the star.

Spectacular scenery and machinery were not the innovations of the eighteenth and nineteenth centuries. The Greeks used machinery, and the masques and court entertainments of James I and Louis XIV used elaborate devices of spectacle. However, as far as we can tell, the Greeks always subordinated their machines or scenic devices to the tragedies themselves. The devices were available to the playwright, who used them when they best served his ends. The English masque was an expensive spectacle restricted to a court audience and often to court participants. From the late eighteenth century to the present, however, three major factors increased interest in theatrical spectacle. First, the almost universal adoption in western theatre of the proscenium stage encouraged a framed action, which could be viewed in the same way by all members of the audience, and which could use a front curtain to conceal changes of scenery. Second, a fast-growing taste for melodrama, which subjugates character and thought to thrills — usually of the spectacular variety—developed in the popular theatre of the eighteenth century and has continued, particularly in the movies, to the present day. Finally, the late eighteenth-century interest in antiquarianism, together with a demand for greater realism in melodrama and a growing interest in the influence of environment and local color, sparked efforts to create realistic spectacle on the stage. The use of gas and then electricity made more realistic effects possible, and new technological devices influenced the conventions of spectacle. All of these led to new kinds of confusion on the stage.

Productions of Shakespeare, for example, attempted to reproduce an actual locale for every scene in the play, forcing the audience to wait for a long time between scenes. Sometimes a lengthy scene change was made for a scene only a few moments long. Consequently, to arrive at a more reasonable playing time, entire scenes were cut from the plays. The original intentions of the plays, then, were sacrificed for spectacle or realism. Even in the modern theatre, where scenes can be shifted very rapidly, scenic effects can obscure the values of the text and often of the performer who tries to interpret it.

The introduction of sensational melodramatic action, encouraged by technological advances and verisimilitude in representation, created the need for designers of scenery, costume, and lighting, as well as technicians to build and manipulate stage scenery. This development tended to swell the ranks of the personnel required to stage a play, and the results were often chaotic without the control of someone in authority.

Yet even while such technical advances were being made, and special settings were often created for each play, until the twentieth century most theatres used stock scenery for all or most of their productions. As far back as the seventeenth century, when in the public theatre little stress was placed on the environment of an action, the same wings and backdrops were used for different plays. Economy and habit continued this practice, even when newer plays required more specific and detailed scenery or designs more congruous with the naturalistic effects created by the performers. "The actor interprets," said Adolphe Appia, "according to his own liking, what the author has written, hence his personal importance on the stage is exclusively inter-pretative rather than technical, with the result that his role is developed according to one conception, while the settings are being painted according to another."[1] Although realism had been introduced to the theatre before Strindberg wrote *Miss Julie* in 1888, he still felt compelled to plead for scenic conventions that would be consistent with the text. He pleads for stage doors which, when slammed, do not "shake the whole house." He complains in his preface to *Miss Julie* of the inappropriateness of stage scenery:

> There is nothing more difficult than to get a room that looks reasonably like a room, though it seems easy enough for the scene painter to provide erupting volcanoes and waterfalls. Granted, the walls must be of canvas, but it is about time we did away with painted shelves and cooking utensils. There are so many other stage conventions we are called upon to believe in that we might be allowed to relinquish our faith in painted pots and pans.[2]

Only a few years later, Strindberg was to require something entirely different in scenery for his expressionistic and dream plays.

It is not surprising that many writers in the past few centuries have preferred to write novels instead of plays, and when some, such as Shelley or Browning, became interested in dramatic writing, they wrote closet dramas. In a theatre where the writer created vehicles for the star or formula plots for melodrama, with little reward or recognition and little opportunity for full self-expression, it is extraordinary that good playwrights emerged at all. When they did, it was most often on the wings of a literary and theatrical revolt such as the romantic and the later realistic movements. During such periods the need for more significant and meaningful content was expressed, and changes from sterile conventions or trivia were urged. But revolt, while healthy and necessary, could not in itself assure the revival of great theatre, which must be the result of a respectful collaboration of script, performer, and scenic conventions.

Many nineteenth-century writers who wished to contribute to the theatre were not, as had been traditional in the past, men who developed in the theatre. Hugo, Zola, Chekhov, and Tolstoy were writers of fiction who became tempted by the stage. Unlike Sophocles, Shakespeare, or Molière, they could not instruct those already involved in the theatre how to put on a play—not even the new playwright's own plays. To make matters worse, the prevalent conventions of acting and stagecraft proved incongruous with the demands of the new writers' plays. The first professional production of Chekhov's *The Sea Gull* was a dismal failure because methods of acting and design were not only inadequate for Chekhov's naturalism but *contradictory* to it. The previous reference to Strindberg's frustrations with the stage set is another example of the writer's problem in the changing theatre of the late nineteenth century. A new and important playwright could not succeed when he could not take charge of a production, or when the acting and scenic conventions of his theatre were not amenable to his play. Unless a new position could be created, a position requiring the full authority of a man of the theatre who might unite all the aspects of modern production by interpretation of a script, theatrical unity could not be achieved.

Another important development, which occurred simultaneously with the blossoming of the director, reinforced his necessity in the theatre. During the last half of the nineteenth century, realism in art and the theatre had taken hold. Realism is related, as are all styles in the theatre, to a way of viewing life and of expressing that view. In art, conventions are used by the artist to express the truth as he sees it. The conventions of realism are the means by which an artist creates the illusion of everyday life. He will avoid obvious exaggeration and distortion in favor of objective reality. Although the choice of subjects for such expression need not be limited, the nineteenth-century realist also believed that the theatre should be concerned with the vital social and domestic issues of the day, with the hope that confrontations with the "facts of everyday life" would lead to social improvement. In the last quarter of the century, realism was carried a step further by the naturalists, who maintained that art should copy science by depicting life "as it is," without direct comment and without the structural artifice of the well-made play (which the realists used). Although naturalism rejected many tenets of realism, both styles emphasized surface, or material, reality.

Soon, a reaction occurred, which denied that the only reality or truth was to be found in an objective view. It maintained that man also has a spiritual and emotional life and that subjective truths are as valid — if not more so—than those of the realists. The neoromanticists, the symbolists, and later the expressionists all maintained that the "inner life" not only should be the main concern of the artist, but could best be expressed in subjective ways: through poetry or by emotional and psychological distortion. Maeterlinck, the Belgian playwright, maintained that truth could be penetrated more through silences than by speech, which according to Maeterlinck is inept. The subjective theatre artists began to look to the past to find conventions that appeared to stress spiritual over material reality, and found them in the Greek theatre, the Elizabethan theatre, and in the Romantic drama of the late eighteenth and early nineteenth centuries. Reinhardt and Copeau broke with proscenium traditions in favor of reconstructed Greek and Elizabethan stages. Rostand and Maeterlinck resorted to poetic diction, and set some of their plays in earlier historical periods.

The realists were not defeated. Some, like Chekhov and O'Casey, integrated some aspects of the subjective theatre, but the thesis play and sordid naturalism became more popular and continued as a mode of expression while the experimentation of the subjective theatre persisted.

The importance of all of this to the modern director is that much of his value—indeed one of his chief functions—is to determine the nature and degree of the reality of each play he directs. The modern theatre today is more complex and diverse than ever before. No longer is it simply a part of a religious festival with *established* conventions. Today, a director may direct any number of plays from the Greeks to the present. He must determine whether to use the original conventions, to modify them, to adapt them to the realistic viewpoint, or to create new conventions that he believes will best penetrate their reality for a modern audience. When he makes up his mind, he must then infuse his fellow artists and craftsmen with his idea, so that the acting, the setting, and the lighting contribute to a stylistic unity in performance.

The breeding ground for this new and important position was the European theatres that contributed to the so-called "Independent Theatre Movement." The movement, whose beginnings are attributed to André Antoine and his *Théâtre Libre* in Paris (1887), represented the concrete efforts of small groups in Paris, Berlin, Dublin, London, and Moscow to establish intimate theatres where serious new playwrights would have opportunities to be heard and seen, and where experimentation with new conventions might be attempted. Most of the ills of the nineteenth-century theatre mentioned earlier were attacked by the leaders of this movement. One mode of attack was to establish the kind of director for which the French playwright Henri Becque called when he said in 1882, "Let us encourage production as much as we can. Let us insist constantly for an outlet and support for this production. Let us demand from our theatre directors more decision and more ability. Let us insist that they be men of artistic imagination rather than men with business preoccupations." [3]

Probably the first distinguished director of Becque's description who was not an actor, writer, or businessman was George II, the duke of a small duchy called Saxe-Meiningen. The Duke (1826–1914) was determined to produce plays in his court theatre without the mistakes and carelessness that he believed to be characteristic of the popular theatre in Europe. With extraordinary versatility he designed his company's sets and costumes and created the composition, movement, and business for each production. The Duke was convinced that all these elements of play production should result from a careful study of the play and should achieve life-like reality. What was important about the Duke's contribution was not merely that his sets and his performers created such an illusion, but that character and environment became dynamically interrelated. The actor performed with and within his set, and related to it as he would to a real room or exterior.

The use of costume followed the same principle. Not only was it to be historically accurate, but a style of movement consistent with the style of the costume was created for the actors. The Duke of Saxe-Meiningen eliminated the star system from his repertory, and emphasized the ensemble—all participants working together not for personal glory but for the total effect of the play. To achieve this end, he demanded frequent rehearsals, in which every action was carefully worked out and in which every character, even individual members of crowds, was expected to be a specific character related to the events taking place on stage. Antoine and Stanislavski, both Independent Theatre directors, saw the Meiningen company perform and acknowledged their debt to its accomplishment.

Although the Duke of Saxe-Meiningen probably was the single greatest influence on the development of the modern director as the controlling force for a realistic ensemble, two other men exerted a somewhat different, but equally important influence on directorial method. Edward Gordon Craig (1872–1966) and Adolphe Appia (1862–1928) were scene designers by occupation, but both men were also theoreticians, conscientiously concerned with defining the nature of the theatrical experience and with realizing this experience on the stage. Craig and Appia opposed the kind of stage realism championed by the Duke of Saxe-Meiningen. Both men were of the subjectivist school and insisted that art is concerned with the inner life rather than with the banalities of external detail. Craig said that the director should avoid "trying to imprison or copy nature, for nature will be neither imprisoned nor allow any men to copy her with any success,"[4] and Appia maintained that "the less the dramatic author makes his characters dependent on the 'indications' in the setting, the more he will be a dramatist."[5] When they speak of interpreting a play, neither man ever refers to specific locales or to minute descriptions of external details. Instead Craig refers to "the entire color, tone, movement, and rhythm," and Appia speaks of the "initial *idea*," and referring to historical plays remarks, "The eternal drama hidden beneath historical customs, events, and costumes must be made visible and audible to everyone."[6]

The means by which Craig and Appia achieved their ends varied, but they shared the technique of using light and three-dimensional nonrepresentational forms on the stage to create an emotional rather than literal environ-

Sketch by Gordon Craig for *Macbeth*, Act I, Scene 5. Courtesy of Peter A. Juley & Son.

ment for the actor. The following statement provides us with an excellent description of the means used and the effect created by Craig's designs:

> The elements of which Craig makes use for his creations are nothing or almost nothing: some screens and some electric lights. He sets upon the stage of his little theatre . . . his small screens, and, while you look on, with a rapid movement of the hand arranges them in a certain way; a ray of electric light comes to strike between those simple rectangles of cardboard, and the miracle is accomplished: you behold a majestic scene; the sense of the small disappears absolutely; you forget the dimensions of the theatre, because of the harmonious relationship which Craig knows how to bring about 'twixt the lights and the lines. Another slight movement of the screens (always before your eyes) and the scene changes and then changes again without the lines and the light effects ever recalling to you that which you have already seen. And thus one passes from the vision of a *piazza*, a street, an imposing portico, to that of a *sala*, a prison, a subterranean dungeon. Craig is a great painter, a great architect, a great poet. He paints with light, he constructs with a few rectangles of cardboard, and with the harmony of his colours and of his lines he creates profound sensations, as only the fathers of poetry knew how to create.[7]

Appia's objectives and the methods he used to achieve them are well expressed in his description of one of his sets, the Elysian Fields in Gluck's *Orpheus*:

> Orpheus travels the underworld seeking Eurydice. The scene in the underworld is made up of complicated sets of stairs, broken by terraces; and the whole is held up by pillars fitted into the supporting walls. Accordingly, the characteristic feature of the underworld is *steps*.
>
> If, then, anyone recalls the music that introduces Orpheus to the Spirits of the Blest, he will understand that only *inclined planes*, without a vertical line of any kind to interrupt them (steps are a combination of horizontal and vertical lines), could in themselves express the perfect serenity of the place. (This refers to the upstage portion of the setting.) Their arrangement is particularly difficult; but, happily, the score gives valuable clues in this respect.
>
> In such a space, physical movement is naturally calm and quiet; and the soft light—with its uniformity and its gentle mobility— transforms the material reality of the actual construction into a kind of rocking movement that is wave-like in its effect. Thanks to the lighting, the characters share in this unreal atmosphere.[8]

The kind of unity for which these men strove was new in the theatre insofar as it was a conscious effort to illuminate the play's atmospheric essence.

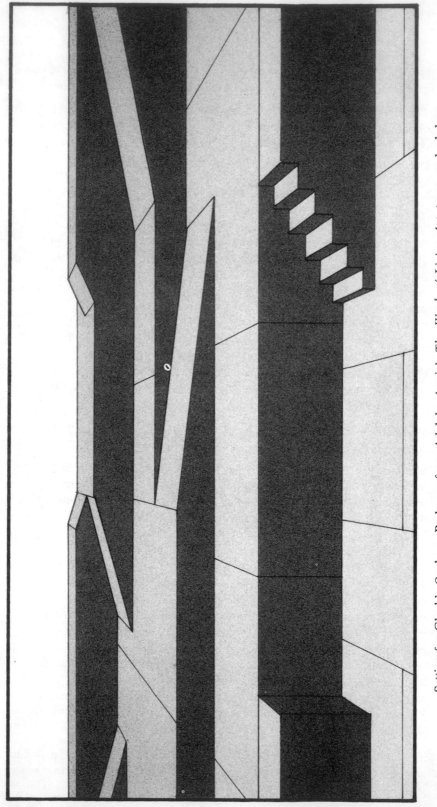

Setting for Gluck's *Orpheus*. Redrawn from Adolphe Appia's *The Work of Living Art*, trans. and ed. by Bernard S. Hewitt, University of Miami Press, 1960.

Atmospheric unity or what might be called the "feeling" of the play becomes as important as the other unities, such as plot, on which a play ordinarily depends. A play tells a story, creates characters, and expresses attitudes about life in a period and a place, but pervading all these, like a mist covering diverse objects in a landscape, is the effect that controls our *feeling* about the play. According to Craig, the only person who might achieve the "emotional design" is the stage director. Other important figures contributed to what has come to be known as "the new stagecraft," but the Duke of Saxe-Meiningen, Appia, and Craig are its pioneers. Directors such as Reinhardt, Stanislavski, and Meyerhold are significant, but their work and their principles are essentially variations and extensions of the basic ideas of the aforementioned about the art of the theatre and the purpose of the director.

Although the battle between the two kinds of reality persisted into the middle of the twentieth century, and the anti-naturalists (chiefly those influenced by Artaud and Brecht) began to dominate the theatre in the sixties, attitudes about the function and importance of the modern director have changed little. Artaud's anti-verbal stance, Joan Littlewood's practice of the director as collaborator and revisor of the text, and the influence of games and improvisations on the development of a production have expanded the director's contribution but not significantly changed his responsibility as the unifying agent of a theatrical presentation. All areas of theatre art are guided by his interpretation of a text into performance, which hopefully will present a clearly articulated design of idea and atmosphere.

NOTES

[1]Adolphe Appia, *The Work of Living Art*, trans. H. D. Albright (Miami Fla.: University of Miami Press, 1960), p. 52.

[2]From the Preface to *Miss Julie*, translated by Brian Johnston at the author's request.

[3]Quoted in Samuel M. Waxman, *Antoine and the Théâtre Libre* (Cambridge, Mass.: Harvard University Press, 1927), p. 95.

[4]Edward Gordon Craig, "The Artist of the Theatre," in Toby Cole and Helen Krich Chinoy, eds., *Directing the Play* (New York: Bobbs-Merrill Company, 1953), p. 128.

[5]Appia, *The Work of Living Art,* p. 44.

[6]Appia, p. 64.

[7]Letter by Filiberto Scarpelli quoted in Janet Leeper, *Edward Gordon Craig Designs for the Theatre* (London: Penguin Books, 1948), p. 19.

[8]Appia, p. 110.

The Contemporary Director

Briefly stated, the task of the contemporary director is to collaborate with actors, designers, and technicians toward the most meaningful theatrical expression of a playwright's manuscript. This means that the director is not an isolated artist, responsible to no one but himself and his viewers. He is responsible to the playwright to create a theatrical experience consistent with the playwright's intentions. He is obliged to stimulate and encourage the creativity of his fellow artists in the direction of the playwright's vision. But none of this is to any avail if the expression of this vision, as guided by the director, does not interest or move an audience.

Because the design and philosophy of this approach to directing is based not merely on the conclusions drawn from the preceding essay, but on assumptions that with careful scrutiny may appear ambiguous and may even be contrary to the attitude of some directors, further clarification is necessary to justify the approach. First, frequent allusions have been made to the playwright's "intentions." How may the director presume to know what those intentions are? Recently, an important international director defended his unique approaches to classical drama by emphasizing the importance of what the play means to "me in my time," maintaining that, because Sophocles and Shakespeare are dead and have left posterity with no explanations of their plays, it is impossible to be sure of their intentions. While there is some justification in defending the subjectivity of interpretation and the contemporary significance of the classics (why perform them at all if this element is not present?), his remark about the mystery of the playwright's intentions could prove misleading. It may give a director *carte blanche* to be careless in his treatment of a play, or to use the play to demonstrate his own virtuosity at the expense of the play's intrinsic unity and design. In fact, it is precisely by thorough exploration of a play's design that a playwright's intentions may be explored. When asked about the intentions of their art, most artists, including playwrights, will point to the work and say, "It is there." In an interpretative work of art, the interpretative artist's duty is to determine what "is there" before or while he attempts to express it. Too often, relying on intuition, inspiration, the urge to make the play as written into something else, or a superficial analysis will result in incongruity, chaos, or, at best, interesting experiments that do not quite hold together. Shakespeare, of course, suffers most because modern directors are inclined to seek fresh and novel, or even startling, ways of interpreting his plays. Basically, nothing is wrong with this provided the inspiration for new insights is justified by the text and the means used to express these views illuminate rather than pervert the text.

It is naive, on the other hand, to assume that there may be only one absolute interpretation of a play. It is the nature of dramatic art that the manuscript, like the score of a symphony, is not complete until it is performed. Even when two directors agree about the genre, style, characterization, and thematic objectives of a play, their productions will vary, because all of these factors may be expressed in a variety of ways. A playscript rarely or never specifies precise ways of expressing its context; cast differences alone will lead to striking variations between several productions of the same play. Any director who has directed the same play twice will admit that, even with no serious changes in conception, the new production will vary in numerous ways from the old. The stage space may be different, affecting composition and movement; much of the older business may be replaced by new inspirations; the temperaments and skills of the new actors will result in quite a different expression of character.

The reader must be aware that there is no contradiction between a director's loyalty to a text and his creative freedom as an interpreter. He is creator and interpreter when his imagination is first stirred by the play he is to direct, then channeled toward the clearest and most exciting illumination of the text.

Another disagreement might occur regarding the sequence of activities in the director's preparation as it is suggested here. What should the director do first? To what extent should his visualization of the play be determined before he begins rehearsals? The *regiebuchs* of Max Reinhardt suggest that most of the play's effects were worked out before rehearsals began. Yet anyone who has experienced a play's progression from script to stage will realize that not everything can be anticipated, and that the collaborative nature of theatre art makes absolute preconceptions impractical. Even a painter or novelist who works by himself most often finds his finished product considerably altered from his original conception. A director begins his work when the play makes its initial impact, during his first reading. He then strives to discover the means of producing that impact on the audience. In the process, through a closer study of the play, and through the creative contributions made by those who work together in bringing the play to life, new discoveries are usually made about the play's potential. Some elements might not be realized until the "completed" production is performed, during which an audience's reaction may reveal more than was recognized by the director and his performers or some unexpected responses indicate incongruities between the text and its interpretation. Practicing directors vary in their methods of developing interpretation. Some prefer to form as complete an idea as possible of meaning and visualization before any meetings with their associates. At the other extreme are directors who like to work spontaneously and experiment fully with design and performers, sometimes until the final days of rehearsal. In between are those who study the text carefully, then flexibly allow ideas to take shape or be altered as the director's experience with his associates dictates.

This book does not necessarily advocate one or another of these approaches. Successful methods vary with the skills of the individual director and with the circumstances of production. A director who must work with amateur actors, a small budget, and limited rehearsal time will probably discover that the spontaneous, experimental approach leads to chaos. Even under ideal conditions, the nature of the play itself may require one particular technique.

In a general discussion of a director's function, however, it is probably best to follow the most logical procedure of preparation. It is more reasonable in a book such as this to cope with the director's problems by dealing with his responsibilities in the most practical way. It is difficult, perhaps impossible, to explain intuition or inspiration in artistic expression. Clearly, however, the interpretative imagination must necessarily be nourished by the fullest awareness of the script's potential. Part of this "awareness" depends on feeling, certainly, but it can be discussed only in objective, analytical terms. This book attempts to suggest some methods of achieving awareness and, as its title suggests, follows a basic Stanislavski philosophy:

> One cannot always create subconsciously and with inspiration: no such genius exists in the world. Therefore our art teaches us first of all to create consciously and rightly, because that will best prepare the way for the blossoming of the subconscious which is inspiration. The more you have of conscious creative moments in your role the more chance you will have of a flow of inspiration.[1]

Stanislavski probably has had as great an influence on modern directing as he has had on acting. The statement quoted above was written for an acting book, and expresses an artistic philosophy that was created to find a way of substituting interpretative integrity and honesty for mannered, affected, or mechanical acting. As this book is being written such tendencies are fairly prevalent. Naturalistic clichés have replaced declamatory ones; in the rebellion against realism, realistic plays are performed expressionistically, just as poetic drama earlier in the century was distorted by the realists. Theatricalism has become an excuse for exhibitionism or novelty; "good taste and caution" are exercised at the expense of a play's power, or shock and sensationalism are emphasized out of proportion to the demands of the text. Imaginative directors, in search of a unifying metaphor, become enamored of an image suggested by only part of a play and try to make it fit the whole, frequently with ludicrous results.

To create "consciously and rightly," then, the director determines what he believes must be expressed, and he must take care that his conclusions emerge from his submersion in the text. What follows is an attempt to demonstrate one method of achieving the submersion that hopefully will lead to a "flow of inspiration."

NOTES

[1]Constantin Stanislavski, *An Actor Prepares,* trans. Elizabeth Reynolds Hapgood (New York: Theatre Arts Books, 1946), p. 14.

The Director and the Text: Internal Investigation

When one has lived for some time in close contact with a work, . . . when one has devoted oneself to a minute analysis of each element before reaching the synthesis of a performance, the universe of this work becomes so familiar to you that it risks the loss of its magic. It would seem that too great an effort of understanding is prejudicial to spontaneity, and that you will forever be prevented from again taking an unsophisticated look at the work in question. For works whose intense radiance persists, it could be said that, on the contrary, the farther one goes in knowing it, the less one understands the origin of its mystery.[1]

Earlier it was maintained that a playwright's intentions are best determined by a careful study of the play itself. Yet, an interpreter can also investigate sources external to the play such as biography, criticism, and history. External investigation often proves indispensible, as another chapter in this book will attempt to demonstrate. But the single most important source for understanding, and the source to which one must return for verification after external studies have been made, is the text. In fact, the director's response to his play will be freer and, in many instances, much deeper if he is able to approach his play without preconceived ideas about its meaning and manner. External investigations, whenever possible, should begin after the director has concluded an intensive internal analysis.

The director's problem, as he tries to determine the meaning and experience of a particular play, is finding a method that will permit and encourage the text to "speak" to him. Many experienced directors shudder when a word such as "method" is used. This is partly because they distrust formulas, especially as every play must be considered unique. Even plays written by the same playwright have their own "lives." Is it not better to work out one's approach to each play on its own terms? In addition many directors prefer to apply their personal and equally unique methods of getting the most out of a play's values, and they are absolutely correct in wishing to do so. Nevertheless, although plays vary, they have in common the fact that they are plays, which employ plots, characters, language, and spectacle. As works of art, they also share the fundamental characteristics of all art—the ordering and designing of experience. Consequently it must be possible to rationally explore all plays by carefully studying how their plots, characters, language, and spectacle are selected, ordered, and designed. There are, of course, different ways of doing this, and it is obvious that one mark of the great director is that he, in his own way, is able to perceive more deeply and imaginatively than others.

No one is able to teach the capacity for insight or the inspiration that makes a fine director, but the following pages contain suggestions for gaining insight into a play through the play itself. We must begin, however, just as the director does, with selection of a play.

NOTES

[1]Pierre Boulez, "Pélléas Reflected," introduction to the libretto of Debussy's *Pélléas and Mélisande,* Columbia Record Album MS 30119.

Selecting the Play

The criteria for the selection of a play will vary with the organization for which the director is working. Indeed, a play may be selected by someone other than the director, after which a suitable director is employed to guide its rehearsals. In the professional theatre this is often the case, and in the community theatre a play selection committee may sometimes choose a play or a season of plays. In almost all circumstances, however, the director is free to accept or reject his involvement with a play on the basis of his subjective response to it. Later we shall see that some objective considerations are also important, but there can be little argument (excepting a tempting salary offer) that the director's personal response to a play should be considered first. No director should assume the responsibility of directing a play about which he is not excited. A director's lack of enthusiasm will affect not only his contribution toward the creation of an effective production, but will undoubtedly infect his cast. Enthusiasm and confidence in rehearsals do not guarantee that a play will please audiences, but a play can hardly succeed without these attitudes, and they will not persist with the cast if the director fails to share them.

The inability of a director to respond appropriately to a play does not mean that it is necessarily a bad manuscript. The fault may be in the director. He may find particular plays personally distasteful; he may be convinced that a play lacks the necessary ingredients of good drama; he may feel comfortable only with particular kinds of plays—it is not unusual for some directors to be considered most qualified to handle comedies, or classical plays, or avant-garde works. Nor is it enough merely to respect a play or to recognize its qualities. Unless the *emotional* urge (and this is just as true of "intellectual" plays) to direct a play exists, the director should refuse to commit himself to it.

Although the strong desire to present a play always should be a qualification for its selection, external considerations may often influence choice. One of the first of these considerations is knowledge of the audience. In the golden ages of the theatre of the past, when audiences were relatively homogeneous, there was a built-in awareness of what the audience would understand and respond to. Today's theatre is much more complicated. Some playwrights write plays for popular tastes while others prefer to experiment or create esoteric dramas for a more limited audience. And, unlike the ancient theatre, the hundreds of theatre organizations in the western world select their repertoire from all the known dramatic literature of 24 centuries. The director's problem in these circumstances is to determine what will first invite, then move and please the potential audience in his community.

The theatre artist is not "prostituting" himself to commerce when he admits that he must have an audience. We may understand and respect Samuel Beckett's reported satisfaction when he looked in on a performance of one of his plays and saw only a handful of people in the audience, but it is simply not in the nature of theatre art to encourage empty houses. Artists create so that their creation will be expressive to someone besides themselves. Drama is a public art, and plays are enacted not for the actors and directors but for the evocation of an audience's response. What are rehearsals all about? They are efforts to find the *best* means of expressing the company's experience of a play to an audience, and the director's task is to identify himself with the potential audience so that he can objectively judge the clarity and effectiveness of the production. A production without an audience is like a doctor without patients.

Of course, a director should not be expected to surrender his integrity to cater to "popular taste." In large cities there are majority and minority audiences, and support for a variety of plays exists. In San Francisco, while *Anniversary Waltz* is enjoying a long run, *Zoo Story* or *Birthday Party* may also play extensively—in a smaller house, to be sure, but the important thing is that an audience is there. In other communities a director who insists on a season of Genet, Gelber, and Beckett (perhaps "lightened" by an Albee) might insure his company's integrity, but he also could be insuring its privacy. In many colleges and communities even some Broadway hits are taboo because of their subject matter. The plays of Tennessee Williams, which now appear tame beside those of Albee and Gelber, are still considered obscene in numerous regions. Directors may choose to give their audience "what it thinks it wants," or they may bravely attempt to educate it to want something better. In any case, the director's choice of plays should not be made without a study of the theatre goers or potential theatre goers in the community.

The college theatre, of course, has a very special kind of audience. Directors in the universities ordinarily will be less concerned with the majority preferences of the adjacent community than they will be with the needs of the college community: its students, teachers, and administrative personnel. One major responsibility that most drama departments assume is the presentation of plays selected from the world's great drama in such a way that the performers and audience may experience a varied mixture each year. Unfortunately, some college directors happily fill their college theatres with the lure of little more than Rodgers and Hammerstein musicals "balanced" by Tennessee Williams and Arthur Miller. In the process they perpetuate the audiences that dictate to the commercial theatre today. On the other hand, it has been argued that the universities, because they need not be concerned with the box office (not always true, by the way), should perform only plays by new playwrights. Advocates of this idea appear to assume that university theatre exists primarily to develop new playwrights. Although encouraging new playwrights should be part of a university's drama program, university theatre also has obligations to the student audience, which justifiably expects to be able to view the great drama that is taught in the classroom, or that expresses the varied views of man's nature which the university presumably investigates.

For repertory companies or university drama departments, which present "seasons" of plays, variety has been mentioned as a desirable objective in the choice of plays. The variety referred to has been limited to periods, but variety exists on other levels as well. Everything else being equal, greater satisfaction is derived by audiences exposed to contrasts. Laughter and tears are equally valid ways of responding to life on the stage, and to limit presentations to one or the other is to limit the potential of audience response. Even theatres that concentrate on a single playwright or motif attempt to achieve variety within their defined scope. Theatres specializing in Shakespeare festivals, for example, generally attempt to vary their seasons with a mixture of the tragedies, comedies, chronicle plays, and dark comedies. It is usually wise to look for variety from season to season also. Established companies should review their past few seasons and ask whether they have neglected some important playwright, period, style, or genre. Have recent playwrights such as Pinter or Stoppard been represented? Have all the comedies been farce or high comedy? Has Molière somehow been forgotten in the past five years?

Another practical consideration in play selection is the physical theatre and its facilities. The stage may be too small for the ship setting of *Billy Budd*; the proscenium may be too low for Juliet's balcony or too narrow for the two rooms in *Come Back, Little Sheba*; the theatre house may be too large for the delicate intimacy of *The Glass Menagerie*. The absence of adequate backstage space or a loft often makes it unfeasible to present a realistic play with numerous scene changes. Some producing companies are restricted to performing all of their plays in the arena style. When such is the case, plays requiring complicated sets, trick effects, or masses of people on the stage must be excluded. Spatial limitations often may lead to ingenious and highly satisfactory solutions, but before deciding to deal with a play the director must anticipate incongruities between its demands and the limitations of his theatre. If he cannot find satisfactory solutions to such incongruities, it would be fairer to the play not to force the issue.

However, one other might be mentioned. In the professional theatre, plays are often selected or written for a star. Sometimes financial backing will depend on the acquisition of a particular performer. A new play may be postponed until the "right" cast is found. In repertory theatres, plays must be selected with an eye toward the size of the company and the particular talents within the company. When the Royal Shakespeare Company, for example, prepares its Stratford season, which usually includes about eight plays, it must be able to suitably cast each play without using any actor in more than three or four of the plays. A director may prefer to give up his production of *Hamlet* if the actor he has in mind is too busy in other productions. In the university, where precasting usually is avoided, directors want to be reasonably sure that there will be enough men on hand for *Othello* or *The Caine Mutiny Court Martial*. Nor are there many directors who would care to risk doing *King Lear* without knowing that a few advanced actors will audition for the play.

Determining Treatment

After a selection has been made, the director should read the play as often as necessary to develop the ideas he believes must be pursued in production. Even before analysis, it is a good idea for the director to record his spontaneous impressions and reactions to the play. Because he necessarily must become involved with details, a director may forget the relationship between these details and the impact they originally were intended to create. With comedy, the director and the cast in the labor of rehearsals often forget the hilarity of their initial response to the play, and are surprised on opening night how much the audience laughs. With a serious play such as Euripides' *Electra*, concern about Greek tragic method, the philosophical implications of the play, and the psychological attributes of the characters may cause the director to forget that the play also contains excruciating suspense, strong pathos, cruelty, and despair. Or the director may be so carried away with tempo, contrasts, lighting, and other effects that he fails to recognize that the Greek tragic method, philosophical implications, and psychological justifications are the basis for these effects and that an inadequate realization of these elements will make all of his efforts shallow and ineffective.

Because meaning cannot really be separated from effect, the director cannot prepare his play in a formalized manner and concentrate on one to the exclusion of the other. He may, in his analysis of character, begin to visualize movement and stage positions, colors, and the necessity for certain set pieces or props. Despite this, in his various readings of the play he must begin to concentrate on certain essentials. At some point he must go through the play to determine the needs of the setting, or pull together all the textual evidence for his fuller comprehension of character. Included in these concentrated studies are two elements that are extremely important in the production of a play because they influence acting, settings, costuming, lighting—in fact, practically every aspect of production. These elements have been called by many different terms. Here they will be called *genre* and *style*.

to recognize the particular qualities and emphases of each comedy he directs. Much of the language and action in Molière's *The Doctor in Spite of Himself* or *Scapin* quite strongly suggests coarse physical comedy, or slapstick, while the same writer's *The Misanthrope* justifies practically none. The directors of various productions of *The Taming of the Shrew* have gone to opposite extremes in some of the Kate–Petruchio scenes. Some have preferred to treat the wooing and the honeymoon scenes as high comedy and have avoided the broad action that is quite clearly indicated in Shakespeare's text. Others have recognized the low comedy qualities of these and other scenes, but have played them so broadly that the high comic qualities of the language have been neglected or obscured. One cannot justifiably impose one's preferences for refinement or coarseness on comedy. If the director has such prejudices, he should direct only plays that suit his tastes.

Mixed Genres.   It was remarked earlier that both comedy and serious drama often contain elements of each other. Ordinarily it is not difficult to recognize the writer's emphasis on one genre or the other, but sometimes scenes or characters in tragedy or comedy assume traits that appear ambiguous or inconsistent with the seriousness or ludicrousness of the play. The greatest danger of classification in art is that once a work is neatly categorized the viewer or interpreter attempts to impose "consistency" on the entire work, as though the neoclassic ideas of purity and the "unities" applied to all periods of artistic endeavor. Most contemporary directors and critics attempt to avoid the extremes of the neoclassic viewpoint. They are aware and respectful, for example, of Shakespeare's tendency to include comic scenes in his tragedies and melancholy scenes in his comedies, but when "tragic" figures become ludicrous, or when situations are treated both seriously and comically—or ambiguously—how often do they attempt to oversimplify or "cover up" for Shakespeare by cutting scenes or by forcing them into a more "consistent" vein? *Antony and Cleopatra* is supposed to be a tragedy, and the hyperboles with which the principals are described contribute to the tragic stature that one expects in the protagonists. But if one reads the play without preconceived notions about the "seriousness" of tragedy and its central figures he discovers that both Antony and Cleopatra have comic foibles that may appear difficult to reconcile with superhuman attributes. Even in productions where these apparent contradictions are permitted to come through, directors invariably cover up the comic elements of Antony's botched suicide (IV, 14) and the comic awkwardness with which his body is handed up to Cleopatra and her attendants (IV, 15). It apparently has not occurred to many that Shakespeare intended such mixed responses. By accepting them his interpreters might realize new significance in such exchanges as:

MECAENAS: His taints and honors
          Waged equal with him.

AGRIPPA: A rarer spirit never
                Did steer humanity. But you, gods, will give us
                Some faults to make us men. . . . (V, 1)

Shakespeare, it might be found, has been more consistent than they have permitted him to be. Still, *Antony and Cleopatra* remains an essentially serious play because of the magnitude of its characters and the seriousness of their suffering. But it is not the same kind of tragedy as *Macbeth* or *Othello,* whose protagonists have very little of the ludicrous about them.

The prevalent genre of contemporary drama is mixed. Chekhov, Pinter, Anouilh, Williams, Ionesco, and Beckett create plays that stimulate complex serious and comic responses. Their plays are not just predominantly serious or comic with an occasional scene that reverses our responses. Pathos, horror, or revulsion are provoked alternately, and sometimes simultaneously, with laughter. It is common knowledge that Chekhov was annoyed at Stanislavski's gloomy treatment of *The Cherry Orchard.* Unfortunately, too many directors have taken categorically Chekhov's corrections, which maintain that the play is a comedy and "cheerful," and neglected the sadness that it surely provokes. Epihodov's accidents and Charlotte's eating of the cucumber are pure comedy, but Ranevsky's tensions in Act III and the leavetaking in Act IV are touching, while the Ranevsky–Trofimov argument in Act III and the Varya–Lopahin "proposal" scene in Act IV are moving and amusing almost at the same time.

Eugene Ionesco tells us of his deliberate intention to fuse genres in his *Notes and Counter Notes:*

> I have called my comedies "anti-plays" or "comic dramas," and my dramas "pseudo-dramas" or "tragic farces": for it seems to me that comic and tragic are one, and that the tragedy of man is pure derision. The contemporary critical mind takes nothing too seriously or too lightly. In *Victimes du Devoir* I tried to sink comedy in tragedy: in *Les Chaises* tragedy in comedy or, if you like, to confront comedy and tragedy in order to link them in a new dramatic synthesis. But it is not a true synthesis, for these two elements do not coalesce, they coexist: one constantly repels the other, they show each other up, criticise and deny one another and, thanks to their opposition, thus succeed dynamically in maintaining a balance and creating tension. The two plays that best satisfy this condition are, I believe: *Victimes du Devoir* and *Le Nouveau Locataire.*[1]

The director's responsibility in his interpretation of genre is to see each unit in the play according to its serious or comic intent. He decides on a predominant atmosphere for the play because one genre is emphasized, but he must never lose sight of shifting responses within the whole.

...architectural stage with its three stage-level openings may have been influenced by Italian Renaissance stages, which imitated the physical plan of the classical theatre.

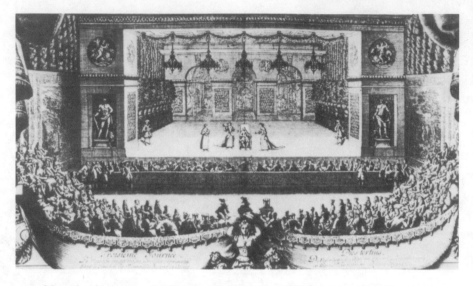

Neo-classic theatre. Setting for Moliere's *Le Malade Imaginaire*. Courtesy of The Rockefeller Collection, Yale Drama Library.

These conventions are important to the interpreter primarily because of their influence on the structure and the spirit of the play. For example, the use of the mask in the Greek theatre perhaps had much to do with the austere limiting of characterization to a single essence, and contributed to a formal rather than a realistic depiction of character. Language, conforming to the visual illusion, then assumes a formal quality and the performer moves in the manner that the language dictates. The result is that a performance of a Greek tragedy will make similar vocal and pantomimic demands *even without the use of masks*. The language of Aeschylus cannot be acted in the manner of Chekhov, or vice versa, even if the plays of each are performed in the physical theatre of the other.

The style of a set is influenced similarly. A thoroughly realistic set is somehow incongruous with artificial language and movement. Put Sophocles' *Oedipus Rex* into a realistic set, and you either make the language incongruous by forcing the characters to relate physically to chairs, tables, doorknobs, and teacups, or you make the realistic set incongruous by ignoring it. The language of a play and the action suggested by it should influence the stylistic treatment of every aspect of play production. A wise director, moreover, tries to understand the text in connection with the conventions that influenced it, for the best way to solve stylistic problems may be emulation or modification of the original convention.

Period Conventions. Just as the artist must create with certain conventions, every civilized age has developed its art of behavior, for which it also establishes conventions. The term *mode* is to behavior what *style* is to drama. In fact the words have been used interchangeably in both art and life. Every organized culture adopts its own acceptable social norms. Its manner of dress, coiffure, speech, dining, and manners all contribute to a distinctive mode of behavior, and all are determined by the culture's conception of man's nature. Restoration drama was written for an essentially aristocratic society. It placed great value on science and reason as opposed to emotion and instinct. Social order like science, it was believed, should be based on laws or rules dictated by reason. Art itself was expected to be guided by rules and tended, as did much of the manners of the time, to be formally decorative. Clothes and wigs were elaborate and ornamental, and demanded that the wearer, if he was not to appear ridiculous, stand, sit, and move in an elegant but seemingly unself-conscious manner. Accessories, such as fans for the ladies or snuff boxes and canes for the men, were handled according to certain regulations, and their uses contributed to the appearance and movement of the bearers. To the modern observer the dress and behavior of the seventeenth-century upper class appears artificial and, therefore, unnatural. But to seventeenth-century man, artifice was a code of behavior that distinguished men from beasts, and naturalness resulted from exercising the code without labor.

The director must acquire knowledge such as this if he is to achieve the appropriate style for plays written in or about ages and cultures other than his own. Every dramatist takes the behavioral modes of his own time for granted and permits them to influence his writing. The richness and fullness of the dress worn by Elizabethan actors undoubtedly made more feasible the richness and fullness of the language in Shakespeare's plays. This makes it of dubious value to perform classical plays in modern dress. The director and the actor must then decide whether to allow vocal and physical expression to be dictated by their contemporary clothing and trappings, or by a language that was written for and influenced by the mode of another age.

Personal Conventions.   One quality that sets the truly great artist apart is that his own individuality emerges even though he conforms to the conventions of his theatre and his time. Mozart is a classicist, Braque is a cubist, and Shelley is a romanticist. Each is so characterized because of the period in which he created, and because each conformed to the conventions that were dictated by stylistic trends. But on hearing Mozart, viewing Braque, or reading Shelley, one is able to identify the artist as well as the general style. This individual quality is not easily defined, but clearly the way that a creative artist uses his art form and its conventions will distinguish him. It might be argued that conformity to conventions can lead only to adequacy and discourages originality, but the geniuses of art rarely have been complete rebels against the traditions they inherited. In fact, the artist who best integrates those traditions may be the most artistically successful. Shakespeare invented no new conventions. Instead he made his age's most exciting use of its given stage, of the dramatic structure that had evolved up to its time,

Michelangelo. *Pieta*. Cathedral at Florence.

weight of the dead Christ is heavy and cumbersome and creates a nearly unendurable tension between the forms. Both of these sculptures convey recognizable aspects of the human form, but because of the combination of nonrealistic details the spectator is forced into an experience of almost metaphysical agony.

In the theatre, the dramatist may exert similar controls through the conventions that he applies to the materials of plot, character, thought, language, music, and spectacle. While all or most of these materials will be developed to be consistent with a particular kind of reality, language usually provides us with our major clue to style. The following statement by George Steiner provides a concise explanation of the relationship between language and artistic reality. After pointing out that the actor and the moral experience of the characters are united to the metric form of Greek tragedy, he says,

> Very early, moreover, the mind perceived a relation between poetic forms and those categories of truth which are not directly verifiable. We speak still of "poetic truth" when signifying that a statement may be false or meaningless by the test of empiric proof, yet possesses at the same time an important, undeniable verity in a moral, psychological, or formal domain. Now the truths of my-

thology and religious experience are largely of this order. Prose submits its own statements to criteria of verification which are, in fact, irrelevant or inapplicable to the realities of myth. And it is on these that Greek tragedy is founded. The matter of tragic legend, whether it invokes Agamemnon, Oedipus, or Alcestis torn from the dead, cannot be held liable to prosaic inquisition. As Robert Graves says, the imagination has extra-territorial rights, and these are guarded by poetry. . . . Where the pressure of imagination is sufficiently sustained, we allow poetry the most ample liberties. In that sense, we may say that verse is the pure mathematics of language. It is more exact than prose, more self-contained, and more capable of constructing theoretic forms independent of material basis. It can "lie" creatively. . . . Prose, on the contrary, is applied mathematics. Somewhere along the line the assertions it makes must correspond to our sensual perceptions. The houses described in prose must stand on solid foundations. Prose measures, records, and anticipates the realities of practical life. It is the garb of the mind doing its daily job of work.[3]

In the theatre, language is spoken aloud. Consequently, in his delivery, the actor must make the distinctions between verse and prose indicated by Steiner. It follows that his physical action must grow out of and support his verbal manner. The stage environment, too, must create a reality consistent with that of the play. For Sophocles' *Oedipus*, a real Theban palace and properties of an *actual* period are less important than a setting which creates the spirit of a noble façade for underlying corruption. Although Ibsen's *Ghosts* also deals with noble façades and hidden corruption, its symbols are rooted in physical realities: the conservatory, red velvet drapes, the orphanage, and venereal disease. To deprive *Ghosts* of its surface realities is ultimately to deprive it of its poetic realities.

The terms presently used to indicate the kind of reality with which art is expressed are *presentational* (or *nonillusionistic*) and *representational* (or *illusionistic*). The conventions of presentational drama lean in the direction of immaterial reality and the frankly theatrical. In representational drama the conventions encourage the illusion of the surface details of everyday life. These terms are very general, and the styles that fall into each classification will vary considerably in their uses of convention. There are different kinds of artifice as well as varying degrees of artifice in presentational drama, just as there are different degrees of realism in representational drama. Greek tragedy and expressionism employ more nonillusionistic conventions than Elizabethan or neoclassic tragedy. Naturalism carries realism to a greater degree of illusion, yet both attempt to suggest material reality.

Mixed Styles.   Just as genres can be mixed in drama, so also can styles. Few theatrical styles are *completely* presentational or representational. Greek

Mixed style. Setting for *The Entertainer* by John Osborne. Design by J. Svoboda, National Theatre at Prague. Courtesy of Art Centrum.

banal and untheatrical limitations of realistic dramas, contemporary directors sometimes attempt to impose presentational conventions on plays that clearly have been conceived as representational. These directors frequently fail because the manner of presentation becomes incongruous with not only the manner of the text but with the meaning, which is the consequence of the marriage between subject and style. *Ghosts*, like *Death of a Salesman*, constantly delves into the past. But whereas Miller's plot and language inform us that the past is enacted, Ibsen's methods dictate the *narration* of the past. Ibsen does not want us to lose sight of the present while characters discuss the past because he wants throughout his play to present the inescapable reality that the past is *in* the present.

Sometimes directors will impose one presentational style on a play whose style may be presentational in a different way. In *Macbeth*, for example, Shakespeare might be said to be using a kind of expressionism when Banquo's ghost appears, because the apparition is visible to no one on stage but Macbeth. But the atmosphere of darkness and the strange, chaotic perturbations of nature do not exist only in Macbeth's mind. Banquo sees the three witches, too. Ross and the Old Man in Act II, Scene 4 witness unnatural events. It is most important to recognize that in the world of this tragedy, abuses against nature may *actually* lead to disorders in nature. The director who insists that the hellish environment is a product of Macbeth's imagination and who styles his play to express this point of view is distorting Shakespeare's intentions.

Some Special Problems in Style.

> It seems to be clear that our modern stage . . . cannot answer the requirements of all the other styles of the past. Its architecture is too different from the original theatrical dispositions, to which the plays of the past are umbilically attached. With the picture frame stage, all plays of the Greek, Shakespearean, or Spanish traditions are distorted and robbed of part of their true reality.[4]

If Michel Saint-Denis' words are taken at face value, then no contemporary director should attempt to produce such plays unless he can find ways of reproducing the original playhouses. But this is virtually impossible. No one is absolutely certain of the nature of the complete physical theatre and conventions of the Greeks or the Elizabethans. Much of what we believe about these structures is based on conjecture. In addition, few professional companies wish to invest a sizeable amount of money in a theatre that is limited to *one* theatrical period, or that desires to ignore modern theatrical innovations such as lights, recorded sound, revolving stages, fly galleries, and painted scenery. It is obviously nonsensical to conclude that if we are unwilling to duplicate the exact conventions in which a play was originally performed that we should no longer produce the play. Saint-Denis, who has successfully staged classical plays in contemporary proscenium theatres, does not limit the meaning of a play's "true reality" to its original conventions. There is, instead, a reality suggested by the spirit of the text, a reality that may be suggested in different ways. The immediacy and the participatory elements of Shakespeare's plays, or the chorus' proximity to its audience during the *stasimon* of Greek tragedy may be felt by the addition of a "thrust" platform, or by creating relative proximities within a proscenium arch when such extensions cannot be arranged. The swiftness of movement so necessary in Elizabethan drama and originally made possible by its permanent architectural setting may be effected by a similar permanent set, by permanent platforms in a "space" setting, or by modern revolving stages. An atmospheric use of light and sound and semi-realistic set pieces may be used to suggest the poetic rather than the realistic qualities of the play (see illustrations, pp. 41, 151, 152, 153).

The greatest fault that may be committed in the staging of classical plays in the modern theatre occurs when the director surrenders to the realistic conventions that have been the mode of the modern theatre for the past

5 Exploring the Design

THE NECESSITY OF EXPLORATION

An unfortunate but common error in interpretation occurs when the meaning of an entire play is determined by the ideas expressed in a single scene or a single speech. A typical example is the one in which *King Lear* is developed along the lines of Gloucester's "As flies to wanton boys are we to the gods; They kill us for their sport" (IV, 1). Obviously, the depiction of human suffering, degradation, and evil in this play makes Gloucester's comment appear to be a useful summary of what Shakespeare intended. Gloucester's lines suggest a meaningless universe where, if God exists, he is capricious. But the play's central characters, including Gloucester himself, suffer for their own sins and, by the play's end, are better human beings for it. Strangely, it is Gloucester who says shortly before uttering the line above,

> I stumbled when I saw. Full oft 'tis seen,
> Our means secure us, and our mere defects
> Prove our commodities.   (IV, 1)

The play's structure, which concentrates on sin and retribution, delineates a world in which good and evil are linked to man's choices and actions, and in which the presence of evil creates such disruption that order cannot be restored until the evil is purged. Had Lear not sinned, or had his intense suffering not led to a recognition of his mortality, Gloucester might be considered correct. Gloucester's line is important, of course, but it must correctly be related to other verifiable aspects of the play before conclusions may be made about its significance.

Another error that leads to distortion of meaning occurs when a director decides that what he believes to be textual omissions or ambiguities must be explained by creating new justifications for characters or by reworking the plot. The following comment on a film version of *Romeo and Juliet* provides a somewhat typical example:

There are a great many "new approaches" to the 1967 version of the classic. For the first time, Juliet's mother is portrayed as a young, beautiful woman . . . whose secret love affair with her cousin Tybalt accounts for the hatred she feels for Romeo, when the latter kills Tybalt. "Why else would Lady Capulet want Romeo's death?" asks the director. "This is the only logical explanation."[1]

Such efforts to improve on Shakespeare's plays usually harm them. If Shakespeare wished Lady Capulet's motives to be incestuous or adulterous, he would have made them clearly and emphatically so. Edmund, Richard III, and Macbeth explain their motives honestly and bluntly to us, and when characters fail to explain themselves directly, their actions and the comments of other characters usually do the job. But when characters are what they are without any explanation of how they got that way, conjecture about causes is irrelevant. All drama was not intended to present studies in abnormal psychology. Lady Macbeth is ambitious for her husband and herself. Her ambitions are strong enough to lead to violence and ultimately to madness. We need not know the hereditary or environmental causes for her ambition, nor need we know the psychological causes of her consciencelessness. The introduction of causal details by Shakespeare or by a cunning director would only diffuse the play and thoroughly alter its objectives (see pp. 63-64).

Often, however, when character justification is logical and clear, it may be so simple that some directors either fail to recognize it or prefer to superimpose a "better" explanation. Anyone who reads *Romeo and Juliet* carefully will observe that Lady Capulet's desire for Romeo's death does have, despite the director's doubts, a logical explanation. Her nephew has been murdered by Romeo. Blood for blood is the creed by which both families have lived for generations, and it has perpetuated the feud between the Montagues and Capulets. Shakespeare never explains how or why the "ancient grudge" began. When we add this omission to the flimsy excuses for the violence in the first scene and the later clashes, it should be clear that such patterns are meant to emphasize "cankered hate" rather than its causes, and the essential meaninglessness of the feud that results in the "fearful passage of their [Romeo and Juliet's] death-marked love." If Lady Capulet needs additional motives for desiring the death of Romeo, then so do all the Capulets and Montagues for their hatred. To give Juliet's mother alone a special reason for hatred is to break the pattern and irony of meaningless hatred and to give her character a disproportionate and melodramatic stress, which contributes nothing to the play's overall intentions.

In the same manner, historical, sociological, and other explanations are imposed on plays whose internal structure suggests none of these. The results are usually distortion, incongruity, and all too often a far less rewarding experience than an imaginative interpretation of the play on its own terms.

Act 1, Scene 3. *A heath.*

 Unit 1 (lines 1–29). The three witches.

  Exposition. Witches 1 and 2 relate their offstage activities.

  Character. Since each boasts of mischievous and wicked accomplishments, we are intended to look on them as instruments of evil. They appear also to have supernatural powers, but not the power to take life.

  Thought. "Though his bark cannot be lost,/Yet shall it be tempest-tost." "Bark" might represent "soul" as well as human life. The witches can create "tempests"—or havoc—but do not have the power to control destiny, though they may be able to foresee it.

  Bridge (lines 30–37). Drum announces Macbeth's arrival.

  Preparation. "The charm's wound up." A ritual is executed in anticipation of Macbeth. The "charm" is the trap by which Macbeth's "bark" will be won or lost.

 Unit 2 (lines 38–50). The three witches, Macbeth, Banquo.

  Forward action. The prophecy is made: Macbeth, thane of Glamis, will become thane of Cawdor, then king of Scotland. In Unit 6, the first prediction will become true, thereby convincing Macbeth and, later, Lady Macbeth that fate has intended their rise.

  Character. The witches' physical appearance is described.

  Language and atmosphere. Repetition of "foul and fair." (See I, 1.)

 Unit 3 (lines 51–69). Same characters on stage.

  Forward action and possible complication. Banquo's future may conflict with Macbeth's.

  Character. Macbeth's reaction to witches is transparent. (Link with Lady Macbeth's admonition in I, 5, "Your face, my thane, is as a book where men/May read strange matters.") Macbeth starts, "seems to fear" the prediction, and is "rapt withal." Note that Banquo "neither beg[s] nor fear[s] . . ."

  Language. Foul and fair suggested by Macbeth's "fear" of "Things that do sound so fair."

 Unit 4 (lines 70–78). Same characters on stage.

  Character. Macbeth's anxiety to hear more, to find out how the witches know and why they have divulged the prophecy.

 Unit 5 (lines 79–88). Macbeth and Banquo.

  Character. The supernatural powers of the witches reemphasized. They vanish "into the air."

  Preparation for possible complication. The men remind each other of their prospective futures according to the prophecy.

  Thought. Question raised, particularly by Banquo, about the reality of the witches.

Unit 6 (lines 89-115). Macbeth and Banquo are joined by Ross and Angus.
> *Exposition.* Recounting of Macbeth's heroic exploits in battle. Announcement that Macbeth has been made thane of Cawdor. The treason of the former thane of Cawdor explained.
> *Forward action.* The witches' first prophecy is validated.
> *Character.* Macbeth is a fearless warrior.

Unit 7 (lines 116–127). Same characters on stage, but Macbeth has an aside, after which he and Banquo address one another.
> *Character.* Banquo has the wisdom to treat this partial fulfillment of the prophecy with caution.
> *Thought.* Macbeth is reminded that the "instruments of darkness" often try to tempt us with "honest trifles." Christian motif of man tempted by devil, but given knowledge to aid him in curbing evil.
> *Language.* "Instruments of darkness" alludes to devil, evil. Repetition of blackness, darkness, night, etc.

Unit 8 (lines 128–147). Same characters on stage, but emphasis on Macbeth's soliloquy.
> *Character.* (1) Macbeth's eager, excited reaction to prophecy fulfillment informs us of his ambition. He considers possibility of murdering for the crown. (2) His conscience and imagination are so strong that the thought of Duncan's murder shakes him violently ("function is smothered in surmise") and forces him to leave the future to chance.
> *Language.* Foul and fair again suggested by the mixed reactions of Macbeth to his promotion, the news of which heightens the possibility of his becoming king. It "cannot be ill, cannot be good." Use of antithesis repeated in "nothing is but what is not." Banquo uses clothing metaphor (lines 145–146), which is repeated throughout the play.

Unit 9 (lines 148 to end of scene). Same characters on stage.
> *Character.* Macbeth forced to cover up true cause of his trance. Unit's essential purpose is to end scene and justify exit.

The values of such a microscopic study of the architectonic unit are two-fold. First, it prevents the interpreter from overlooking the least detail in the play's structure, and from directing each scene from too general a point of view. Too often in the theatre certain scenes are glossed over or prove to be nonorganic, even obtrusive, because the director has not mined their potential. Expository scenes tend to suffer the most this way because they often appear to be dull, but necessary. The director's tendency is to "animate" these scenes with a great deal of external business and movement. How often this occurs in the plays of Ibsen and Pirandello, where a closer analysis of expository scenes may reveal subtle suggestions about character and character relationships— even hints about the major ideas of the play! The opening scene in *Ghosts* is an example. It is rich in its preparation for almost all the things that the play

..., and later, his qualities as a king are expressed. Except for the political murders, Scotland's dissolution under Macbeth is not shown, and England's Edward never appears. Is the exposition concerning chaos in Scotland intended only to justify the rebellion against Macbeth? Why the absent Edward, and why has Shakespeare selected these special attributes to characterize him?[5] These elements of exposition ordinarily are not cut from the play when it is performed, but often their importance to the play is neglected, and potential stimuli to a more meaningful and imaginative treatment of the play are thwarted.

While the expository materials in *Macbeth* have not been scrutinized exhaustively, the examples above should demonstrate the kinds of questions that need to be asked about the playwright's handling of exposition: To what degree does exposition dominate the plot? Why has the playwright included these specific expository materials? Why has he chosen to make certain events take place offstage?

Forward Action. In most plays there is a logical, causal progression of events, which explains and justifies the play's development from beginning to middle to end. A play begins with a status quo in the lives of its characters or in the condition of the community that the characters inhabit. The status quo is upset, sometimes at the play's very beginning, by the discovery of some event; the characters respond to the new circumstances, and in the course of the play, their actions are complicated by new discoveries and new reversals, which ultimately bring about their victory or defeat. The forward action of a play is made possible by preparation, complications, and fulfilled action, which in turn may bring about new complications.

Preparation. The first witches' scene in *Macbeth* prepares the audience for their meetings on the heath with Macbeth, which will occur in Scene 3. We also are prepared to link the evil witches, who in the first scene remark "Fair is foul, and foul is fair" (line 11), with Macbeth, whose first lines in the play are "So foul and fair a day I have not seen" (I, 3, line 38). The prediction of the witches in Scene 3 prepares us for Macbeth's startled reaction to the awarding of the title, and to Macbeth's conclusions about the witches' veracity. Their prophecy about Banquo's heirs inheriting the throne prepares us for Macbeth's concerns after he wins the crown. In Act III, Shakespeare carefully prepares us for Banquo's murder. Macbeth's seemingly casual questions about Banquo's and Fleance's plans for the day and, more directly, his scene with the two murderers prepare and direct the audience to the murder in Act III, Scene 3. Lady Macbeth's sleepwalking scene and later references to her "illness" make it possible to accept the news of her death without improbable surprise. This does not include all the instances of preparation in *Macbeth*, but should demonstrate how different parts of a play are linked together, giving importance in retrospect to what originally may have lacked significance. Recognizing a writer's method of preparation will also make the director aware of a pattern or design in plotting, which should contribute to meaning. The director is then in a better position to reinforce these points for the awareness of the audience.

Complications.   *Macbeth* begins in turmoil, but before the third scene has ended, it appears that the disruption to the state of Scotland may have been settled. In the new status quo, the enemy has been conquered and Macbeth has achieved glory for his valor. Before Macbeth is rewarded, however, the first complication to the new status quo is suggested by Macbeth's soliloquized admission that he covets the throne. Now complications may be viewed in two ways: those threatening the good of Scotland, and those threatening Macbeth's security. By the conclusion of Act I, Lady Macbeth has persuaded Macbeth to kill the king, which will create further chaos in the state, but Macbeth's wishes are hindered by the prophecy regarding the succession of Banquo's heirs, by Duncan's naming of Malcolm as next in line, and by Macbeth's own qualms about regicide.

In Act II, after the murder has been committed, the concentration of complications is directed toward Macbeth's security and peace of mind. Even before the murder, there are suspenseful obstacles to the success of its execution. Macbeth has failed to leave the daggers at the scene of the crime and the grooms must be disposed of if they are not to be questioned.

The action of Act III dwells on the obstacles confronting the protagonists after the murder. Macbeth is so tormented by the prophecy concerning Banquo's heirs that he orders the murder of Banquo and his son, but Fleance escapes and Banquo's ghost returns to haunt Macbeth. Because of his public reaction to the ghost, Macbeth's officers begin turning away from him. Until Act III, Macbeth has had things his way, but regicide not only has made life almost unbearable, it begins now to bring about consequences that jeopardize Macbeth's crown and safety. We are prepared for the major reversals in the play in Act III. Fleance's escape, Banquo's ghost, and the fact that the "bloody cousins are bestowed in England and Ireland," combined with Macduff's self-exile to England, are to be the beginning of the end for the bloody couple.

Macbeth appears in but one scene in Act IV, which concentrates on intensifying the complications toward Macbeth's security. We learn that many Scots are beginning to rebel against the tyrant, and that the English forces have agreed to assist Malcolm. In Act V all events lead to the eventual destruction of the Macbeths. Lady Macbeth becomes ill, further desertions occur, forcing Macbeth to fight from the fortified Dunsinane rather than the field, and the enemy approaches in force. But Macbeth believes he will win because of the prophecies about Birnam Wood and the impossibility of Macbeth's death at the hands of any man born of woman. What appear to be elements in his favor, however, point to his defeat when Birnam Wood moves, and Macbeth learns that Macduff was "untimely ripp'd" from his mother's womb.

Fulfilled Action. In the course of a play, certain ends are usually accomplished, but except for completed goals that occur at the conclusion of a play, completed actions usually serve another purpose, contributing to further complications. In *Macbeth*, the first battle is completed and the rebels are overcome, but victory creates the possibility of another rebellion and even worse disorder. Macbeth and Lady Macbeth plot to murder Duncan and win the throne. They succeed in doing this only to find that they have created greater turmoil. To overcome the threats to his security, Macbeth succeeds in one bloody act after another, but each one makes his allies turn against him while his enemies become more strongly united. Macduff's intense determination to conquer Macbeth is spurred finally by the completed action of the murder of his family.

This structure not only moves the plot forward, but can also create a pattern, as in *Macbeth*, where each of his successes proves to be another step toward doom. Indeed the structural pattern demonstrates precisely that assassinations do not "trammel up the consequence and catch with [their] surcease success."

Crisis.   A dramatic "crisis" is analogous to a medical crisis. The critical moment in a disease is the point at which the condition of the patient will turn toward either recovery or death. In a play, the critical moments occur when a choice or occurrence will force the action or the fortunes of the characters to go one way or the other. Just as in real life, the crises manufactured in drama are heightened, highly significant moments filled with suspense. Melodramatic plots abound with crises, usually for the sake of tension and suspense, but in plays that emphasize character and ideas, the critical points may also form patterns that intensify our responses to character and thought. *Macbeth* begins and ends with a crisis involving the fate of both Scotland and Macbeth. The difference between the two crises is that in the beginning the victory of Scotland depends on the good and valiant Macbeth, while at the end the salvation of Scotland depends on the defeat of the evil Macbeth. In retrospect the two crises represent the action of the play, our shifting responses to Macbeth, and the relationship between the treatment of character and the political concerns of the play.

Ordinarily plays are structured so that their action leads to a final or major crisis, while, along the way, smaller though significant crises may occur. One of the most important small crises in *Macbeth* occurs in Act I, Scene 7, when Macbeth leaves the banquet tormented by the prospect of Duncan's murder. After concluding his soliloquy, "If it were done when 'tis done," it appears that he has made up his mind to "proceed no further in this business" (line 31). But then Lady Macbeth begins to work on him. Their ensuing argument creates a crisis. Will Macbeth succumb to his or to Lady Macbeth's conception of what "become[s] a man"? Shakespeare has prepared us for this moment by Macbeth's previous vacillations and horror of the deed, and by Lady Macbeth's concerns for her husband's "nature," which is "too full o' the milk of human kindness / To catch the nearest way" (I, 5, lines 19–20). Since the murder is committed in the following scene, the confrontation in Act I, Scene 7 between husband and wife clearly represents a major turning point in the play. The futures of Scotland, Macbeth, and Lady Macbeth are to be determined by the outcome of their argument. It is of paramount importance for the director to recognize that not only must he express the suspense of this scene and make the audience agonizingly concerned with the question "Will Macbeth or won't he?" but he also must be concerned with the elements of thought and character that both intensify and are intensified by the tensions of the crisis.

Climax.   The term "climax" in drama is comparable to its use in real life when we refer to experiences involving an active release of tension. "Explosion" is an appropriate synonym for climax, since the latter invariably involves a bursting point for accumulated tensions. When the clock strikes the final note of midnight at the end of the year, our society is expected to "cut loose" and purge the inhibitions and tensions of the old year, so that it may freshly be reborn at the beginning of the new year. The difference, of course, between climaxes in art and life is that in life we cannot always control climactic moments, whereas the structure of a play usually leads us through a series of carefully planned explosions to a final burst, stronger than any of the previous ones. Our interest and involvement in a play are developed and sustained by the success of the writer in structuring action that rises and falls but always moves toward an ultimate peak, a culminating point, near its end. The director's responsibility is to recognize how the action of a particular play builds, and to express through action and stage effects the appropriate degrees of release at the climactic moments of the play.

Macbeth, one of the most melodramatic of Shakespeare's tragedies, abounds in climaxes, many of them violent. One of the strongest and earliest of these occurs after the murder of Duncan. The killing of Duncan and his guards might have afforded Shakespeare with a climactic scene, but Shakespeare preferred to place the bloody murders offstage, building instead to the moment of Macduff's discovery of the bodies and the chaos and excitement that follows. Shakespeare's dialogue clearly demands much shouting.

> Ring the alarum bell. Murder and treason!
> Banquo and Donalbain! Malcolm! Awake!
> Shake off this downy sleep, death's counterfeit,
> And look on death itself! Up, up, and see
> The great doom's image! Malcolm! Banquo!
> As from your graves rise up, and walk like sprites,
> To countenance this horror! Ring the bell.   (II, 3, lines 79–85)

Bells ring, other characters race on stage partially clothed, and Lady Macbeth faints.

The play's major climax, the culminating point for all of its action, occurs in the last act, building from Macbeth's discovery that Birnam Wood actually has moved, to the battle scenes, and culminating with the triumphant exhibition of the tyrant's head after he has been slain offstage. It is interesting to note that the great Japanese director Kurosawa found Shakespeare's climax too tame, and in *Throne of Blood*, his film adaptation of *Macbeth*, showed Macbeth being pierced by hundreds of arrows until he looked like a human porcupine.

Not all climaxes from *Macbeth* are violent or physically as active as these two examples. An important climax and a culminating point for the first act of the play occurs even earlier than Duncan's murder. The crisis previously described, in Act I, Scene 7, where Macbeth and Lady Macbeth argue about the immediate murder of Duncan, explodes into climax at the point at which Lady Macbeth finally convinces him of its justification. Throughout the act doubts and misgivings have been expressed by Macbeth, until a decision *must* be made. The decision itself climaxes this particular line of action, and it is clear that Shakespeare intended an air of exultation and excitement by his use of such lines as,

> Bring forth men-children only,
> For thy undaunted mettle should compose
> Nothing but males.   (I, 7, lines 72–74)

and by the excited rapport between the husband and wife during the conspiratorial dialogue that ends the scene.

As in the case with crisis, the climaxes in a play are not developed merely for effect. There are far too many instances in modern drama where the director's interest in "theatricality" leads him into such an overelaboration of the "big scenes" that they lose all meaning, despite their impressiveness. Climaxes are as much a part of telling the story as any other aspect of plot, and often include revelations of character and thought that are intrinsic to the total design of the play.

Resolution.   In essence, the previously discussed "completed actions" of a play are the same as "resolutions," which are the answers to the questions raised by the play's complications. However, the distinction between *completed action* and *resolution*, as the terms are used in this text, is that the former refers to the creation of new conflicts by the way in which previous conflicts have been solved, while the latter refers to the final answers to the play's major complications. In *Macbeth*, many complications standing in the way of Macbeth's ambitions are resolved as the play progresses, but before the play is half over, we are made aware that a pattern has formed in which each of Macbeth's "successes" is really propelling him toward disaster. The major question of the plot becomes "To what end will the killing of his king bring Macbeth?" Essentially, the question is posed in the witches' prophecies to Macbeth and Banquo when, although the murder of Duncan is not mentioned, we are prepared for Macbeth's fruitless successes. Shakespeare forces our retrospective awareness of this by a second meeting of Macbeth and the witches just past the halfway point in the play, and by the final resolution of the prophecies of Birnam Wood and Macbeth's invulnerability to man born of woman. The resolution of *Macbeth*, then, concerns the final explanation of the witches' ambiguous predictions and the final consequences of Macbeth's criminal actions. What must not be overlooked, however, is the question raised at the beginning of the play, referred to regularly throughout the play, and finally resolved with the defeat of Macbeth. This is the question of the fate of Scotland, whose disintegration is inextricably linked to Macbeth's decisions and actions and whose salvation is made possible by the death of its tormentor. The major resolutions in Macbeth occur when the fates of Macbeth and of Scotland are determined.

The Super-Objective. This term originated in Stanislavski's first translated publication, *An Actor Prepares,* in which two chapters, "Units and Objectives" (VII) and "The Super-Objective" (XV), combine to explain the theory of the super-objective. Since then, directors and theorists have tended to use the term according to their own interpretations of its meaning. Despite Stanislavski's clear projection of the idea and purpose of analysis and synthesis, there is some confusion about the application of the term *super-objective*. Stanislavski is addressing the actor, and alternates between the objectives of characters and the main line of the play's action. Often, in fact, his examples of a play's super-objective prove to be the objective of its protagonist. Secondly, Stanislavski appears to alternate between a theme or a moral statement of a play and its main line of action, although this may be the result of the assumption that each will embody the other.

Harold Clurman translates Stanislavski's term as "super problem," but prefers in one essay to use Boleslavski's word "spine," and defines it as the "basic action of the play," or the play's "core."[6] In a later essay, Clurman shifts to the term "main action,"[7] but obviously is referring to the same principle. Clurman's summary explanation most closely explains what *super-objective* or its synonyms mean to most contemporary directors:

> All of this finally resolves itself into one question the director must ask himself: *What is the basic action of the play?* What is the play about from the standpoint of the characters' principal conflict? Every plot has a superficial resemblance to innumerable others. To give his play its specific meaning, the director must decide what fundamental desire does the plot of his play symbolize, what deep struggle gives it shape and direction. What is the play's *core*? For Gordon Craig, *Hamlet* is a story of a man's search for the truth. Saroyan's *My Heart's in the Highlands*, to its New York director, was the story of people eager to give things to one another—lovers all, in a sense. For me, Odets' *Night Music* had to do with the search for a home. Whether these formulations are correct or not, the point is that the director's most important task at first is to find the basic

line of the play . . . in one way or another, the director must be inspired in his actual stage "effects" by the "spine" which he has chosen for the play. It is the basis of the whole production.[8]

Regardless of Stanislavski's ambiguity in his explanation of the super-objective, it is clear that its importance lies in creating some kind of unity and synthesis, or sense of direction ("line of action"), out of the division created by breaking the play into units. Although he is speaking to the actor, Stanislavski could just as well be addressing the director when he says:

> The part and the play must not remain in fragments. A broken statue, or a slashed canvas, is not a work of art, no matter how beautiful its parts may be. It is only in the preparation of a role that we use small units. During its actual creation they fuse into large units. The larger and fewer the divisions, the less you have to deal with, the easier it is for you to handle the whole role.[9]

A play that is derived from history, such as *Macbeth,* might be concerned with any number of different actions or have any one of a number of purposes. It might be concerned with the life and times of King Macbeth and his wicked queen, or with the history of the struggle for Scotland's throne. Plays, however, are rarely this general, and a playwright, to create an absorbing "two hours traffic of our stage," is more likely to use history or biography toward certain ends in the framework of a concentrated "main" action, or super-objective. One method of accurately determining the super-objective is to proceed as we have done thus far: break the play into units, abstract the action or plot objectives, and determine the patterns created by these objectives. In *Macbeth*, the act divisions that have been applied provide us with a good way of synthesizing scenes into larger units, which then may be further synthesized into a conception of the play's super-objective.

Act	Action Objectives	Main Action
I	To defeat the enemy.	To pave the way for the
	To punish traitors and reward the valor of Macbeth.	murder of King Duncan by Macbeth.
	To provide hope for Macbeth's ambitions.	
	To overcome Macbeth's qualms about regicide.	
II	To kill Duncan.	To kill Duncan and remove
	To conceal evidence and shift the blame.	all obstacles to Macbeth's assumption of the throne.
	To throw suspicion on Malcolm and Donalbain.	

III	To eliminate Banquo.	To keep the throne securely.
	To initiate revolt against Macbeth (Fleance's escape, Macduff's desertion, reports of preparation for war in England and Ireland).	To begin counter-movement against Macbeth.
IV	To prepare Macbeth for his defense of the throne.	To justify the mounting opposition to the tyranny of Macbeth's kingship.
	To destroy the enemy, even their innocent families.	To unify the opposition.
	To strengthen opposition: Macduff's thirst for revenge; alliance with Edward.	
V	To build confrontation of battle. To remove all hope of earthly contentment for Macbeths (ultimately, death of Lady Macbeth and despair for Macbeth).	To defeat the Macbeths and restore the crown to its legitimate source.
	To eliminate hope of survival for Macbeth (desertions, Birnam Wood, Macduff—a man not "born of woman").	

When the five main actions are related the play's common denominator of action becomes the struggle for the throne of Scotland. For a "line of action," the struggle may be interpreted in two ways, one moral and one political. The moral action is stressed when the action is viewed as the rise and fall of the protagonist. Macbeth's major objective, as shall be discussed later, is "to capture and subsequently retain the throne with security." Macbeth's objectives closely define the main action of the play, except that the play moves beyond Macbeth's objectives to include his destruction, and in its plot structure to show the moral implications of Macbeth's desires. In the play, Macbeth commits a crime and wins the throne, then multiplies his crimes to protect his position, only to be defeated and punished at the end for his tyranny. There are no further complications after Macbeth's execution —action terminates with the death of Macbeth. Viewed this way, the play's action appears to be structured to emphasize an essentially moral action— one of crime and punishment, which might be summarized by Macbeth's

> . . . we but teach
> Bloody instructions, which being taught, return
> To plague the inventor. This even-handed justice
> Commends the ingredients of our poisoned chalice
> To our own lips.   (I, 7, lines 8–12)

Shakespeare's tragedy, however, is concerned in its overall action with more than the sin and punishment of Macbeth. The play's initial action deals with the military defense of Duncan's right to the throne, and proceeds to his brief victory: almost immediately, the plot moves on to his death and the crowning of his murderer. From this point until Macbeth's defeat the play concentrates on Macbeth's efforts to remain king of Scotland and his opponent's efforts to depose him. There is one more scene after the death of Macbeth, during which a new king is hailed. Viewed this way, the plot of *Macbeth* is designed to emphasize political action, the importance of which is further emphasized by the fact that the objective of every major character in the play is in some way related to the struggle for kingship.

The moral and political objectives of the play have been separated only for analysis. The action is actually a synthesis of the two; the play's political and moral objectives are fused into an action that depicts the effect of politics on morality, and the effect of morality on politics. In other words, *Macbeth* is not designed simply to depict the rise and fall of an evil and ambitious man and his partner in crime, nor is it organized only to depict a political struggle of which the Macbeths are a part. Instead the play's action follows the progression of the moral dissolution of both Macbeth and Scotland because of a struggle for power to the eventual restoration of political and moral order. Indeed the play's action may be said to be summarized by the spectacle and diction of its final scene (actually, its resolution), when Macbeth's bloody head is viewed against the patriot's acclamation of the victorious Malcolm, "compassed with [his] kingdom's pearl," and the pronouncement that "the time is free."[10]

CHARACTER

Before considering a directorial method of exploring character in drama, something should be said about the director's responsibilities in character and character development. Normally, one would think that characterization is principally the actor's job. In one sense, of course, it is. Ultimately, the actor is the sole expressor of character. However, the director may contribute to the selection of character attributes. The overt means of achieving this will be considered in the chapter that discusses working with the actor and the ensemble. Our concern at this point is with the director's preliminary work. First it should be recalled that this chapter is investigating the play's design. It is inconceivable to do this without a thorough consideration of character. Drama alone of all the arts must be concerned with the actions of men. Plays with the most simply developed characters still must depend on the selection of those attributes of character that make credible the development of a story dealing with human action. Through recognition of patterns formed by specific character traits and by the emphasis or lack of emphasis on character development, a director is able to relate character to the play's design as a whole. In other words, if a director is to control a play's unity, he must develop a clear conception of the relevance of all characters to that unity. The previously stated example of a Lady Capulet motivated by her love for Tybalt is a distortion that not only gives her a disproportionate emphasis, but creates a new myriad of relationships based on adultery which have little to do with the main action and themes of *Romeo and Juliet*.

Similarly when an actor is allowed to "steal" a scene, or a whole play, it frequently suggests that he has been permitted to make his role more important or more precocious than the writer had intended. To believe that the porter's role in *Macbeth* was created so that the groundlings could enjoy one of their favorite clowns rather than to contribute to the play's design is to place suppositions about theatrical history over the play's internal structure. Playing up the comic virtuosity of the actor for its own sake will clutter rather than illuminate the tragedy. An audience that departs with only the memory of that "funny drunk" will not have experienced Shakespeare's *Macbeth*. Unbelievable as it may seem, a recent professional production of *Hamlet* was dominated throughout by the feathered white satin-clad presence of Osric!

Conversely, directors often minimize, even cut out completely, the roles of some characters in the plays they direct. When a director is unable to justify the third murderer in *Macbeth*, the simplest solution is to cut him out altogether, thereby losing an important comment on the distrust and tyranny of Macbeth. Because they believe that the Malcolm–Macduff scene in Act IV, Scene 3, is too long and dull, many prominent directors have cut it down to its supposedly essential functions: Macduff's discovery of the slaughter of his family, and the strengthening of opposition to the protagonist. But what is lost? First, it can be a really interesting scene if played with a realization of its relevance to the political design of the play; perhaps more important, it is the only scene that clearly develops Malcolm's character. Without it, the final scene of the play loses its value, excitement, and even meaning, when a "faceless" Malcolm wins the prize.

An obvious, but somewhat easy to overlook, justification for a director's thorough investigation of the characters in a play is the fact that he is responsible for casting the play. The failure to have a good idea of what he is looking for may cause him major regrets when he discovers in the midst of rehearsals that he has made serious mistakes (see Part V, Chapter 1).

The Nature of Character in Drama. In dealing with character in plays, the director must first try to avoid imposing preconceived ideas or prejudices about human behavior. In the modern world, we tend to seek psychological motives for all behavior. It is difficult for us to accept the fact that a man may be evil simply because he has that inclination, that a miser or a religious hypocrite need not have his excesses explained, or that a novice nun can place her virginity above her brother's life and still win our sympathy. If we seek satisfactory causes for Macbeth's ambition and early conscience, or for Lady Macbeth's ambition for her husband and utter disregard of morality, we will be disappointed. This does not mean that Shakespeare has created unsatisfactory characters, nor does it mean that the director should help out such an "unenlightened" playwright with additional dialogue, or with "significant" signs of some special neurosis. In many of their plays, Ibsen, Strindberg, O'Neill, and Williams are interested in exploring what made the characters the way they are. Shakespeare and Molière generally are more interested in what they are and where it leads them. But all of these dramatic artists are concerned primarily in creating and developing characters that function in the play. Even in plays about the lives of real persons, biography for its own sake is rarely the objective. Instead, the playwright may invent and distort to emphasize the nature of a particular struggle or to relate some aspect of a life to a broader theme. Shakespeare's histories, as well as *Macbeth,* chiefly are concerned with actual persons and events, but they never become loose biographies that attempt to recreate the entire lives of characters or historically authentic events. Instead, these plays select and organize character through moral and political concerns theatrically conceived. The only valid way of comprehending the playwright's intentions in his creation of character is to study carefully the traits that are established in the play, to observe how these traits form patterns for each character, and to determine how such patterns relate to those of other characters in the play.

Finding Patterns of Characterization. Clues to characterization may be found in expository passages where the past life of a character might be narrated, in descriptions of the character by other characters in the play, and in what the character says and does. Probably the most thorough method of accumulating these clues is to review all discoveries about character in the "beats" or units of the play. If the units have been properly analyzed, many suggestions about character that might have been overlooked will be revealed. In *Macbeth,* Act III, Scene 3, a third murderer appears. Shakespeare is not particularly interested in defining him except as a murderer, but we are reminded that originally only two murderers were assigned to the disposal of Banquo and Fleance.

[*Enter three murderers*]
1. MURDERER: But who did bid thee join with us?
3. MURDERER: Macbeth.
2. MURDERER: He neds not our mistrust, since he delivers
    Our offices, and what we have to do,
    To the direction just.

In a footnote to this scene, one editor[11] has remarked, "The presence of the third murderer is not explained, but he is presumably 'the perfect spy o' the time' " (see III, 1, line 130). The other two murderers are surprised to see him, and are suspicious at first. But why has Macbeth found it necessary to send him? It is not unreasonable to conclude that because two murderers can do the job as well as three Macbeth has in truth mistrusted the first two and has sent a third as a spy. The sole purpose of the third murderer is to emphasize this development in Macbeth. To prove that this is no accident, Macbeth himself is made to comment after the banquet, "There's not a one of them [nobles of Scotland] but in his house/I keep a servant fee'd" (III, 4, lines 131–132). Shakespeare takes no chances on his audience missing the fact that Macbeth is turning into a first-rate tyrant. But most character suggestions are less subtle than this, and the unit method demonstrates quite nicely the mosaic fashion in which a writer's development of a character may be achieved.

Patterns Formed by Objectives. Perhaps the most important consideration in dealing with character in drama is to recognize that we are not dealing with portraits, nor with purely narrative description, but with characters in action or, in some plays, with characters in reaction. Physical action is not as important in great drama as behavioral action—that is, characters who are depicted in the process of choosing, resisting, struggling. A character is set into action by desire. He wants something or he desires to resist something, or he desires not to desire. But he cannot perform an action without either conscious or unconscious desires or motives. Dramatically, it is not enough to define a character by a collection of adjectives, such as (for Macbeth) ambitious, "full of the milk of human kindness," imaginative, having a strong conscience, fearful. These terms are apt, but they fail to indicate the active nature of the character; they fail to provoke the motives and justifications (sometimes called the *subtext*) that provide dimensional meaning to each scene in which the character participates.

The following abstract from Act I, Scene 3, of *Macbeth* illustrates the sense of motive or desire that lurks beneath the lines of the protagonist:

Dialogue	*Subtext for Macbeth*
MACBETH: So foul and fair a day I have not seen.	*How strange that on a day of victory, the air should appear so foul. Or, how unusual, or unreal, the atmosphere appears. Sees witches to whom Banquo refers and is struck by their peculiarity, too.*
BANQUO: How far is't called to Forres? What are these So withered, and so wild in their attire, That look not like the inhabitants o' the earth And yet are on 't? Live you? Or are you aught That man may question? You seem to understand me By each at once her choppy finger laying Upon her skinny lips. You should be women, And yet your beards forbid me to interpret That you are so.	

Dialogue	*Subtext for Macbeth*
MACBETH: Speak, if you can. What are you?	*I* want *to know who and what you are.* *(See Banquo's next speech to determine Macbeth's outward reaction, which is transparent because of the unexpected revelation by the witches.)*
1. WITCH: All hail, Macbeth! Hail to thee, thane of Glamis!	*"Thane of Glamis." Yes, that I am. Interesting that they should know.*
2. WITCH: All hail, Macbeth! Hail to thee, thane of Cawdor!	*"Thane of Cawdor"? What do they mean?*
3. WITCH: All hail, Macbeth, that shalt be king hereafter!	*"King hereafter!" How do they know that is what I want? Are they qualified to predict such things?*
BANQUO: Good sir, why do you start, and seem to fear Things that do sound so fair? I' the name of truth, Are ye fantastical, or that indeed Which outwardly ye show? My noble partner You greet with present grace and great prediction Of noble having and of royal hope, That he seems rapt withal. To me you speak not. If you can look into the seeds of time And say which grain will grow and which will not, Speak then to me, who neither beg nor fear Your favors nor your hate.	*I want to hear what they tell Banquo.*
1. WITCH: Hail!	
2. WITCH: Hail!	
3. WITCH: Hail!	
1. WITCH: Less than Macbeth, and greater.	*Why are they speaking in riddles?*
2. WITCH: Not so happy, yet much happier.	
3. WITCH: Thou shalt get kings, though thou be none.	*Banquo "get kings"? Will he stand in my way?*

Dialogue	*Subtext for Macbeth*
So all hail, Macbeth and Banquo!	
1. WITCH: Banquo and Macbeth, all hail!	
MACBETH: Stay, you imperfect speakers, tell me more, By Sinel's death, I know I am thane of Glamis, But how of Cawdor? The thane of Cawdor lives, A prosperous gentleman, and to be king Stands not within the prospect of belief, No more than to be Cawdor. Say from whence You owe this strange intelligence? Or why Upon this blasted heath you stop our way With such prophetic greeting? Speak I charge you.	*They are leaving. I want them to stay. I want to test them—to find out if what they say can be counted on. I want desperately to know!*
[Witches vanish.]	
BANQUO: The earth hath bubbles as the water has, And these are of them. Whither are they vanished?	*Oh, no! They're gone! Please come back!*
MACBETH: Into the air, and what seemed corporal melted As breath into the wind. Would they have stayed!	*How Strange! If only they stayed a moment longer. Will I see them again?*
BANQUO: Were such things here as we do speak about? Or have we eaten on the insane root That takes the reason prisoner?	
MACBETH: Your children shall be kings.	*I want Banquo to believe that I am pleased about their prediction concerning him. Will he get in the way?*
BANQUO: You shall be king.	

Dialogue	*Subtext for Macbeth*
MACBETH: And thane of Cawdor too. Went it not so?	*They also said "Cawdor."* *Think it's a joke?*
BANQUO: To the selfsame tune and words. Who's here?	
[Enter Ross and Angus.]	
ROSS: The king hath happily received, Macbeth, The news of thy success. And when he reads Thy personal venture in the rebels' fight, His wonders and his praises do contend Which should be thine or his. Silenced with that, In viewing o'er the rest o' the selfsame day, He finds thee in the stout Norweyan ranks, Nothing afeard of what thyself didst make, Strange images of death. As thick as hail Came post with post, and every one did bear Thy praises in his kingdom's great defense, And poured them down before him.	*I cannot rid the witches'* *prophecy from my mind. Try not* *to appear distracted.*
ANGUS: We are sent To give thee, from our royal master, thanks, Only to herald thee into his sight, Not pay thee.	
ROSS: And for an earnest of a greater honor, He bade me, from him, call thee thane of Cawdor. In which addition, hail, most worthy thane! For it is thine.	*"Thane of Cawdor"! They were* *right! How I hope they were* *right! Can they really predict* *the future? What about the* *kingship?*
BANQUO: What, can the devil speak true?	

| *Dialogue* | *Subtext for Macbeth* |

MACBETH: The thane of
    Cawdor lives.
    Why do you dress me
In borrowed robes?

What are the facts?

ANGUS: Who was the
    thane lives yet,
But under heavy judgment
    bears that life
Which he deserves to lose.
    Whether he was combined
With those of Norway, or did
    line the rebel
With hidden help and vantage,
    or that with both
He labored in his country's
    wreck,
    I know not.
But treasons capital, confessed
    and proved,
Have overthrown him.

MACBETH: [*Aside.*] Glamis, and
    thane of Cawdor.
The greatest is behind.
—Thanks for your pains.—
Do you hope your children
    shall be kings,
When those that gave the
    thane of Cawdor to me
Promised no less to them?

*So! It was true! One of the
difficult hurdles to the kingship
overcome!*

*But I must not let Banquo think
I am over-eager. I want him to
believe I am as much concerned
about his part in this.*

BANQUO: That trusted
    home,
Might yet enkindle you unto
    the crown,
Besides the thane of Cawdor.
    But 'tis strange.
And oftentimes, to win us to
    our harm,
The instruments of darkness
    tell us truths,
Win us with honest trifles, to
    betray 's
In deepest consequence.
Cousins, a word, I pray you.

*Yes, the crown! (From here,
Macbeth becomes preoccupied
with this idea and his thoughts
progress into the soliloquy that
follows.)*

MACBETH: [*Aside.*] Two truths
    are told
As happy prologues to the
    swelling act

*Two of their statements have
been proven true. This makes
me optimistic about the*

Dialogue	*Subtext for Macbeth*
Of the imperial theme.—	*Kingship—*
I thank you, gentlemen.—	*I had better thank them for the*
[*Aside.*] This	*news—How shall I take this?*
supernatural soliciting	*Is it good or bad. Can't be bad*
Cannot be ill, cannot be good.	*if it has partially gotten me what*
If ill,	*I want. But if it's good, why am*
Why hath it given me earnest	*I so appalled at the picture of*
of success,	*Duncan bloody and dead?*
Commencing in a truth? I am	*I wish I could dispose of these*
thane of Cawdor.	*visions that seem to overwhelm*
If good, why do I yield to that	*my desires. The murder that I*
suggestion	*imagine has so much power to*
Whose horrid image doth	*disrupt me that I believe it might*
unfix my hair	*prevent me from actually*
And make my seated heart	*doing it.*
knock at my ribs,	
Against the use of nature?	
Present fears	
Are less than horrible	
imaginings.	
My thought, whose murder	
yet is but fantastical,	
Shakes so my single state of	
man that function	
Is smothered in surmise, and	
nothing is	
But what is not.	
BANQUO: Look how our	
partner's rapt.	
MACBETH: [*Aside.*] If chance	*Perhaps—I wish it could be so*
will have me King, why,	*—I won't have to kill. Let*
chance may crown me,	*chance decide.*
Without my stir.	

In this scene, Macbeth's fundamental desires are quite clearly delineated. He is ambitious. He wants to be king of Scotland. The witches' prophecy has brought his secret ambitions to the surface; they have begun to win him to their "harm," whereby, as Banquo's reaction to these evil spirits suggests, "The instruments of darkness tell us truths,/Win us with honest trifles, to betray 's/In deepest consequence."

The analysis of character should proceed this way throughout the play, and each scene should provide us with a conclusion concerning the character's objectives until, when we have concluded our analysis, we are ready to synthesize all of the major objectives of a character into a recognizable pattern. Until the murder, Macbeth's overwhelming desire is to secure the throne. After the murder, as he already has given his "eternal jewel" to "the common enemy of man," he acts unscrupulously to protect his new-won position.

Patterns Formed by Response to Obstacles. Obviously, even in a concentrated, heightened form such as drama, it would be shallow to believe that a character is defined merely by his desires. A man can be ambitious, but not be a Macbeth. Sophocles' Antigone and Molière's Alceste both wish to cling to a principle without compromise, but they are quite different in character, and we respond by admiring the one and laughing at the other. Men share common desires, but their natures are determined not merely by what they want, but by how they cope with the obstacles that stand in their way. This is particularly relevant in drama where men's actions, the essential ingredient of conflict, are the result of man responding to obstacles. Just as the dramatist will create a pattern that forces us to recognize a character's motives, he also will create a pattern of responses to whatever may stand in the way of the character's goals. Character then becomes the consistency of responses to obstacles. A man is shrewd if he consistently uses his wits to get his way, bestial if he relies on physical force, unscrupulous if he disregards morality, a coward if he runs away, stupid if he miscalculates with ludicrous regularity, will-less if he does nothing, choleric if he rages, weak and contemptible if he whimpers with self-pity, and so on.

In *Macbeth*, the central character is complex because his desires pull him in different directions. His major obstacles reside within himself. His desire to become King of Scotland triumphs over his inclinations to avoid the criminal means that appear necessary if he is to achieve his goal. In his very first scene, he shudders at the images of murder, and agrees to allow "chance" to find the way. Until the murder is committed, Macbeth fluctuates between conflicting desires, the more evil of which is spurred by his determined wife. It actually is necessary to study the conflicting desires as objectives and obstacles at the same time. But it is sufficient to begin with his desire for the throne, and to observe the following obstacles, which are clearly and consistently drawn:

1. *Imagination.* "Present fears/Are less than horrible imaginings." His visions of the "horrid image," or of "Heaven's cherubin horsed/Upon the sightless couriers of the air" are vivid enough to give Macbeth pause and temper his ambition early in the play. The dagger speech beautifully expresses his inability to control the power of his imagination. "Mine eyes," he must admit, "are made the fools o' the other senses," and he extends the darkness of his particular intent to "the one half-world" where "Nature seems dead, and wicked dreams abuse/The curtained sleep."

2. *Conscience.* Shakespeare leaves little doubt in the reader's mind that Macbeth is fully aware of the evil of murder, especially regicide. Act I, Scene 7, does little to advance the plot of the play; instead it emphasizes the great

71

struggle within Macbeth between success and the numerous sins he would be committing. He is Duncan's kinsman, and his host "who should against his murderer shut the door,/Not bear the knife myself." In addition, Duncan has been a good king. Macbeth has no provocation to remove him except "vaulting ambition," which is scarcely a moral justification for regicide.

3. *Transparency.* "Your face my thane," says his wife to Macbeth, "is as a book where men/May read strange matters." Later, aware of this problem, Macbeth reminds himself to "mock the time with fairest show./False face must hide what the false heart doth know."

4. *Integrity.* All of the preceding "obstacles" must be considered a part of Macbeth's finer qualities as a man before he totally submits to the "imperial theme." At first we are told of a man who is a great warrior, loyal to his king and courageously risking his life in battle to defend Duncan's rule. Lady Macbeth fears his nature:

> It is too full o' the milk of human kindness
> To catch the nearest way. Thou wouldst be great;
> Art not without ambition, but without
> The illness [wickedness] should attend it. What thou wouldst highly,
> That wouldst thou holily—wouldst not play false,
> And yet wouldst strongly win.   (I, 5)

5. *Fear.* It is interesting that Macbeth, the great warrior, should shudder at the vision of another killing. His imagination linked with conscience "shakes" his inner "state of man." Less admirable is his fear of the consequences of the act. He is aware of a universal moral order that goes beyond civil law. While willing to risk salvation in the next world (hardly an admirable trait to the Elizabethan Christian), he worries about the "judgment here" and about "this even-handed justice/[which] Commends the ingredients of our poisoned chalice/To our own lips." In the same soliloquy, his imagination creates the image of all nature informing the world of the "horrid deed."

Because all of these obstacles are internal, representing for the most part Macbeth's better nature, the obstacles themselves contribute to the formation of Macbeth's character. At first he is not a wicked or ruthless man. Ambition burns more strongly in him than in others, but temptation in itself is human and harmless as long as one is able to keep it under control. But Macbeth loses control to forces that, when scrutinized, tell us even more about the character as Shakespeare has created him.

1. *Opportunity.* We may assume that Macbeth has always been ambitious, but he has done little to satisfy that trait. The witches' prophecy provides the spark. Macbeth believes that his ambition is justified by the forces of "fate and metaphysical aid" as Lady Macbeth suggests. The prophecy

provides confidence, and fate seems to have offered the perfect opportunity for Duncan's murder. The king, with complete trust in his noble subject, decides to honor Macbeth with an overnight visit in his household.

2. *Lady Macbeth and her challenges.* Even with opportunity, however, Macbeth appears to have decided by the end of his soliloquy at the opening of Act I, Scene 7: "We will proceed no further in this business." The rest of this scene is crucial, not simply because it determines the fate of every important character in the play, but because it examines the means by which Lady Macbeth is able to combat all of Macbeth's arguments and better judgment. These means, used by a woman who understands her husband, reveal to us additional facets of Macbeth's character.

From her first appearance, Lady Macbeth is clearly confident of her ability to influence her husband. We see his devotion as he confides fully in her and addresses her as "my dearest partner of greatness," "my dearest love," "love," "dear wife," and "dearest chuck." But Macbeth is not a will-less or henpecked husband. Lady Macbeth must rely on more than his love or the strength of her determination over his. She must persuade him and, to do so, appeals to a weak chink in his armor: the challenge to his manhood. She begins by contemptuously accusing him of cowardice, using unflattering images of drunkenness and comparing him to the "poor cat i' the adage," who would eat fish but not wet her feet. Playing on his devotion to her, she suggests that his love must be as undependable as is the discrepancy between his ambition and his will to satisfy it. Macbeth responds with exactly the right answer when he defends his manhood on moral grounds: "I dare do all that may become a man./Who dares do more is none." But Lady Macbeth will have none of this. A man, she suggests, keeps his promises (no matter how immoral) to his wife, and is brave enough to go after what he wants (no matter how immorally): "When you durst do it, then you were a man,/And, to be more than what you were, you would/Be so much more the man." She then follows this up brilliantly by using herself as an example. She chooses the most womanly of all female acts, "giving suck," and insists that rather than break a promise, she would "while [her baby] was smiling in my face,/Have plucked my nipple from his boneless gums/And dashed the brains out."

Macbeth now weakens and needs only to be reassured that the plan will succeed; this Lady Macbeth achieves with skill. No football coach ever gave a better pep talk during half-time. Macbeth, inspired, contributes to the male references of the scene when he says admiringly, "Bring forth men-children only,/For thy undaunted mettle should compose/Nothing but males." After this, Macbeth needs no more prompting from his wife for the kill.

Although Macbeth is aware of the nature of sin and guilt, ultimately he lacks the will and moral fiber to overcome temptation. The single scene in which he submits to the false logic of his wife and allows erroneous conceptions of manhood to replace his professed Christian values completes for us the character of Macbeth before the murder.

Significance of Change in Character.   Growth and change by characters in drama vary in degree according to the play and the overall intentions of the playwright. In many melodramas, characters do not change, although their circumstances do. In tragedy, change most frequently occurs near the end of the play when a final catastrophe is accompanied by new self-awareness. In *Macbeth*, however, the central character achieves his chief ambition before the play is one-third completed, and already has expressed full awareness of the nature of his crime and its possible consequences.

New obstacles present themselves after the coronation of the Macbeths. They consist of:

1. The prophecy concerning Banquo's line.
2. Macduff's escape.
3. The military attack against Macbeth's reign.
4. The moving of Birnam Wood, which shakes Macbeth's faith in the witches' prophecy.

With the fact of the murder replacing Macbeth's apprehensions of it, his character begins to change. His new objective is to keep the prize he has won. Now the obstacles are chiefly forces outside rather than within Macbeth, and his manner of dealing with these new forces as the newly crowned king of Scotland reveals a Macbeth in the process of significant alterations.

At the beginning of Act III, Macbeth has become worried and sullen. He is now prepared, *without qualms*, to protect his position. He also begins to act alone, no longer confiding his plans to his wife. In response to the "threat" of Banquo and Fleance, he employs assassins to murder them. There is no hesitation now, no troubled conscience—although he retains a degree of sensitivity and remorse when he admits his fall from grace with "mine eternal jewel/Given to the common enemy of man." The apparition of Banquo's ghost is an extension of his former conscience and imagination, but this is to be the last sign of those qualities. With Macduff's escape, he is determined to act without scruple or hesitation, and orders the cold-blooded murder of Macduff's wife and children. By the last act, Macbeth's dehumanization is complete:

> I have almost forgot the taste of fears.
> The time has been my senses would have cooled
> To hear a night-shriek, and my fell of hair
> Would at a dismal treatise rousè and stir
> As life were in 't. I have supped full with horrors.
> Direness, familiar to my slaughterous thoughts,
> Cannot once start me.   (V, 5)

When informed of his wife's death, he responds that she would have died sooner or later and broods on life as a "tale told by an idiot." Despair, the deadliest of the seven sins, has gripped him; he has "risked the life to come" and is losing. He can no longer command the loyalty of his troops because of his cruel, tyrannical treatment of them. Regardless of his "I 'gin to be aweary of the sun,/And wish the estate o' the world were now undone," the last prediction that has not yet been proven false, his invulnerability to any man of woman born, sparks his determination to fight on. But with the discovery that Macduff "was from his mother's womb/Untimely ripp'd," Macbeth completely loses his confidence, and has no alternative but to fight a last desperate battle with his adversary. In the play's beginning, we were presented with a warrior who fought bravely and loyally for his king; at the play's end, we perceive the same man fearing to fight ("it hath cowed my better part of man!") and finally doing so because he fears even more the consequences of not fighting. This must generate echoes of Act I, Scene 7, where the nature of "man" had been argued. The play delineates, morally, spiritually, even militarily, the unmanning of its central character. Lady Macbeth, to strengthen her resolve, had demanded in her first scene, "unsex me here," and in Act I, Scene 7 she further defeminizes herself when she places a criminal promise above her functions as a mother. Macbeth, in submitting to her argument, only succeeds in "unsexing" himself, as the consequences of his choice reveal.

Spine.   Almost all plays share the kind of character progression that has been demonstrated with *Macbeth*. A character is shaped by the consistency of his desires and the pattern formed by his manner of responding to obstacles. In *Macbeth*, Shakespeare intends with his central character to delineate the moral and spiritual disintegration of a noble man. This conception of the character's purpose is important for the director to know, but it is not useful to the actor unless it is stated in terms of an action that pulls together, or fuses, all of his objectives in the play. When his characteristics are viewed separately, a character may become too diffuse. The actor may capably perform the separate emotions and attitudes of his character, but the character will be disconnected and lack an identity, unless he can find a way of relating all qualities to a consistent line of action. The action that gives a character his essential unity has been called by names, including "spine," "inner motivating force," and "super-objective."

In *Macbeth*, it was observed that Macbeth's major objectives are divided into two parts. In the first two acts, he wants to become king, and in the balance of the play he wants to protect the crown he has criminally managed to win. These objectives may be combined into a statement such as "I wish to gain the crown and never relinquish it under any circumstances," but this neglects one of Macbeth's most characteristic needs. From the first, he is obsessed with safety. To paraphrase his qualms, something like the following might emerge: "If only I could become king without these horrible visions!" "Never mind eternity, what about the consequences here?" "If we fail?" (I, 7) And following the murder: "To be thus is nothing,/ But to be safely thus" (III, 1). "Banquo and Fleance threaten me. Eliminate them. Don't trust anyone: use spies; get spies to spy on spies." "Macduff threatens me. Get him out of the way and destroy his family, too." "Find the witches again to see if you are safe." "Birnam Wood and no man of woman born! I can do anything for I am protected!" As the play begins, Macbeth is a soldier who fights without fear for his personal safety. However, his direction, as far as the play is concerned, begins with his response to the witches' tempting words. From then on, his ambition is accompanied by the equally strong desire to be safe. A more accurate statement about spine by the actor playing Macbeth would probably be "I wish to capture and subsequently retain the throne without endangering myself." Another way of stating this, which would include Shakespeare's moral concerns, might be: "I must overcome 'all that may become a man.'" This has an ironic validity that encompasses Macbeth's progression throughout the play. He must sacrifice his Christian scruples to become king; but he has failed to anticipate that his loss will be permanent; he has failed to anticipate the beast to come.

Physical Characteristics. The physical aspects of character are also important and must be related to those characteristics influencing and influenced by behavior. This will be dealt with in a later chapter about casting the play.

Finding the Pattern in Character Relationships. A character or a point of view may sometimes be illuminated by an awareness of the writer's use of contrast or parallels between the various personages in his plays. In *King Lear*, Goneril and Regan are contrasted to Cordelia, as is Edmund to Edgar. Lear and Gloucester are paralleled as erratic parents whose misfortunes result from their relationships to their offspring. Because these are the major characters in the play and the comparisons are obvious as well as important to plot and character, a vital aspect of Shakespeare's intentions clearly was to deal with parent-child and sibling relationships. Molière frequently selects characters to represent two extremes, with a normative character in between. In *The Misanthrope*, Alceste stands at one extreme as the rebel against a corrupt society, while Célimène and most of her admirers are its most typical representatives. In between are the moderates, Philinte and Eliante, who are aware of the excesses of the fashionable life of the court but who sanely attempt to live with it. A deliberate pattern is created to deal with the complex issues of the rebel and society.

Several such patterns already have been suggested for *Macbeth*. Macbeth's moral awareness is contrasted to Lady Macbeth's determination to suppress it. His sensitive and imaginative responses to murder and regicide are balanced by her callousness, his "weakness" by her demon-strength. Although Lady Macbeth's function in the plot is to propel her husband toward crime, it is apparent that Shakespeare has gone beyond plot necessities in creating her. The "male" motif so strongly developed in *Macbeth* is amplified by the delineation of her character.

> Come you spirits
> That tend on mortal thoughts, unsex me here,
> and fill me from the crown to the toe topfull
> Of direst cruelty!   (I, 5)

She has defeminized, "unmanned" herself here, and will use this commitment to infect her husband. She represents early in the play the self-dehumanization to which Macbeth will be subjected later in the play.

The Macbeth–Lady Macbeth design might be sufficient to inform us that Shakespeare is vitally concerned with the nature of man and of evil, but the briefest analysis of the remaining major characters in the play demonstrates that their character traits are selected and designed on a similar basis. Of the remaining characters, Shakespeare emphasizes the three men most closely related to the throne: Duncan, Banquo, and Malcolm. He appears to be concerned principally with the character of kings or those who aspire to that position. They form a pattern for an "imperial theme." Duncan is as uncomplicated a character as one may discover in drama; he is little more than a good, venerable old king. Banquo and Malcolm are developed more, but not to the extent of comparable roles, such as Claudius or Gloucester, in other plays. Banquo accompanies Macbeth in the first confrontation with the witches. On one level this is necessary because the prophecies include the information that Banquo and his descendants will threaten Macbeth's claim to the throne of Scotland. But Shakespeare does more than this, and we must inquire about his motives. Banquo, unlike Macbeth, is aware of the possibility of deception when dealing with such spirits. Only a corruptible man will rationalize that their predictions are the absolute workings of fate, will justify evil means in seeking an "inevitable" end, or will be encouraged by beings who could well be employed by the "fiend/That lies like truth." Banquo's morally correct reaction emphasizes Macbeth's morally corrupted judgment. To be sure that we do not miss the point, Shakespeare plots another scene between Banquo and Macbeth, in which Banquo responds to Macbeth's hint, "If you shall cleave to my consent, when 'tis,/It shall make honor for you," with

> So I lose none [honor]
> In seeking to augment it, but still keep
> My bosom franchised and allegiance clear,
> I shall be counselled.   (II, 1)

Malcolm is developed purely as a potential king who concentrates solely on the virtues and responsibilities of the true monarch. Act IV, Scene 3, is lengthy, but does little to advance the action of the play. It reveals how, in a time of treachery, the wise king must test even his allies. In the process it enumerates the qualities of the true king, qualities that Malcolm pretends to lack in testing Macduff's allegiance to goodness. Note how this also reiterates the repeated theme of deception in the play.

During this scene, a character who never appears is made an important part of the discussion. Shortly after Malcolm's reference to the "devilish Macbeth," a doctor enters to announce a "heavenly" cure made by Edward, King of England.[12] There follows a glowing report of the actions, which "speak him full of grace." Later in Act V, Scene 2, the healing image is repeated, but this time in terms of the cure for the "illness" that Macbeth has perpetrated against Scotland. "Meet we," says Caithness, "the medicine of the sickly weal,/And with him pour we in our country's purge/Each drop of us." To which Lennox replies, "Or so much as it needs/To dew the sovereign flowers and drown the weeds." Thus Edward's virtue is linked to Malcolm's and contrasted to Macbeth's wickedness. Finally, in relating the moral nature of man as it is developed in Macbeth as well as in other characters to the moral responsibilities of the ideal monarch, we are guided toward the political-moral principle, which forms one of the "higher purposes" of character in this play.

The value of such investigation of character by the director of *Macbeth* cannot be overestimated. Recognizing the design created by character traits contributes mightily toward conclusions about the playwright's intentions, but the process also makes the director aware of the special significance of each character, which ultimately will contribute toward appropriate expression in performance.

LANGUAGE

. Language is the source of a play's dramatic expression. Combinations of words in the dialogue may be merely literal, that is, they may be created in the simplest, most direct fashion to tell a story. But we have observed the important relationship that exists between language and style, and the manner in which the various theatrical modes of expression are inspired by the writer's use of language. Of additional importance to the director is his awareness of the relationship between language and mood, language and character, and language and thought.

Language and Mood.   We usually are informed about the locale or environment in which the action of a play is set by allusions in the dialogue. "This castle hath a pleasant seat," says Duncan as Act I, Scene 6 of *Macbeth* begins. Many writers attempt to suggest more than a mere physical environment, however. They are often more concerned with emotional climates, with atmospheres that enhance the mood or feeling in which a scene takes place. The colors, the shapes, and the manner of illumination of a setting, whether presentational or representational, will be influenced by the atmospheric suggestions of the language. Through the same stimulus, the visual and audible effects of the action of each scene should be controlled by the director for their atmospheric qualities as well as for their contributions to plot or character.

Few plays compare with *Macbeth* in the creation of deliberate atmospheric effects through language. Duncan's simple statement informing us where he is also informs us how pleasant it is: "The air/Nimbly and sweetly recommends itself/Unto our gentle senses," to which Banquo adds:

> This guest of summer,
> This temple-haunting martlet, does approve
> By his loved mansionry that the heaven's breath
> Smells wooingly here. No jutty, frieze,
> Buttress, nor coign of vantage but this bird
> Hath made his pendent bed and procreant cradle.
> Where they most breed and haunt, I have observed
> The air is delicate.   (I, 6)

In the modern theatre, light and sound might be used to reinforce the sweet and gentle atmosphere that is suggested. The characters are stimulated by such an environment as well as by their victory and their expectations of a loving welcome and longed-for comfort. Actors and director must strive to bathe this brief scene with warmth and conviviality. To regard this scene in isolation would be to miss the more dynamic and significant aspects of its mood.

The play begins with the witches' exposition of "fog and filthy air," and moves to the bloody and violent atmosphere of war, then returns to the witches' meeting with Macbeth, who pronounces, "So foul and fair a day I have not seen." From here we move to the more joyous atmosphere of victory and then to the misleadingly pleasant environs of Macbeth's castle. The first act seems to move from foul to fair, but the scene of Duncan's arrival is only deceptively fair. It has been preceded by Lady Macbeth's reference to "this night's great business;" the "pleasant seat" proves to be deceptive, for it will be the gate to hell. Indeed, the language from this point contains repeated references to hell. "Hear it not, Duncan," says Macbeth of the ringing bell, "for it is a knell/That summons thee to Heaven, or to Hell." The owl shrieks, the crickets cry. The porter is a parody of the porter at hell's gate. The hellish chaos that invades the earth with the murder of Duncan is expressed in Ross's conversation with the Old Man in Act II, Scene 4:

> Thou seest the heavens, as troubled with man's act,
> Threaten his bloody stage. By the clock 'tis day.
> And yet dark night strangles the traveling lamp.
> Is 't night's predominance, or the day's shame,
> That darkness does the face of earth entomb
> When living light should kiss it?

The rest of the play is "murky," shrouded by images of darkness, death, and gloom. Its color is red, the image of blood, repeated again and again against the blackness. No setting, no lighting effect could ever hope to match the feeling created by Macbeth's

> Now o'er the one half-world
> Nature seems dead, and wicked dreams abuse
> The curtained sleep. Witchcraft celebrates
> Pale Hecate's offerings, and withered murder,
> Alarumed by his sentinel, the wolf,
> Whose howl 's his watch, thus with his stealthy pace
> With Tarquin's ravishing strides, toward his design
> Moves like a ghost. Thou sure and firm-set earth,
> Hear not my steps, which way they walk, for fear
> Thy very stones prate of my whereabout,
> And take the present horror from the time,
> Which now suits with it.   (II, 1)

More will be said later about the relationship between atmosphere and meaning.

Language and Character.   In most plays with well-drawn characters it is possible to recognize which character is speaking even if the name of the speaker is concealed. Status and education will be revealed principally by the grammar, vocabulary, and precision of the speech given each character. In Shakespeare, verse and prose are often used to differentiate the noble from the common man. The drunkenness and coarseness of the porter in *Macbeth* requires one of the few uses of prose in the entire play. Emotion versus cool-headedness, wit versus dullness, verbosity versus brevity are all aspects of character that are structured by the language provided characters in drama. Compare Macbeth's emotional, image-packed speeches in the first third of the play to Lady Macbeth's unimaginative, coldly calculated language.

Changes in a character may be identified by significant changes in his manner of speech. Lady Macbeth moves from a controlled blank verse to the irrational prose of her sleepwalking scene. Macbeth, when he gives up his soul, loses the capacity of conscience or imagination (possibly his good angels—the better part of man) to fight evil. His language loses its former capacity for metaphor, striking images, and allusions. The Macbeth who says in Act V, Scene 3, "The mind I sway by and the heart I bear/Shall never sag with doubt nor shake with fear," and who curses an innocent servant with "The devil damn thee black, thou cream-faced loon!/Where got'st thou that goose look?" is a different Macbeth than the one who complained to his wife in Act II, Scene 2, "Methought I heard a voice cry 'Sleep no more! /Macbeth does murder sleep'—the innocent sleep,/Sleep that knits up the raveled sleeve of care."

Another quality of language may be of great importance to the director in stimulating the actor. He may encourage the actor to allow himself to be affected physically, emotionally, and vocally by the images created by language. A recent trend in interpreting Shakespeare and poetic drama has been to insist that the actor read his lines as swiftly and as neutrally as possible, so that the words themselves may affect the audience. There are, at the root of this approach, certain attitudes. One is that it is old-fashioned and "hammy" for the actor to "color" words. Another is that, in poetic drama, such coloring can only be distracting because emotions and images are best conveyed by the words themselves, unhampered by inflection, tone, or any of the other methods used by the actor to suggest feeling or attitude. One has only to witness such attempts at "neutrality" to realize how dull and unexciting they can be. Even reading Shakespeare silently, one hears in his inner ear the vocal qualities of the poetry. An actor always expresses. If he chooses neutrality in a line reading, then the listener assumes a neutrality of attitude on the part of the character. If the lines indicate strong emotions but are read neutrally, the only consequence will be contradictions that confuse the audience. The character of Macbeth is *not* neutral during his vivid, horrid imaginings, and the words will *not* take care of themselves without an accompanying sense of the actor believably responding to those imaginings.

A director can help an actor considerably by providing images that may stimulate the appropriate feelings or expression in a scene. In Chekhov's *The Three Sisters*, characters come in from the cold in the second act, and in the third act everyone is tired and exhausted because of a fire in the middle of the night. Although a good actor's sense and emotion memory should serve him, the director suggests consistency by the degree of heat or exhaustion, and aids the actors in finding and selecting the *kind* of reactions that will be varied and appropriate. One of his methods, rather than demonstrating with gestures or vocal techniques, is suggesting actual experiences and qualities that may stimulate cold and exhaustion. Even the best actors may benefit from proddings to their sensory and emotional recall. The beauty of dramatic poetry is that the dramatist himself provides unique and provocative images in his language to which the actor should respond. Frequently, the director must remind an actor that he is not visualizing or experiencing the images, causing his reading to be dull or meaningless. "What do these words make you *see*?" the director first asks the actor; then, "How does what you see make you feel?" Then "What does what you feel make you want to do?"

When Shakespeare wrote Macbeth's soliloquy in Act I, Scene 7, he could have created a much simpler and more direct statement. Beginning with line 12, "He's here in double trust," Macbeth might have said, "There are good reasons for my not killing Duncan. I am his relative and his subject. As his host, it would not be proper. Besides he's been a good king, and it wouldn't be long before everybody knew I killed him. My only justification is ambition, which will probably lead to no good end." But Shakespeare, in getting these points across, is not satisfied with mere argumentation. Instead he loads the speech with images and metaphors. One of his reasons, of course, is to characterize Macbeth's way of thinking through his problem and to probe Macbeth's feeling about the problem. The actor and director should work on this speech by concentrating as carefully as possible on the images created by the language, then allowing their impact to create honest responses to them (Table 2).

Language and Thought.   With the exploration of the ways in which language is used to influence character and mood, it should be apparent that language at the same time contributes to our feeling and awareness of the writer's thought—his emphasis upon attitudes about life, or a world view. In many contemporary realistic or naturalistic plays that are dominated by attitudes, opinions, or ideas concerning man's relationship to his cosmos or some aspect of it, thought is expressed directly in the arguments of the characters. In *The Caine Mutiny Court-Martial,* for example, arguments during the trial and Greenwald's long lecture in the banquet scene include direct statements about the meaning of responsibility during war. Of course, all aspects of the play's structure are directly related to this, but the playwright resorts to direct argumentation and rhetoric, too. In some other plays indirect argumentation is stressed. The naturalist usually prefers to avoid presenting a structured thesis so as to create the illusion of life untampered with. Chekhov's characters often argue at some length about the meaning of life, but they are either wrong, or rationalizing, or too impotent to practice what they preach. It is rare, too, that Chekhov, when he permits certain arguments to become part of the pattern of his plays, provides us with any solutions. What comes through is a sense of the imperfection of man: his lack of will, his self-contradictions, his inability to communicate effectively, the discrepancy between his ideals and his ability (or even desire) to act on them.

Although prose plays such as Ibsen's *Ghosts* use patterns of words, images, and metaphors to deepen our responses to their thought, such methods naturally are more predominant in poetic drama. Studies of the contribution of language patterns to the meaning of a play are fairly recent and began with the exploration of Shakespeare's imagery. But this method of dramaturgy was used in the earliest extant tragedies. In his *Agamemnon*, Aeschylus uses consistent metaphorical patterns, such as the allusions to trapping. His principals are compared to animals such as eagles and lions, and he relates these repeatedly to traps, lairs, nets. When these are considered in relation to what happens in the play, our awareness of fate, morality, justice, and world order is poetically intensified. The language has deepened our feelings, our subjective awareness, of Aeschylus' world view in a manner that the same story dramatized in straightforward prose could not.

To illustrate, some of the language–thought patterns in *Macbeth* will be discussed. It should be kept in mind, however, that such discussion cannot fully be developed in a directing text. Entire books deal with the language of single plays of Shakespeare, and *Macbeth* has been the subject of numerous articles probing its imagery. Here, rather than dealing with every language pattern in the play, certain emphatic language–thought patterns will be noted and their significance stressed.

In Act V, Scene 1, the doctor attending Lady Macbeth states that "unnatural deeds/Do breed unnatural troubles." He is in effect summarizing the intent of the play's action and character depiction. At the same time his use of "unnatural" echoes the play's many allusions to nature: to the nature of man, and to the connection between his nature and the nature of the cosmos. Repeated references, both literal and figurative, to darkness (night, blackness, death), to sleep, and to sickness may be channeled into the broader stream of a conception of nature.

The repeated references to what was called "the male motif" were noted previously in the discussion of character. Lady Macbeth "unsexes" herself when she sacrifices her natural function as a woman, which is not merely biological, but essentially moral since she wishes her unsexing to fill her with "direst cruelty." She asks that "no compunctious visitings of nature [natural pity]/Shake my fell purpose." We have seen how this relates to the argument about "what becomes a man," and have noted the pattern of dehumanizing action, or the consequences of the complete rejection of Christian criteria for man's nature. In the process, the characters submit themselves to the power of darkness. Macbeth appeals, "Let not light see my black and deep desires"; Lady Macbeth demands "the blanket of the dark" and "thick night" to hide their evil deeds; Macbeth orders a "sealing night" to "scarf up the tender eye of pitiful day" (II, 2) and observes a moment later that "good things of day begin to droop and drowse/While night's black agents to their preys do rouse." In this pattern, blackness, darkness, and night representing evil are summoned willfully by the protagonists to replace the natural with the unnatural, to replace "fair" with "foul."

The Macbeths' success in this regard has unnatural consequences, which are expressed partly by their evolution into monsters, but are most subjectively expressed by the play's sleep imagery. "Wicked dreams abuse the curtain'd sleep" (II, 1); "Sleep no more! Macbeth does murder sleep" (II, 2). "They sleep/In the affliction of these terrible dreams/That shake us nightly," and Macbeth observes ironically, "Better be with the dead,/Whom we, to gain our peace, have sent to peace,/Than on the torture of the mind to lie/In restless ecstasy" (III, 2). He "lack[s] the season of all natures, sleep" (III, 4), and paralleling "Macbeth shall sleep no more," Lady Macbeth is ultimately tortured into somnambulism ("a great perturbation in nature"). This meaningful and apparently deliberate design should enrich the potential for characterization, but it also demonstrates that Shakespeare is concerned with delineating man's loss of inner peace when he surrenders his better nature.

The torment of sleeplessness is represented, too, as a kind of sickness of the spirit. "More needs she the divine than the physician," says Lady Macbeth's doctor. The sickness of the spirit of the usurper, the criminal king, creates, quite clearly, the sickness of the kingdom. Another doctor is

TABLE 2

THE ACTOR'S RESPONSES TO MACBETH'S SOLILOQUY

The Speech and Its Images	Visualizing or Thinking	Responding
He's here in double trust.	See Duncan in your mind's eye—perhaps as he enjoys your hospitality in the next room.	Growing conviction, perhaps disappointment, at these strong arguments.
First as I am his kinsman and his subject / Strong both against the deed. / Then as his host, / Who should against his murderer shut the door, / Not bear the knife myself.	See yourself defending Duncan, perhaps with a sword. See the knife—or the same sword in your own hand—in a different light, not for Duncan's defense but to be plunged into him.	
Besides, this Duncan / Hath borne his faculties so meek, hath been / So clear in his great office,	See Duncan again, but now in all his purity and sweetness. An image of Christ—or of a *similar* person of goodness in the actor's own experience.	A sense of admiration, but with regret—"If only this man was not too good to kill!"
that his virtues / Will plead like angels trumpet-tongued against / The deep damnation of his taking off.	The actor must see the angels, must hear the loud shrill blast of trumpets arousing the populace. He must also recognize that this is the response of heaven to taking a life without permitting Duncan a final confession.	A beginning of awe and fear at the vision. Physically Macbeth begins actually to see above him what he is describing.

And pity, like a naked new-born babe,
Striding the blast, or Heaven's
    cherubin horsed
Upon the sightless couriers of the
    air,
Shall blow the horrid deed in every
    eye,
That tears shall drown the wind.

See the heavens open up, the naked new-born babe, or the typical cherubin of Renaissance painting, riding on gales of wind, forcing by their sound and fury hordes of people to respond to the murder of Duncan with an even louder keening.

The images and sounds have become so vivid that they almost blind and deafen the awestruck, fear-ridden Macbeth.

Macbeth must subdue his imagination, and pull himself together. Then acknowledge the consequence of his vision.

Pause before next line.

        I have no spur
To prick the sides of my intent, but
    only
Vaulting ambition, which o'erleaps
    itself
And falls on the other.

Envision a horse as his "intent," his inability to "spur" it on. Instead he as the rider makes the error of overleaping, and collapsing on the other side.

Quietly, keenly depressed and disappointed at the justice he has forced himself to recognize. Bitterly ironic.

introduced in Act V to report on Edward's miraculous cures, and, as it has previously been noted, the metaphor of sickness and healing is applied to governing. The good ruler is the doctor who must get rid of the infection (the tyrant) by his medicine (might and right) and restore good health to the body (Scotland). With this metaphor, Shakespeare illuminates the relationship between the ruler and his country, between his spiritual health and the spiritual health of those he governs.

Shakespeare does not limit the play to the political consequences of the actions of men; he also includes the cosmological consequences. "Nature" is extended to include the forces of nature operating in the universe. The elements, the normal functionings of the physical world, are so linked to man's action that the malfunctioning of man's nature, especially when he occupies a position of political responsibility, may be followed by a malfunctioning of the natural environment. Just as it has been demonstrated that the natural functions of man—such as sleep—may be disturbed by his moral behavior, *Macbeth* is filled with examples of how the natural world may be disrupted by "unnatural deeds." Of course Macbeth is thinking figuratively when in Act I, Scene 7 he speaks of the operation of supernatural forces setting loose the elements to expose "the deep damnation of of his [Duncan's] taking off," but later events in the play indicate a literal belief in the relationship between metaphysical and natural forces.

It might be argued that like the dagger he sees before him, the disruption of nature occurs principally in the imagination of the sinner, but the most unnatural events are witnessed by other characters in the play. After the murder but before its discovery, Lennox informs Macbeth:

> The night has been unruly. Where we lay,
> Our chimneys were blown down, and as they say,
> Lamentings heard i' the air, strange screams of death,
> And phophesying with accents terrible
> Of dire combustion and confused events
> New-hatched to the woeful time. The obscure bird
> Clamored the livelong night. Some say the earth
> Was feverous and did shake.   (II, 3)

In Act II, it is apparent that the only function of the Old Man is to contribute to the atmosphere of a world of whose present chaos a man of at least seventy cannot recall a parallel. (Lennox earlier remarked, "My young remembrance cannot parallel/A fellow to it.") He and Ross describe the perturbation of nature, and it is Ross who expresses the causal connection between them and "man's act":

> Ah, good Father,
> Thou seest the heavens, as troubled with man's act,
> Threaten his bloody stage. By the clock 'tis day,

And yet dark night strangles the traveling lamp.
It 't night's predominance, or the day's shame,
That darkness does the face of earth entomb
When living light should kiss it?

OLD MAN: 'Tis unnatural,
Even like the deed that's done. On Tuesday last
A falcon towering in her pride of place
Was by a mousing owl hawked at and killed.

ROSS: And Duncan's horses—a thing most strange and certain—
Beauteous and swift, the minions of their race,
Turned wild in nature, broke their stalls, flung out,
Contending 'gainst obedience, as they would make
War with mankind.

OLD MAN: 'Tis said they eat each other.   (II, 4)

Such language contributes to the violent atmosphere that distinguishes *Macbeth,* but it also has meaning. Just as the events of the play are concerned with the pattern of sin and punishment, the atmosphere of the play is created by language that reflects causal effects in a moral universe.

No discussion of the language patterns in Macbeth can be complete without reference to its repeated use of antithesis, particularly in the repetitious description "foul and fair." Strung throughout the play are phrases such as the following: "Nothing is but what is not," " 'tis day/And yet dark night," "lies like truth." Such attention to antithesis textures the play with irony, a quality that is created also in its action and characterization. One of the most brilliant uses of irony is established early in the play when Duncan announces that he is transferring the title, thane of Cawdor, from an executed traitor to Macbeth, and adds, "What he hath lost noble Macbeth hath won." We learn shortly that Macbeth has won more than Cawdor's title; he has also inherited his treacherous character.

Irony inevitably reminds us of life's deceptions, but frequently in literature it may be used for the sake of cleverness or to enrich a particular observation. Works such as *Oedipus, Ghosts,* and *Macbeth* are deeply concerned with deception in human life and with the discrepancy between illusion and reality. The language of all three of these plays is suffused with antithesis and double entendre. At the very beginning of Macbeth, the witches tell us that "fair is foul, and foul is fair." Significantly, the next time we are reminded of this is when Macbeth appears and says on his first line, "So foul and fair a day I have not seen." Thus, creatures of evil are linked to a man who has been described as noble and good. In addition, the repetition impresses on us the fact that the atmosphere may appear fair and foul at the same time. As the play develops, we discover that like the "sweet air" outside Macbeth's castle, fair appearances may conceal foul realities. It is "fair news" that Macbeth is to become king, but "foul" in the sense that he must use "foul" means and must "foul" his soul eternally to achieve his ends. After the murder, Lady Macbeth assures her husband that "a little water clears us of this deed," but she dies lamenting, "Will these hands ne'er be clean?"

Directly and indirectly, the theme of deception reappears regularly throughout the play. Macbeth is deceived by prophecies that seem fair but prove to be foul: He can be killed by "none of woman born," and "never vanquished" until Birnam Wood moves to Dunsinane Hill. The world, this play informs us, is filled with deception—much of it in nature. But man also has as great a capacity to deceive. Macbeth reminds himself that "false face must hide what the false heart doth know" (I, 7), and tells Lady Macbeth that "we/Must lave our honors in these flattering streams/And make our faces vizards to our hearts,/Disguising what they are" (III, 2).

Because of the alliance between deception and tyranny, to avoid evil and pursue the good men must use extreme caution in choosing their allies and companions. This is made explicit in the Malcolm-Macduff scene in Act IV, Scene 3. Perhaps more difficult is man's capacity or will to resist the "fair" temptations of the devil. Macbeth, too late, begins "To doubt the equivocation of the fiend/That lies like truth" (V, 5). Too late he realizes that his submission to foul forces for the sake of a fair future has "cowed [his] better part of man!" adding, "And be these juggling fiends no more believed/That palter with us in a double sense" (V, 8). Macbeth knows that man is given "his better part" to cope with temptation, and the audience has seen the manner in which the "better part" of Banquo responded to the possibility of deception by "the instruments of darkness."

Thus the ironic language of the play combines with action and character to explore moral choice and action as they relate to the treacherous deceptions that surround us on every side and exist even within us.

THOUGHT

"All the parts of the poem . . . are parts not only of an action but also of the symbolic structure of perspective and belief—of the poet's world view, his affirmations or denials, his lament or his prophecy."[13]

It has been suggested in the discussion of language that arguments, ideas, the "poet's world view," are often stated directly in the course of a play. "Unnatural deeds/Do breed unnatural troubles," and Ross' "Thou see'st the heavens, as troubled with man's act,/Threaten his bloody stage" are examples of typically direct argument in *Macbeth*. It also was suggested at the beginning of this chapter on analysis that although it is possible for one line, one scene, or one character to illuminate a play's intent, it often is dangerous to draw conclusions based on the mere abstraction of such statements. When, however, patterns of ideas emerge from a study of action, character, and language, the interpreter is on surer ground and direct arguments such as the two above may be viewed in their proper perspective. The term *thought* applies to the ideas, values, and attitudes that emerge from "all the parts of the poem."

Before illustrating the manner in which the director may draw conclusions about thought that should influence his treatment of nearly all aspects of theatrical expression, a warning must be given about the tendency to summarize a play's intentions in a single statement, most often referred to as the "theme" of the play. To say *Macbeth* tells us that "crime does not pay" is not incorrect, but is an obvious oversimplification that relegates this masterpiece to the realm of the crime story with a "message." To direct it with such a point of view would be to subjugate its richness and complexity to melodrama. There are interesting plays organized around as basic and simple a theme as "crime does not pay," but tragedies such as *Oedipus* and *Macbeth*, as classically uncluttered and direct as they are, contain rich veins of meaning that are constantly being mined. This is why they are the subject of constant reevaluation by critics, scholars, and thoughtful theatre artists. Such plays do not say one thing but many things, and in the process the things they say all seem to belong together.

The analysis of the parts of *Macbeth* has made it abundantly clear that, while there is a strong and carefully structured plot line, Shakespeare's concerns are with more than an exciting tale. We have seen how the causal aspects of the action itself stress the moral dissolution of its central character and his country. We have seen how Shakespeare selected and developed his characters not merely to advance his plot of regicide and retribution, but to deal intensively with man's nature; how, in the struggle between good and evil, a man may deceive himself and surrender his soul for a crown, and how such a surrender may destroy him spiritually and physically. We have also seen in the selection of character attributes of the major characters in the play an emphasis on political man, clarifying the distinctions between good and bad rulers and their effect on their country's order. We have observed how Shakespeare moved beyond story and character delineation to create a pervasive atmosphere for his play, which broadens the spectator's experience of the cosmological extension of man's action. The play also is about a marriage, and the relationship between the sexes. It raises questions about fate and free will, and the problems of choice in a world filled with deceptive appearances.

The miracle is that with these apparently multiple concerns, the play perfectly exemplifies dramatic order, unity, and concentration. Perhaps the reason for this is that all of the play's concerns emerge from a particular world view. In this world view, the conception of the universe is moral, embracing and linking man's government of himself and his country to a higher order that cannot permit evil continually to perpetuate itself. This is medieval Christian doctrine, of course, and no part of the play remains unaffected by it. Religious criteria are behind the development of plot and character, and the uses of language through metaphor, as well as its contribution to the play's atmosphere, are based on Christian assumptions, as are the supernatural aspects of the play. Frequent references to grace ("deep damnation," "mine eternal jewel") to "heavenly" virtues as opposed to "devilish" behavior, to "Hell," powers of darkness, and the foul "fiend" contribute to the unmistakable religious conception of the play.

Yet, a director need not view or express *Macbeth* as a Christian morality play. One director may emphasize the play's religious motifs through visual symbols on the stage, but another director may find the politics of the play more relevant to his time. One need not be a Christian to appreciate or to represent the major concerns of this play. Most of us understand the nature of tyranny, of the human personality confronted with temptation but frightened by the prospect of criminal violence and its possible consequences. We are, Christian or not, concerned with the problem of choice in a world filled with deceptive appearances and, whether or not we believe in cosmological order, we can accept symbolically the atmospheric reverberations of evil.

This chapter has discussed the director's preparation through an internal analysis of a play. One may disagree with the interpretation of *Macbeth* as it has been presented. Much, of course, has not been explored. There are, too, other methods of interpretative analysis. What is important, however, is that the director pursue some sort of exploration so that he may see the play's parts in relation to the whole, and the whole as the pattern of its parts. When he has done this, he may be further assisted by exploring aids external to his reading of the play, and finally have a substantial and germane foundation for expression.

NOTES

[1]Marika Aba, "Wherefore Art Thou, Zeffirelli?" *Los Angeles Times,* November 12, 1967, Calendar Section, p. 15.

[2]Music is the one ingredient that was an integral part of the Greek theatre, but has not been a necessary part of the theatre of subsequent eras. It might be argued that the rhythms of a play are comparable to those of music, but such rationalizations are unnecessary. Drama can be created without music, but music is an important part of much drama, and its inclusion distinguishes theatre even further from its literary relatives.

[3]John Dietrich, *Play Direction* (Englewood Cliffs, N.J.: Prentice-Hall, 1953).

[4]For an explanation of the contribution of Act II, Scene 4 to the scheme of *Macbeth,* see pp. 86-87.

[5]See p. 78.

[6]Harold Clurman, "Principles of Interpretation," in John Gassner, *Producing the Play* (New York: Holt, Rinehart and Winston, 1953), pp. 272–273.

[7]Harold Clurman, "Some Preliminary Notes for *A Member of the Wedding,*" in Toby Cole and Helen Krich Chinoy, eds., *Directing the Play* (New York: Bobbs–Merrill Company, 1953), pp. 311–320.

[8]Gassner, *Producing the Play,* p. 277.

[9]Constantin Stanislavski, *An Actor Prepares,* trans. Elizabeth Reynolds Hapgood (New York: Theatre Arts Books, 1946), pp. 108–109.

[10]That is, "Liberty is restored," according to G. B. Harrison, ed., *Shakespeare, The Complete Works* (New York: Harcourt, Brace and World, 1952), p. 1218.

[11]Harrison, p. 1203.

[12]Some scholars maintain that the inclusion of Edward is Shakespeare's gesture toward his own king, James I, who supposedly had similar healing powers. This may be so, but it does not affect the explanation above.

[13]Robert B. Heilman, *Magic in the Web* (Lexington, Ky.: University of Lexington Press, 1956), p. 12.

III

Supporting the Text: External Investigation

Books quoted in the programme: W. H. Auden, *The Dyer's Hand* (Faber); A. C. Bradley, *Shakespearean Tragedy* (Macmillan); Cleanth Brooks, *The Well Wrought Urn* (Dobson); John Russell Brown, *Shakespeare. The Tragedy of Macbeth* (Arnold); W. C. Curry, *Shakespeare's Philosophical Patterns* (Louisiana); Willard Farnham, *Shakespeare's Tragic Frontier* (C.U.P.); Henri Fluchère, *Shakespeare* (Toulouse); G. Wilson Knight, *The Imperial Theme* (C.U.P.); L. C. Knights, *Some Shakespearean Themes* (Chatto); Jan Kott, *Shakespeare Our Contemporary* (Methuen); A. P. Rossiter, *Angel with Horns* (Longmans); Arthur Sewell, *Character and Society in Shakespeare* (C.U.P.); E. M. Tillyard, *Shakespeare's History Plays* (Chatto); D. A. Traversi, *An Approach to Shakespeare* (Sands); *Tynan on Theatre* (Pelican); John Wain, *The Living World of Shakespeare* (Macmillan); Sybil and Russell Thorndike, *Lilian Baylis* (Chapman and Hall).[1]

Research may clarify what appears obscure; it may reinforce conclusions drawn in analysis or inspire more penetrating insights into the play's structure and meaning. Different plays require different kinds of research. A knowledge of both the Elizabethan stage and the sources of *Macbeth* and *Twelfth Night* is helpful in interpreting these plays, but *Twelfth Night* does not require the awareness of political philosophy and Christian doctrine that *Macbeth* demands, while a contemporary play such as *Barefoot in the Park* makes few research requirements at all. The play itself will dictate the kind and amount of external investigation needed, but areas of exploration that are fundamental to most dramas include the playwright, the play's sources and evolution, its history, internal problems, records of previous productions, criticism, and milieu.

[1]From the program of the Royal Shakespeare Theatre production of *Macbeth*, directed by Peter Hall in 1967.

6 The Playwright

HIS PERSONAL LIFE

More often than not, our knowledge of the playwright's life is not particularly useful to a clearer understanding of his play. The little we know of Shakespeare's life is valueless in this respect. His supposed poaching, his marriage to a woman older than himself, the willing of his "second best bed," and even suspicions of homosexuality (based on interpretation of the sonnets rather than on biographical fact) contribute nothing of value to our understanding of his work. Knowing or suspecting that Christopher Marlowe was an atheist conceivably could lead to a misinterpretation of *Dr. Faustus*, which is structured on and supports accepted Christian doctrine. On the other hand, Strindberg's life, especially as revealed in his autobiographical novels such as *The Son of a Servant* and *Confessions of a Fool*, illuminates the ambivalent view of women, the battle between the sexes, madness, the class system, and much more of the subject matter of his plays. To know Jean Genet's life, his criminality and perversion, their causes and their influence on his world view, is to better understand his brilliant but difficult and complex plays.

Arthur Miller's *After the Fall* obviously contains much that is autobiographical. Later historians and analysts will no doubt remind readers of this fact, and future directors who are interested in reviving the play will feel obliged to relate its characters and events to Miller's life and times. Such a practice no doubt illuminates our impressions of the play, but it has dangers. The play should not be viewed purely as a self-confession when it is, according to Miller's own insistence, much more than that, for then our familiarity with the real-life qualities of several of its characters can distort Miller's manipulation of those characters for artistic and thematic purposes. Nevertheless, the play unquestionably is related to specific details of Miller's personal experience. An awareness of Miller's relationship to his parents, to his wives, and to his political enemies and allies may benefit the director's overall view of the play and its characters.

THE PLAYWRIGHT'S COMMENTARIES AND OTHER WORKS

Many artists, including dramatists, refuse to comment on their creations, arguing that the work of art must speak for itself, and of course they are correct. The work of art must stand for itself for two reasons. First, it is its own justification for being: if the artist believed he could express his ideas or feelings in another way, he probably would have done so. Second, the viewer responds to the work of art, not to what is said about it. If our appreciation of a Picasso painting depended on verbal explanations, the painting would be a failure; it would have failed to convey itself as a painting. An audience viewing a play by Shaw should not be expected to enjoy *Pygmalion* any less for not having read his lengthy preface. But dramatic art is interpretative, and if playwrights choose to write about their plays, the director must familiarize himself with their views, which often illuminate their intentions. Unquestionably, the discovery of Chekhov's insistence that *The Cherry Orchard* was a comedy led directors to lift the play out of the pall of gloom with which Chekhov's plays used to be staged. Ibsen's own comments on the ludicrous intentions in *An Enemy of the People*, especially in his treatment of Peter Stockman, should make it apparent that the play is concerned with something more complex than ecological problems or a simple attack on the majority. (Miller's adaptation of this play makes Stockman a tragic hero, and the resulting play has quite a different viewpoint than the original.) In *Candida* the treatment of Candida and Marchbanks as well as Shaw's ending have baffled many critics and directors, but familiarity with Shaw's own hints in various essays and letters may lead to satisfying solutions for the director. The same playwright's views on socialism, sex, and evolution (the "life force") are expressed in his essays and should be read to strengthen our understanding of the themes and references in his plays.

Much of today's theatre is moving in new directions and breaking with traditional dramatic structure and purpose. To avoid imposing the wrong interpretative methods on plays, the director must find guidance in articles and prefatory or autobiographical essays. Ionesco clarifies his intentions regarding style, genre, and structure in *Notes and Counter Notes*, a collection of many of his articles and speeches. Brecht has contributed numerous explanations of his epic structure and alienation techniques. Genet's autobiographical novels, *A Thief's Journal* and *Our Lady of the Flowers*, must be considered essential reading in attempts to interpret the ambiguities of *The Maids, The Balcony*, and *The Blacks*.

Among the best sources of information regarding the playwright's concerns are the themes and variations that have been expressed in his other dramas. Although *Macbeth* is not strictly a chronicle play, it parallels in many ways the characteristics of the histories. Conceptions of the nature of the ideal ruler, of the moral consequences of irresponsible rule or regicide, are as much a part of *Macbeth* as of the histories from *Richard II* to *Henry V*. The relationship between political order and cosmological order is a persistent theme in the histories as well as in tragedies such as *Hamlet, King Lear*, and *Macbeth*. The gardener's speech in *Richard II* (III, 4) where an analogy is drawn between the duty of the gardener and the duty of the prince, between the consequences for the garden and for the state, expresses a point of view that is relevant to the political morality of *Macbeth*. So is the oft-quoted speech of Ulysses on "the specialty of rule" in *Troilus and Cressida* (I, 3). These examples may illuminate or confirm our conclusions regarding the connection between political and natural disorder in *Macbeth*.

In the same way, we find repeated in Brecht's plays the principle that survival in a corrupt world requires corruption, in Ibsen's dramas the theme of self-realization and arguments about the value of illusion, in Tennessee Williams' dramas characters repeatedly shattered by materialism, urban loneliness, and the loss of a gracious and elegant gentility. The plays of many writers repeat or build on specific motifs, and our response to each may be intensified by our familiarity with the others.

7
The Play's History

All plays have a "history." Even when a director works on a completely new play, there is a past to be explored. The "pastness" of a new play is in its origins and development. If the director is fortunate enough to be working with the playwright or to be able to correspond with him, he may inquire about its evolution to its present form. He may ask about the initial source of the play, why the playwright wished to explore it, and what influenced him in its structuring. William Gibson's recounting of the evolution of *Two for the Seesaw* in his *The Seesaw Log* shows how a play develops from its inception, and the forces that determine its ultimate shape. A director unquestionably is in a better position to explore the playwright's intentions when he has had the opportunity of working directly with him. A majority of directors, however, do not have such an opportunity and are more often involved with productions of previous successes whose creators are no longer available for direct comment. But, frequently, a play's development may be reconstructed from available evidence, adding something to our awareness of the playwright's intentions. Such evidence includes source materials, text variations, and the play's relation to a milieu.

SOURCE MATERIALS

A play may be related to recognizable sources such as historical events (Shakespeare's histories, *Danton's Death, The Crucible*), biography *(Abe Lincoln in Illinois, The Miracle Worker, The Great White Hope)*, mythology (plays from Aeschylus to Sartre and O'Neill that reinterpret the Atreus and other legends), or adaptations from novels or other plays (*Twelfth Night, The Caine Mutiny Court-Martial, West Side Story, The Threepenny Opera*). Comparing such plays with their sources will reveal what the playwright has retained and rejected, how he has rearranged the chronology of events, added fictional characters or situations, provided psychological justifications that may be unknown to historians but necessary for dramatic probability, and used original language to indicate an interest in something more than mere history, biography, or story-telling. Previously it was stated that a play-wright's intentions may be determined by a careful study of his design; now we may add that his intentions also may be revealed by the manner in which he has redesigned the sources from which his play has emerged.

For these reasons it is foolish to dismiss the contribution of Shakespearean scholarship to the creative interpretations of his plays. When such scholarship contributes to an awareness of Shakespeare's creative use of his materials and to a better understanding of his purposes, it cannot help but stimulate the imaginative expression of the plays in the theatre. Shakespeare's sources for *Macbeth* are several, but the most important is from Raphael Holinshed's *The Chronicles of England, Scotland, and Ireland* (1587). Shakespeare actually molded together two separate historical events as narrated by Holinshed. The first was the murder of King Duff by Donwald in 968, and the second was the killing of King Duncan by Macbeth nearly a hundred years later. Shakespeare fused the two events because they were so similar, and because each could contribute particular characteristics to the single story. The existence and influence of Donwald's wife in the earlier history contributed to the creation of Lady Macbeth and her influence in the murder. The first narrative also emphasizes the chaos in nature that follows the murder of the king. For the most part, however, Shakespeare adheres closely to Holinshed's depiction of Macbeth's history, in which the three witches and Banquo appear and in which the Malcolm–Macduff scene in England has been followed very closely. As faithful as Shakespeare has been to his sources, however, his omissions, additions, and modifications redesign Holinshed's history into quite another experience. Holinshed's Duff has had relatives of Donwald executed, and Duncan in the later story is depicted as a weak king. Shakespeare eliminates such justification for Macbeth's deeds, preferring that his motives be based purely on ambition. He also omits references to the historical Macbeth's early cruelty and his tendency to send the heads of his victims to the king, preferring to start his play with a protagonist whose evils will evolve only after an intense internal struggle. Omitted, too, is the historical evidence that for several years after the murder of Duncan, Macbeth's rule was effective and just. Shakespeare prefers to depict Macbeth as immediately hardening into a cruel tyrant.

Although Holinshed describes characters, Shakespeare goes far deeper in their delineation: Macbeth's transparency and his struggle with conscience and imagination, Lady Macbeth's rejection of her sex and her methods of influencing her husband, Banquo as a contrast to Macbeth, and the deterioration of Lady Macbeth's mental health and her ultimate demise are all Shakespeare's contribution. Although in Holinshed, the unnatural consequences of unnatural deeds are reported, Shakespeare extends this idea to embrace the action and atmosphere of the entire play. Shakespeare parallels Holinshed's political morality (it is extraordinary how much of the language and spirit of the Malcolm–Macduff scene he retains), but comparing the history and the tragedy reveals that Shakespeare's interest in political morality is extended to include an examination of human evil from temptation to damnation; he has striven to create the experience of a hell on earth, painted in chiaroscuro and splotched with blood. Shakespeare's use of his sources is conscious and deliberate, and examination of his dramatic and thematic intentions may add to or reinforce our conclusions about the play's meaning.

TEXT VARIATIONS

On occasion varying versions of the same play are published. *Cat on a Hot Tin Roof* has two versions of the third act, one being the act originally created by Tennessee Williams, the other a new version which the director, Elia Kazan, persuaded Williams to write. When Arthur Miller revived *The Crucible* for an off-Broadway production that he directed, he added a new scene to the play, which appeared in a subsequent printing. Such variations occur far less frequently in contemporary drama than in the plays of the sixteenth and seventeenth centuries, and only a foolish director neglects such variations. One outstanding example, of course, is *Hamlet*, three different versions of which were published in 21 years. The first quarto (1602) is presumed to be from the prompt book or the memory of the actor playing Marcellus. A second quarto, the most complete text, appeared the following year and may have been taken from Shakespeare's own copy. In 1623, the first folio edition appeared. It is believed that this version was a more recent production of the play, perhaps with revisions made by Shakespeare himself. It is agreed that while there are differences between the second quarto and the first folio, both of these are preferable to the pirated first quarto.

Directors have found the first quarto of significance, however, because certain stage directions do not appear in the other versions of the play. But much of the first quarto is of lesser quality and includes, among other differences, serious changes in the sequence of scenes, such as the following:

Second Quarto, First Folio	*First Quarto*
1. "Fishmonger" sequence (II, 2)	"To be or not to be"
2. "Rogue and peasant slave" (II, 2)	"Nunnery" scene
3. "To be or not to be" (III, 1)	"Fishmonger" sequence
4. "Nunnery" scene (III, 2)	"Rogue and peasant slave"

Obviously each order will create a different response from the viewer, and directors have often scorned the authorized sequence for the sequence in the first quarto or for new combinations that satisfy them more. While modern editors adhere to the accepted versions, they too vary in their selection from the differences between the second quarto and the first folio. Most directors, too, even if they prefer the authorized first folio, are reluctant to surrender the "How all occasions do inform against me" speech (IV, 4), which does not appear in that edition of the play. Therefore, the director must be familiar with both, so that he may make his own choices.

This is a good example of the role of scholarship in the art of directing. The scholar uses his discipline to clarify the text. As this also happens to be the director's task, scholarly consensus will often prove indispensible to him in discovering the existence of discrepancies such as those concerning *Hamlet*, and in making the correct choices.

MILIEU

Plays, directly or indirectly, are influenced by values and customs of the time and place in which they were written and produced. Although the dramatic intentions of plays are not always concerned primarily with the religious, philosophical, political, or psychological problems of the times, the most trivial and least morally concerned play invariably implies certain standards of virtue and evil, patterns of accepted or deviational behavior, and the customs of the society with which it is dealing. Agatha Christie's *The Mousetrap*, an extraordinary commercial success in London, makes no pretense to be anything more than an ordinary murder mystery, whose objective is to create suspense and provide the audience with an evening of chills and thrills. It is not structured to provide us with significant insights into twentieth-century morality. But it does assume that crime is wrong and does not pay. It provokes sympathy for certain characters, suspicion and dislike for others. The people in the play speak, dress, and practice customs characteristic of the contemporary British middle class. All this requires no special investigation by a contemporary director, but if for some reason the play were revived two hundred years from now, a director might well be compelled to review the cultural milieu in which it was set. This is not to say that contemporary plays require no such exploration now. Serious dramas are often directly concerned with the experiences of modern life, and with a perspective in which those experiences are viewed. The plays of Sartre put his existential views into action, and it is important to be familiar with those views and their causes if the plays are to be directed with the necessary vision. The absurd or the comic–tragic world view are not new: Euripides, Shakespeare, Webster, Chekhov in other periods and civilizations expressed them. But the modern absurdist depiction of mankind differs because it is relevant to twentieth-century conditions. Two world wars, the "death of God," Buchenwald, the persistence of tyranny and corruption, the ultimate weapon—all must be taken into account in preparing to perform the plays of Beckett, Ionesco, Brecht, or Dürrenmatt. As this is written, there is a movement toward a more political theatre whose involvement and commitment requires a thorough awareness of the cultural revolution, its causes, and proposed solutions.

Just as a later age will need to research the conditions of our mid-century if it is to meaningfully revive the works of our current movements, it is valuable for us to recognize comparable conditions (emphasizing, of course, those conditions that are the concerns of the play) when we produce plays of the past. Euripides' intentions, for example, become less ambiguous if we know what was happening to the Athens of his time, and the manner in which his plays responded to conditions that Aeschylus did not live to see. Familiarity with the influence of Sophistic thought, its relativist point of view, and its rejection of traditional morality will contribute strongly to our recognition of the futility and despair that dominates the conclusion of *Electra* and permeates *The Trojan Women*. *Hippolytus*, perhaps the most controversial of his plays, makes better sense and loses the inconsistency caused by allegorical explanations when it is viewed in terms of relativist thought. The moral decay of Athens and the tragedy of a useless war contribute to Euripides' philosophy and to the materials of his plays.

In previous sections of this book, the religious and political aspects of *Macbeth* were stressed. Recognition of the former is hardly possible without some understanding of Christian doctrine. Without it, we lose not merely the importance of such phrases as "mine eternal jewel [grace]/given to the common enemy of man [the devil]," but the significance of Macbeth's struggle, which is based on a Christian view of the human condition: what "becomes" a man, the nature and consequence of sin, the dreadful implication of despair. The discussion of thought in *Macbeth* demonstrated how a play's values may be determined by its structure rather than by external processes, yet a reader unfamiliar with the Elizabethan world view might overlook, or lack the "frames of reference" necessary to recognize what is in the play. The resulting production usually concentrates solely on a character study of ambition, or creates an atmosphere whose sole value is melodrama. Portions of the play such as the Old Man–Ross sequence or the Malcolm–Macduff scene are cut because they seem irrelevant, and the golden triumph of the restoration of order at the play's conclusion is not fulfilled.

A specific example of the value of exploring milieu can be made with Shakespeare's use of the witches in *Macbeth*. Our understanding of their nature and function is important not simply to determine what they signified to their original audience, but to better deal with the problems of fate and free will that their presence creates, and that is so much an issue in determining how the characters in the play are to be interpreted. At issue, also, is the objective reality of the spiritual forms in the play. Are the witches, the dagger, Banquo's ghost visible to the audience, thereby suggesting that they are not merely figments of Macbeth's imagination? Today it is difficult for us to accept the reality of supernatural demonic forces in the universe, and so their presence in twentieth-century productions of *Macbeth* may create the effect of a melodramatic fairy tale, where audience disbelief is supposed to be suspended as it is titillated by spooky spirits in a ghost-story atmosphere. Or, when the writer's intentions are viewed more seriously, we are asked not to view the irrational forces in the play as real, but rather as symbols of fate or predestination, or as expressionistic manifestations of Macbeth's conscience or guilt or inherent evil.

To assist ourselves in resolving the problems created by differences between sixteenth- and twentieth-century beliefs, and to avoid prejudiced or distorted interpretations of *Macbeth*, we must learn something about "that mediaeval ontology which he [Shakespeare] and his age had more or less consciously assimilated." This quotation is taken from an article by Walter Clyde Curry, "The demonic Metaphysics of Macbeth."[1] This kind of scholarship can be of great value to the director who does not have the time and opportunity for primary source investigations. "Philosophy, theology, and religion have joined themselves with theosophy, theurgy, and thaumaturgy, with superstitious legend, classical and folk mythology, black magic, and other occult sciences in creating for the Renaissance mind a spiritual world of evil intelligences."[2] Evil in Shakespeare's time was subjective and nonsubjective, "that is to say, evil manifested itself subjectively in the spirits of man and objectively in a metaphysical world whose existence depended in no degree upon the activities of the human mind."[3] The subjective evil is based on sin, original or otherwise, while objective evil is manifest in "the malignant activity of demons or fallen angels."[4] Curry also describes medieval notions of fallen angels, who are not naturally joined to bodies. They are spirits who can appear in any desired form and who can emulate human voices and be heard by human ears. They have clairvoyant powers and can influence humans by persuasion or by provoking the passions, but "cannot plant thoughts in the mind."[5] Their function in the cosmic order "is to participate in the working out of man's destiny. . . . God disposes that they provide opposition to the good in man, so that, through exercise in fighting against evil, the human soul may indirectly be perfected into salvation."[6]

Shakespeare's audience would understand and accept the notion of the objective appearance of metaphysical forces. "Here, then, were terrifying creatures, created by a contemporary public at the most intense moment of witchcraft delusion, which Shakespeare found ready to his hand. Accordingly he appropriately employed witch-figures as dramatic symbols, but the Weird Sisters are in reality demons, actual representatives of the world of darkness opposed to good."[7] That audience was aware, too, of the possibility of free will and how it is related to fate, and how these conceptions are related to a moral order—a cosmology—in which demonic spirits played an important role. With information such as this the director returns to the play and tests these concepts in its structure and language. He will then be able to confirm, add to, or reject the conclusions that emerged in his analysis as opposed to more contemporary conjectures.

NOTES

[1]Walter Clyde Curry, "The Demonic Metaphysics of Macbeth," Chapel Hill, 1933, p. 32.

[2]Curry, pp. 8–9.

[3]Curry, p. 5.

[4]Curry, p. 14.

[5]Curry, p. 19.

[6]Curry, p. 16.

[7]Curry, pp. 6–7.

Internal Problems

Even in the less controversial texts of Shakespeare there are differences of opinion about punctuation and the precise meaning of words and phrases that ultimately must result in decisions concerning the actor's delivery. The New Variorum editions of Shakespeare are very helpful in this respect. They print a traditional version of the text with numerous notes elucidating it and often with varying interpretations of different parts of the play.

PUNCTUATION

The following example from Act I, Scene 7 of *Macbeth* demonstrates how different editions of a text may vary, and how such differences may influence interpretation:

If it were done, when 'tis done, then 'twere well,	*If it were done when 'tis done, then 'twere well*
It were done quickly: If th' Assassination	*It were done quickly. If th' assassination*
Could trammell up the Consequence, and catch	*Could trammel up the consequence, and catch*
With his surcease, Successe: that but this blow	*With his surcease, success, that but this blow*
Might be the be all, and the end all. Heere,	*Might be the be-all and the end-all—here,*
But heere, upon this Banke and Schoole of time,	*But here, upon this bank and shoal of time,*
Wee'ld jumpe the life to come.[1]	*We'd jump the life to come.[2]*

A lengthy footnote in the New Variorum argues the pros and cons of placing a period at the end of the first line, and ignoring the colon after "quickly." Note also the difference between the reading of "that but this blow/ Might be the be all and the end all. Heere,/But heere . . ." and "that but this blow/Might be the be-all and the end-all—here,/But here . . . ."

Later in the scene when Macbeth asks "If we should fail?" Lady Macbeth in the first folio edition responds with "we fail?" as an interrogation.

Later editions use an exclamation point. Even if an interrogation point is explained as the folio's equivalent to an exclamation point, the decision will have to be made between a response that suggests the impossibility of failure (we fail?) or one that admits the possibility (we fail!) followed quickly by reassurances that with the proper courage they will succeed.

VOCABULARY

Every word of a play must be understood by the director and the actor. Such a statement may be so obvious that its inclusion in a text seems foolish, but it is too often an unfortunate fact that the actor and director do not bother to investigate the meaning of words. In contemporary plays, slang, colloquialisms, foreign words and phrases, or recognizable terms with meanings different from their current use must be carefully researched. In the aforementioned scene from *Macbeth* (I, 7), Macbeth's soliloquy alone contains at least six phrases that are either unfamiliar or subject to different interpretations.

Note that "Banke and Schoole" in the New Variorum text becomes "bank and shoal" in modern editions. "Banke" may mean "school-bench" which, with "Schoole" and the later "teach bloody instructions" gives the figure of speech some consistency. The resulting meaning is explained by H. Elwin as "if here only, upon this bench of instruction, in this school of eternity, I could do this without bringing these, my pupil days, under suffering, I would hazard its effect on the endless life to come."[3] But another meaning is possible if "Shoal" is, as Theobald suggests, "Shallow," a "narrow Ford of humane life as opposed to the great Abyss of Eternity,"[4] and if bank is literally interpreted as the edge of the water. Then Hunter's reference to the image as that of "the isthmus between two eternities"[5] has relevance. For the actor, whose expression is influenced by images, it is obvious that the two interpretations will evoke different expressions. The director might base his decision on his belief that a modern audience would more quickly grasp the meaning of bench and school than bank and shoal.

In Shakespeare's plays some words have connotations that we no longer recognize. In the seventeenth century, the word "fool" could, in addition to its common meaning, be a term of endearment. When King Lear uses the term in Act V, Scene 3, he may indeed be referring to Cordelia. Such an interpretation can be supported for several reasons. First, it has been conjectured that because Cordelia and the fool never appear on stage at the same time, they may have been played by the same actor. More significant for a pattern of meaning is the association that is created by the use of "fool" to Cordelia. It makes us aware of the parallel between the two characters: except for Kent, they are the only characters in the play who show their love of Lear by being absolutely honest with him.

One of the more controversial problems in Act I, Scene 7 of *Macbeth* involves Macbeth's willingness to "jump the life to come" if "this blow/

Might be the be all and the end all." "Jump" means "risk" or "hazard." Is Macbeth willing to risk the rest of his life on earth if the murder is successful? Or is he willing to risk eternity for the security of his remaining years? Critics have disagreed about these two interpretations, and the director must choose between them. One method of making a decision might be to relate this sequence to the language, arguments, or idea patterns in the rest of the play. In our own analysis several conceptions would appear to favor the risk of eternity rather than life here on earth. It was observed that Macbeth constantly is concerned with his safety; his tyranny after the murder of Duncan is motivated by the fear of "bloody instructions" returning "to plague the inventor." We have also noted the frequent references to grace and eternity, and Macbeth's despair at the loss of his "eternal jewel." A Christian who would be willing to "jump the life to come" and mean eternal life already is guilty of despair. In this manner a director may, by relating parts to the whole, make choices that contribute to a consistent interpretation.

TRANSLATIONS AND ADAPTATIONS

If the director is familiar with the original language of a foreign play, he should compare the translation with the original. The reasons for this are fairly obvious. The translation may have deleted or added words or speeches; it may have ignored language patterns such as imagery, or characteristic modes of speech for a character; in attempting to make the play more relevant to the ears of an audience of a different country or time, it may have become too colloquial, or in attempting to be as literal as possible, it may not be colloquial enough. Translations of Greek tragedies are particularly suspect of the latter. Nineteenth-century translations of Greek tragedy tend to be literary rather than dramatic, while many twentieth-century translations are so colloquial that the tragedies lose their essential style and dignity. Aristophanic comedy poses an additional problem. The topicality of these farces is incomprehensible to modern audiences, and their earthiness was too offensive for Victorian tastes. If topical references are to be made meaningful, up-to-date translations are necessary or the director must make the adjustments himself.

When the director is not familiar with the original language, he should compare available translations, study the differences, and consult with someone who knows the language before deciding which translation is the more appropriate. One of the most interesting modern examples of a text whose translations provide drastic differences for the reader is Dürrenmatt's *The Visit*. Maurice Valency's English translation introduces Claire Zachanassian with the following description:

> *(From the right* CLAIRE ZACHANASSIAN *appears. She is an extraordinary woman. She is in her fifties, red-haired, remarkably dressed, with a face as impassive as that of an ancient idol, beauti-*

ful still, and with a singular grace of movement and manner. She is simple and unaffected, yet she has the haughtiness of a world power. The entire effect is striking to the point of the unbelievable.)[6]

In a different translation, by Patrick Bowles, Claire's entrance is described as follows:

(Enter, right, CLAIRE ZACHANASSIAN. Sixty-three, red hair, pearl necklace, enormous gold bangles, unbelievably got up to kill and yet by the same token a Society Lady with a rare grace, in spite of all the grotesquerie.)[7]

The differences in age and physical appearance are extreme enough to demonstrate that one of these versions is a corruption of the original text. In Act II, the following lines are heard from offstage in the Bowles version:

VOICE OF CLAIRE ZACHANASSIAN: Baby, pass me my left leg.
VOICE OF BUTLER: I can't find it, Madam.
VOICE OF CLAIRE ZACHANASSIAN: On the chest of drawers behind the wedding flowers.[8]

The Valency version omits this, as it does Claire's cigar smoking and her fondness for whisky—"neat."

Clearly, Valency's translation is a softer, less grotesque portrait than that of Bowles. Which is truer to Dürrenmatt? Which is more appropriate to the intentions of the play? These are questions that the director of an English version of *The Visit* must answer before he chooses a translation.

NOTES

[1]Horace Howard Furness, Jr., *Macbeth: A New Variorum Edition of Shakespeare* (Philadelphia: J. B. Lippincott, 1873), pp. 67–71.

[2]Modernized edition based on Folio 1. Harrison, G. B., ed., *Shakespeare, The Complete Works* (New York: Harcourt Bruce & World, 1948).

[3]*Ibid.*, pp. 96–97.

[4]*Ibid.*

[5]*Ibid.*

[6]Friedrich Dürrenmatt, *The Visit,* adapted by Maurice Valency in Haskell M. Block and Robert G. Shedd, eds., *Masters of Modern Drama* (New York: Random House, 1962), p. 1137.

[7]Friedrich Dürrenmatt, *The Visit,* trans. Patrick Bowles (New York: Grove Press, 1962), p. 17.

[8]*Ibid.*, p. 41.

Records of
Previous Productions

Unless a play has been recorded on film, records of previous productions do not ordinarily recapture the entire spirit of those productions. Even a completely detailed prompt book cannot recreate the tone of voice, the tempo and rhythm, the manner of execution of visual expression, or the immediate emotional impact of the production on which it is based. Nevertheless, serious investigations of previous productions may illuminate the particular value of certain scenes or sharpen our conception of character; the director may even find himself confronted with a totally new insight into the experience of the play.

Before the age of electronics enabled us to record plays or parts of plays on film or on phonograph records, the only sources available were reports by eye-witnesses, usually critics, of actual performances. The major plays and productions of the twentieth century probably have received more journalistic reviewing than those of any other period in theatrical history. It would be difficult not to find reviews of an important twentieth-century theatrical production in newspapers and magazines. Critics such as Stark Young and Kenneth Tynan have published collections of their selected essays of performance criticism. These critics indicate their ideas about the plays and how a production has failed or succeeded in expressing those ideas. In the process they discuss how the direction, the design, and the acting either illuminated or muddied the play's intentions. They also may describe bits of stage business to provide the reader with an idea of the style or kind of invention that characterized a particular production. The following excerpts from a review by Kenneth Tynan of Laurence Olivier's *Macbeth* (1965) illustrate this point.

> He [Olivier] begins in a perilously low key, the reason for which is soon revealed: This Macbeth is paralysed with guilt before the curtain rises, having already killed Duncan time and again in his mind. Far from recoiling and popping his eyes, he greets the air-drawn dagger with sad familiarity; it is a fixture in the crooked

furniture of his brain. Uxoriousness leads him to the act, which unexpectedly purges him of remorse. Now the portrait swells; seeking security, he is seized with fits of desperate bewilderment as the prize is snatched out of reach. There was true agony in "I had else been perfect"; Banquo's ghost was received with horrific torment, as if Macbeth should shriek "I've been robbed!" and the phrase about the dead rising to "push us from our stools" was accompanied by a convulsive shoving gesture which few other actors would have risked. . . .

The witches' cookery lesson is directed with amusing literalness; the Turk's nose, the Jew's liver, and the baby's finger are all held up for separate scrutiny; but the apparitions are very unpersuasive, and one felt gooseflesh hardly at all. On the battlements Sir Laurence's throttled fury switches into top gear, and we see a lion, baffled but still colossal. "I 'gin to be a-weary of the sun" held the very ecstasy of despair, the actor swaying with grief, his voice rising like hail on the crest of a trapped animal. . . .

. . . The midnight hags, with traditional bonhomie, scream with laughter at their own jokes: I long, one day, to see whispering witches, less intent on yelling their sins across the country-side. The production has all the speed and clarity we associate with Glen Byam Shaw, and Roger Furse's settings are bleak and serviceable, except for the England scene, which needs only a cat and a milestone to go straight into *Dick Whittington*.[1]

Observations of performances, while more preponderant in our time, are not limited to this century. We are able to go back to the first great western tragic dramatist, Aeschylus, to find a useful comment about the effect of a production. It was reported that the chorus of Furies in *The Oresteia* (458 B.C.) was so horrible that children died and pregnant women miscarried. No doubt that is an exaggeration but it tells us how far Aeschylus intended to go in creating an effect which in the text is merely suggested. We have eyewitness accounts of Shakespearean productions from his own time to the present. An astrologer named Simon Forman wrote a description of a performance of *Macbeth* at the Globe in 1611. Earlier, probably in 1607, a character in Beaumont's *The Knight of the Burning Pestle* comments on the stage business of Macbeth's reaction to Banquo's ghost. Our knowledge from such observations and from available prompt books may contribute weightily to our awareness of the kinds of stage problems that particular scenes present and how various directors or actors have dealt with these problems. In a well-researched book, *Shakespeare and the Actors*, Arthur Colby Sprague describes how stage business has been used in many prominent productions to cope with the theatrical problems of Shakespeare's plays. The banquet scene in which Banquo's ghost appears poses many problems and provides a stimulus for a variety of expressive business. One major problem of the scene is the appearance and disappearance of the ghost. In Simon Forman's description, Banquo's ghost actually appears and sits behind Macbeth. Later, however, a controversy arose concerning the dramatic effectiveness of a real versus an imagined ghost. Another controversy involved the method of entrances and exits used for the ghost. In some productions a trap door is used; in others the trap is used in combination with conventional entrances and exits through the wings. In yet others, the ghost enters unobtrusively with the guests and his appearance is concealed until Macbeth notices him. Edmund Kean provided an interesting, remarkably modern method of handling this scene in the mid nineteenth century. When Banquo first was seen as a ghost his head was illuminated with a pale blue light. Upon its reappearances, the ghost was discovered within a pillar that suddenly had become illuminated.

The various responses by Macbeth to the appearance of the ghost begin with the description in *The Knight of the Burning Pestle* when Jasper says,

> I'll come in midst of all thy pride and mirth,
> Invisible to all men but thyself,
> And whisper such a sad tale in thy ear
> Shall make thee let the cup fall from thy hand,
> And stand as mute and pale as death itself.   (V, 1, lines 25-29)

Sprague provides us with accounts of the manner in which performers in the eighteenth and nineteenth centuries, including Garrick, Holman, Kemble, Kean, Macready, Forrest, and Irving, responded to the ghost, some of them making their response one of the emotional high points of their productions. A more recent work, Dennis Bartholomeusz' *Macbeth and the Players*, is devoted completely to the history of important interpretations of *Macbeth*. It is a well-documented book with some fascinating details ranging from text alterations to business innovations by the play's stars.

If prompt books are available they should be studied. Biographies of actors and directors contain informative materials about the artists' approach to their roles. Mrs. Siddons' accounts of her approach to Lady Macbeth are illuminating. A contemporary director or actor does not have to imitate the method of expression in such scenes, although if he believes that one of the methods cannot be bettered, he surely can adopt it. Imitation of specific business, however, is not the purpose of such inquiry. Its value is the way in which a setting or a piece of business may illuminate ideas and character.

NOTES

[1]Kenneth Tynan, *Curtains* (New York: Atheneum, 1961), pp. 98-99. There are reviews of other *Macbeth* productions in this book.

Criticism

In the previous chapter the expression of other dramatic artists was emphasized. Other sources of value may be found in critical studies of the texts
themselves, studies that may be termed "literary" but nevertheless have the
capacity to provide the *raison d'être* for dramatic expression. Critics such as
Eric Bentley and Robert Brustein offer splendid insights into character and
meaning in twentieth-century drama. George Bernard Shaw's essays in *The
Quintessence of Ibsenism* still are considered to be among the best discussions
of Ibsen's plays. Martin Esslin's *Theatre of the Absurd* probably did more
to clarify the purposes of our mid-century avant-garde theatre than any other
work. His book on Bertolt Brecht is of great help to directors who have been
unable to otherwise familiarize themselves with Brecht's objectives and his
techniques. The director should also use articles in learned journals that
emphasize or include essays on dramatic art and literature.

No director should consider his preparation complete until he has
read available studies of plays from the "classical repertoire" that he may be
planning to stage. To consider productions of Greek tragedy without con-
sulting the works of Gilbert Murray or H. D. F. Kitto, among others, would
be a deprivation that a director can ill afford. Books and articles probe the
works of almost every great playwright of the past. For Shakespeare, there
is so much valuable material that a director's chief problem consists in
deciding which of the many critical works he should select for study. In
addition to the extraordinary number of publications on Shakespeare's plays
today, much of the important critical work on Shakespeare was written before
the twentieth century. Samuel Johnson, Coleridge, Hazlitt, and DeQuincey
are only a few of the prominent English writers who scrutinized the work of
their famous countryman. Who can dismiss the porter scene in *Macbeth* as
mere comic relief, after having read Thomas DeQuincey's article "On the
Knocking at the Gate in *Macbeth*"?

Criticism of the text touches on many areas that may prove important
to a director. Although the terms *tragedy* and *melodrama* in themselves

contribute nothing to expressive interpretation, discussions that try to determine such classifications provide helpful observations about our responses to characters and about the kind of impact that the play should have. Questions about the extent of our "pity and fear," our identification with a protagonist, our degree of admiration for his "stature" or "nobility," or of our sense of loss at his demise are very important, whether or not they lead to conclusions about the play's literary classification. In *Macbeth*, it is vital for the director to determine how much, if any, sympathy or identification he wishes the audience to feel for Macbeth and Lady Macbeth. His conclusions will determine how he casts the play, and how the characters appear in facial expression, movement, makeup, and costume.

> Let your Macbeth be chosen for the nervy, fiery beauty of his power. He must have tense intelligence, a swift leaping, lovely body, and a voice able to exalt and to blast. Let him not play the earlier scenes like a moody traitor, but like Lucifer, star of the morning. Let him not play the later scenes like a hangman who has taken to drink, but like an angel who has fallen.[1]

A. C. Bradley in his impressive and influential *Shakespearean Tragedy* insists that "The way to be untrue to Shakespeare here, as always, is to relax the tension of imagination, to conventionalize, to conceive of Macbeth, for example, as a half-hearted cowardly criminal, and Lady Macbeth as a wholehearted fiend."[2] Bradley does not ignore their evil, but supports their "sublimity" with references to their support and love for one another, their mutual suffering, Macbeth's "imagination of a poet," and his "inner being . . . convulsed by conscience."[3] Bradley reminds us that after the murder, when his imagination becomes quiescent, Macbeth becomes domineering, even brutal, or he becomes a cool pitiless hypocrite. But this is offset by his will to live: "The forces which impelled him to aim at the crown re-assert themselves. He faces the world, and his own conscience, desperate, but never dreaming of acknowledging defeat."[4]

This kind of criticism corresponds very closely to directorial thinking when a director must be concerned with his handling of character and its importance to the consistency of his interpretation. Twentieth-century studies of Shakespeare's use of language and imagery have proven to be extraordinarily influential to directors' thinking, especially in scenery and costume design. It was observed previously in the internal analysis that language patterns may contribute to our awareness of a play's design and intention as well as to a predominant mood or atmosphere. Later, in a discussion of costume design, Caroline Spurgeon's book *Shakespeare's Imagery* and articles by Cleanth Brooks and Alan S. Downer are cited for the way in which their studies of clothing imagery may be used in a production to poetically dramatize character and meaning.

NOTES

[1]John Masefield, *A Macbeth Production* (London: William Heinemann Ltd., 1945), p. 31.

[2]A. C. Bradley, *Shakespearean Tragedy* (London: Macmillan, 1951), pp. 349–350.

[3]Bradley, pp. 352-353.

[4]Bradley, p. 360.

Milieu within the Play

Previously, milieu was discussed as the period in which the play was created. Internal milieu refers to the period in which the play has been set. Sometimes the two periods correspond, as has been the case with most twentieth-century realistic dramas. Playwrights of past periods were inclined to set their plays in periods and places other than their own. Exceptions have occurred in plays of the past: Aeschylus departed from the usual conventions of Greek tragedy, which dealt with Homeric legend, when he wrote a tragedy (*The Persians*) about the recent Persian wars. Shakespeare's only example of England "here and now" was *The Merry Wives of Windsor*. The theatrical conventions of Aeschylus and Shakespeare were such that except for certain historical accuracies, realistic depictions of a milieu were not considered to be of great importance. In Athens, setting and costume were designed for tragedy rather than for a specific time or place and resembled the architecture and clothes of the contemporary Greece. In Shakespeare's theatre, the same set served all plays, and costumes were contemporary, although items of clothing suggesting the past were on occasion worn over the contemporary costume used by the actor. Anachronism did not appear to disturb anyone.

The modern theatre, however, has tended to emphasize environmental realism. We would not dream of performing Bolt's *A Man for All Seasons* in contemporary costume with twentieth-century decor. We feel obliged to research as thoroughly as possible the life and times of Sir Thomas More, even though Robert Bolt has written his play for dramatic rather than historical purposes, and for its relevance to the problems of the mid-twentieth century. And, despite the lack of such emphasis in the Athenian or Tudor periods, the modern director and designer must determine what period they wish to suggest when they stage plays from these eras. Should *The Oresteia* be performed in a Mycenean environment, in the manner of the Athenian theatre of the fifth century, or in modern dress? Should *A Midsummer Night's Dream* be performed in the Athenian environment of the story, in Elizabethan costume, in a combination of both, or in the period of the Restoration? Shall we stage our *Macbeth* in the protagonist's historical milieu or that of James I?

Such decisions will be a matter for later discussion. The point to be made now is that whatever decision is made milieu research will be necessary. Homer and mythology must become as familiar to us as to the Greek audience when we deal with Greek tragedy, and we must investigate the costumes, architecture, furniture, customs, and accessories of whatever period we decide to place our play (unless we attempt to be purely abstract in our presentation, or experiment with a "rehearsal" type of performance in modern dress as was attempted in the John Gielgud production of *Hamlet* starring Richard Burton). If *Macbeth* is to be set in the time and place of the real Macbeth, the costumes, armor, and accessories of the eleventh century must be researched. We must try to discover modes of greeting, soldier's salutes, and ceremonial customs of the time. In the banquet scene, tables, chairs, receptacles for food and drink, and eating habits of the period should be explored.

There are plays whose contexts represent so fully the parallel between internal and external milieu and which are so intended to mirror the times that it is impossible to conceive of them as taking place in any other period or locale than their own. Restoration comedy is such a representation. *Within* the play, the externals of behavior are so important that we must not only, in performing them, understand them—we must be capable of recreating the manner in which they were performed. How to walk, stand, sit, greet members of the same or the opposite sex, take snuff, manipulate fans, dance, sing, comprehend "studied negligence" in the practice of all of these, as well as recognize the influence of the style of Restoration stage conventions on movement and delivery—all of these require study that goes beyond the text, yet is intimately connected with it. The diaries and commentaries of observers of behavior in the court of Charles II, such as Ward or Evelyn, must be studied as must the portrait painting of the time. While other period plays may require more or less intensive study of modes and manners depending on each play's emphasis on custom and style, Restoration comedy requires a maximum study of the smallest details of external behavior. In an excellent article about the acting of Restoration comedy, N. W. Henshaw suggests that "The task of the director and the actor is to translate the world of the play into terms the audience can understand. Such a translation depends on a thorough comprehension of a somewhat alien way of life. A director is well-advised to immerse himself [and his actors] in the verbally and graphically expressed thoughts of the people who lived that alien life."[1]

NOTES

[1]N. W. Henshaw, "Graphic Sources for a Modern Approach to the Acting of Restoration Comedy," *American Educational Theatre Journal*, Vol. 20 (1968), p. 168.

Preparation for Expression: Working with the Designers

"The director is an artist, good or bad, since he creates a theatrical body for the idea he has from the play."[1]

Once the director has explored all avenues of investigation that contribute toward his knowledge and feelings about the play, he is ready to prepare his interpretation for theatrical expression. At this point, his independent work virtually has ended, for theatrical expression is ultimately the result of the director's collaborative efforts with other theatre artists, principally designers and actors.

Ideally, these other contributors to the play's final expression also are interpretative artists. They hopefully will bring to their first meetings with the director their own independent explorations of the text. They, like the director, should have developed a knowledge and feeling about the play on which to base the creativity and invention which will evolve as discussions and rehearsals progress. Because theatre art is a result of the collaborative effort of independent minds it often can be a frustrating experience. But for this same reason it can be very rich. The experience is frustrating when one or more of the collaborators lacks the integrity or the skill to contribute meaningfully to interpretation, or when differences in interpretation and its expression cannot be reconciled. Might it not be simpler to allow the director to be the sole interpreter and expect the designers and actors to base their artistic endeavors on his study and insights? This is not uncommon practice. One school of directing advocates such control by a director. Sometimes, when an experienced director works with inexperienced personnel he has no alternative. But when competent designers and actors are involved, the entire creative experience potentially becomes richer and more satisfying for all concerned. Truly creative artists of any kind are more strongly stimulated and their work is better integrated when it is at least in part the result of their own convictions. The director's task is to pull the endeavors of all the artists into a unified and consistent whole.

Of course, disagreements will occur. They should be discussed. All parties should respectfully listen to and weigh the arguments. The final decision is the director's since it is his responsibility to coordinate and move the production in a meaningful and unified direction. But the director should be guided by this objective rather than by the dictates of his ego, or by the necessity to assert his leadership. The actor and designer must submit in controversies when it is demonstrated that their suggestions may deviate from or confuse major interpretative concepts. Mutual respect for the others' intellect and creative capacities establishes the ideal atmosphere for the collaborative art that is theatre.

The following chapters are devoted to explaining and demonstrating the ways in which the director works with designers and actors. The philosophy underlying their relationship is based on the previous introductory remarks. The director must be the final judge of the interpretative core of the play and the means used to express it, but it is best to work in an atmosphere of creative collaboration, in which the ideas of the designer and actor are permitted the fullest possible expression.

NOTES

[1]Stark Young, *The Theatre* (New York: Hill and Wang, 1958), p. 85.

The Director
and the Design Staff

In the modern theatre, design covers five areas. Setting, properties, costumes, and lighting are all aspects of visual design. From the earliest dramas, audible design also has played an important role. Greek and Elizabethan drama used original instrumental music and song, and modern drama often has incorporated a "score" as well as special sound effects.

There is not necessarily a separate designer for each of these areas: scenery, properties, and lighting are often designed by a single individual; the set designer on occasion has created the costumes. Whatever the number of persons involved, the five areas of design must be coordinated toward a unified effect. To achieve this, frequent conferences between the director and the designers are necessary to establish the relationship among all aspects of design. For example, costume colors must be coordinated with set and light colors; music must be composed with the same justification for style, period, and atmosphere as the set and costumes. The sequence of procedure will vary depending on the manner in which a director and the design staff prefer to work. The following section suggests several possible procedures.

1. At the initial meetings, practical considerations external to the play but which will affect the approach to the play's design may be discussed. Factors such as budget and the limitations and problems presented by the theatre, auditorium, and equipment are considered. Realistic evaluation of the budget will prevent much wasted effort and disappointment. It is helpful to know at once if elaborate sets and costumes are possible, or if the designers must direct their imaginations toward more economical and simplified methods of expression. Would it be feasible, for example, to consider a revolving stage with many levels for *Macbeth*? Or should the setting be kept to a minimum while costumes and lighting are emphasized? What spatial and sight line problems do the stage and auditorium present? If the theatre has a balcony, is the proscenium arch high enough so that actors on tall platforms may be seen? How deep may the set be planned before creating too wide a gulf between actor and audience? Will the stage permit a thrust acting area?

Is there sufficient depth and wing space for the storage of wagon stages? Is there a fly gallery and a counterweight system so that sets may be flown in and out? What lighting effects may be achieved with the available electrical power, switchboard capacity and control, and number of instruments? The director must be as aware of these problems as the designers, or he may waste his time and theirs with visualizations that are not physically or financially feasible.

However, a counter argument is that the imaginations of all parties should be given free reign, that in the early stages their thinking should exclude practical considerations and concentrate on more abstract concerns such as a style for the play, design metaphors, and atmosphere. The belief here is that the details mentioned previously tend to limit and narrow the creative process, which if first allowed free reign may eventually be modified, without losing the essential subjective qualities, to suit practical limitations. If the artistic staff agrees that this method is best, then initial talks should concentrate on the interpretative aspects of the play.

2. Whenever interpretative aspects are to be discussed, sufficient time should be given each artist to think deeply about the play and its impact on him. The director, who must make the final decisions, usually acts as a chairman for the discussions, and must determine whether he should first present his views, or first listen to the views of the others and then discuss his own in relation to the suggestions that have been made. Rather than taking turns, another procedure is to open the entire matter to free discussion. The director may ask questions about style, visual images, and emotional overtones; the replies may lead into discussions in which he may or may not participate. Some directors may wish to explore as fully as possible the views of others, then weigh them against their own views before committing themselves. Some designers prefer the stimulus of the director's convictions before committing themselves.

If time permits, no decisions need to be made at the first such meeting. Each artist leaves with a better idea of what the others are thinking and begins to relate their suggestions to his own. Each may begin to think, using stage images relevant to the intellectual and emotional aspects of interpretation that have been discussed. Further meetings should then lead to an agreed interpretation which is sufficiently clear for the designers to begin work on their first sketches. At ensuing meetings, where sketches and renderings, colors, and swatches of materials are studied by all members of the artistic staff, the real theatrical communication begins. Rough sketches, water color renderings of sets and costumes, models, and lighting plans show the participants whether they have been thinking, talking about, and feeling the same things. Modifications usually are made at the suggestion of the director, and sometimes one idea after another may be rejected until one that is satisfactory to director and designer is created. It is a trying period when egos are ruffled and tempers often flare, but as long as there is give and take, as long as rejections are justified and positive suggestions are made, control may be maintained without a permanent loss of morale. No designer wants a director to tell him how to design sets or costumes, but neither can confusing or vague suggestions help him, and he will not be content with a series of "No, that's not it . . . ." responses without clarification.

Design aspects of a play should be finally decided before the sets and costumes are constructed. Exceptions in the professional commercial theatre may be sanctioned. If financially and physically possible, it probably is best to admit it when the designs are not working and to rebuild and restage the play. There is a certain integrity to admitting to one's mistakes and attempting to avoid an artistic failure. But educational, community, and many repertory theatres do not have the time and money to do this. Mistakes are more likely to occur when a purely intuitive approach is used by the director and the designers, or when there has been a failure in successful communication between them. Sometimes the intuitive, or "let's find out about this play as we work on it," approach is very exciting and successful, but it is more subject to chance and miscalculation than the principle of preparation that this book advocates.

Of course, some kinds of changes are possible before opening night. Set colors may be changed, moveable pieces may be rearranged, reasonable additions to a set may be made, and lights may be refocused or relighted. If he works with a model and an accurate ground plan in early rehearsals, the director will be able to request changes, alterations, or additions before it is too late.

3. When rehearsals begin, it is a good idea for the director to request that the designers attend some of them, particularly early runthroughs. The light designer will be able to see exactly where the important light areas are located by studying composition and stage action. The set designer will be able to inform the director about the feasibility of some action, and correct or discuss any misconceptions the director may have had about entrances and exits, levels, sight lines, and set limitations. The costumer may get new ideas for some of his designs by watching the actors' business and movement. Often he can be a great help in advising the actors how to anticipate the management of costumes, which may not be worn until dress rehearsal.

The technical rehearsal should be attended by the entire design staff, which should sit close enough to the director to discuss problems that arise as the rehearsal progresses. Most often some of the staff will be too busy completing details backstage, but they should attempt whenever possible to go "out front" and view the progress of the play. The director may, if he does not wish to use the time during the rehearsal, make notes and discuss these later with the design and technical staff.

Finally, at the dress rehearsal, of which there may be more than one, the entire artistic staff should sit back and view the play as a performance. They still will need to take notes so that final problems may be discussed and worked out after the rehearsal. The procedure of the artistic staff continuing its work together even after design decisions have been made cannot be over-emphasized. All too often in both amateur and professional theatre, designers ignore what is done with their contributions to the play, or believe that nothing more can be done with a design after the director has approved it. How many scene designers have been appalled by the misuse of their conceptions, or by the incongruity between the statements made by the set and by the acting? How many costumers wish that they had spent more time in the auditorium when on opening night they observe actors who make the costumes look bad because they do not know how to move in them?

The wise director knows how much richer the play may be when he has the constant advice and continued contribution of the design staff. He should insist on a continuous, dynamic relationship with it from the initial discussions to the opening performance.

13
The Director and the Design

In the previous chapter, an attempt was made to clarify the kinds of relationships that exist between the director and the design staff. The concern of this chapter is to concentrate on the specific methods and justifications of determining the design aspects of the play. It was stated previously that designers rarely wish to be told *how* to design a play. They prefer to discuss the play's needs and interpretation with the director, after which they will suggest the actual execution—subject of course to the director's approval. Because this book chiefly is concerned with the director rather than the designer, it will emphasize the director's role in the evolution of a design rather than its execution.

The preparation for a design involves two major stimuli—the "functional" demands of the play and the appearance and impact of the set, or the "interpretative" aspects of the design.

FUNCTIONAL DEMANDS

The director must work through the entire play several times with the sole purpose of determining its functional or practical demands of set, properties, costume, lighting, and sound. An efficient way of doing this is by making a careful and thorough chart itemizing design necessities for each scene (see Table 3). The advantages of this system are twofold: first, it compels the director to recognize in detail the functional needs of the play's design and, second, it provides the stage manager and property master with a scene-by-scene breakdown of design details so that they may at least simulate such details for rehearsals. In organizing his chart, the director must be aware of the following functional requirements demanded by each design aspect of the play.

Setting and Locale.   Is the play localized in a specific city or country? Is there a particular environment for the play: in someone's home, on a battlefield, in a seaport? Is there an interior or exterior locale: does the play take

TABLE 3

MACBETH: BASIC FUNCTIONAL REQUIREMENTS SETTING

Scene	Locale	Entrances and Exits	Special Requirements
I, 1	Unspecified exterior. A place for the witches.	One ent., one exit. Could be the same.	Possible trap for disappearance.
I, 2	Exterior. Battle area near Forres. Duncan's camp site.	1. Ent. of Duncan 2. Ent. of bleeding Sergeant 3. Ent. of Ross from Fife 4. Exit of Sergeant to surgeon—could use Duncan's ent. 5. Exit of Ross to Macbeth—could use Sergeant's ent.	None.
I, 3	A "blasted heath."	1. Ent. of witches from 3 different directions 2. Ent. of Macbeth and Banquo 3. Ent. of Ross and Angus from Duncan 4. Exit of witches 5. Exit of foursome to Duncan	Possible trap for disappearance of witches.
I, 4	Exterior of Duncan's palace at Forres.	1. Ent. of Duncan, Malcolm, etc. 2. Ent. of Macbeth, Banquo, etc. 3. Exit of Macbeth, then others to Inverness	None.
I, 5	Exterior of Macbeth's castle at Inverness.	1. Ent. of Lady M. from castle 2. Ent. of messenger from Forres 3. Ent. of Macbeth from Forres	None. "This castle hath a pleasant seat." (I, 6)

Scene			
I, 6	Same as I, 5.	4. Exit messenger into castle 5. Exit Macbeth and Lady M. into castle	Same as I, 5.
I, 7	Interior. A hall or room adjoining banquet chamber. Inverness.	1. Ent. of Duncan and party from Forres 2. Ent. of Lady M. from castle 3. General exit into castle 1. Ent. of servants from kitchen 2. Ent. of Macbeth, then Lady M. from banquet chamber 3. Exit of servants then Macbeth and Lady M. to banquet chamber	At least one door.

COSTUMES, ACCESSORIES

Scene	
I, 1	Witches: "so wild in their attire," "filthy hags."
I, 2	Soldiers' garb. Shields. Attendants. Torn and bloody costume for bleeding sergeant. Define royal family. Special garb for Duncan, incl. crown.
I, 3	Macbeth and Banquo in armor. Possible clan identification.
I, 4	No new characters.
I, 5	Lady Macbeth: nothing specified. She is a noble & wife of Macbeth. Possible clan design. Messenger of Macbeth's employ.
I, 6	No new characters. Possible that Lady M. will add cloak or some special garment to greet king.
I, 7	Macbeth now is host. Change from military garb to nonmilitary dress.

PROPERTIES

Scene	Stage	Hand
I, 1	None specified.	None specified.
I, 2	None specified.	Attendants & soldiers, banners, cross, armor, swords.
I, 3	None specified.	Pilot's thumb. Swords.
I, 4	None specified.	Same as I, 2.
I, 5	None specified.	Letter.
I, 6	None specified.	Torches.
I, 7	None.	Torches. Trays with food, drink, utensils.

TABLE 3 (cont'd)

Scene	LIGHTING	MUSIC & SOUND
I, 1	Daytime. "Fog and filthy air." Possible supernatural effects for witches. Lightning.	"I come, Graymalkin." "Paddock calls." Thunder.
I, 2	Daytime.	"Alarum within" for entrance of Duncan.
I, 3	"Set of sun." Witches vanish "into the air"—possible lighting effect?	Thunder. "A drum, a drum!" Thunder for vanishing of witches?
I, 4	Unclear as to time of day. No torches specified. Could be following day.	"Flourish" for Duncan's entrance and exit.
I, 5	Daytime. Lady Macbeth says, "Come thick night."	None specified.
I, 6	Evening. Torches specified. Still enough visibility to see martlet's nest.	Flourish for Duncan's arrival. Bird sounds.
I, 7	Night. Interior. Torches carried by servants—can put torches on walls for Macbeth scene that follows.	Folio suggests oboes. Could indicate festivity in banquet chamber by music, voices.

place in a particular room of a dwelling or in the garden, in the headquarters of the army commander or in a fox hole, on the beach or inside a ship's cabin?

Macbeth takes place in Scotland and in England, and the play's locales are divided into numerous interior and exterior environments, some specifically defined and others more vague. Clues for locale in Shakespeare are to be found in the dialogue and occasionally in the stage directions of the original quartos, or the first folio. Stage directions in later editions are made by editors using the same kinds of supposition that today's director might. *Macbeth* in the folio text contains no stage direction for locale. A director should, whether or not he plans to stage the play with realistic scenery, seek clues for locale within the text and check various modern editions for suggestions. How the designer is to treat locale will depend on stylistic decisions, which will be discussed later. But if a realistic treatment is chosen, then each locale, the heath, the battlefield, the interior and exterior of Macbeth's castle, the English court must be fully represented by the sets. If a nonrealistic approach is desired, then the director and designer may decide to partially suggest locale, or, by not suggesting locale at all in the set, to place the illusion of locale on the actor's imaginative response to place. We know, for example, that the setting for Act I, Scene 3 of Macbeth is a heath before sunset because in Act I, Scene 1, the witches tell us so, and because Macbeth refers to "this blasted heath." In addition, we know that because Macbeth and Banquo are traveling to Forres, the setting is an exterior. Macbeth also refers to the day as "foul and fair." From this, and from the stylistic consistency desired, the designer may try to create a thoroughly realistic illusion of a Scottish heath structured somehow to justify the "foul–fair" allusion or, by the use perhaps of one gnarled tree and a crag or two, merely suggest the heath. Or the scene may be played in open empty space, where the actors' responses to an imagined foul–fair environment, plus the previously supplied information about a heath, may create an environment in the imaginations of the audience. But the director must consider carefully and thoroughly all suggestions of locale, so that they may contribute to his imaginative creation of an environment.

Setting and Ground Plan.   A ground plan is a map of the use of stage space. It is a bird's-eye view of the setting, revealing the size and shape of the ground space on the stage, the location of doors, windows, fireplaces, staircases, platforms, the arrangement of furniture and set pieces such as trees or boulders. The director is not obliged to provide exact dimensions, but should be able to specify whether the play requires small or large acting areas, or a combination of both. The interior set of *The Lower Depths* must suggest a crowded oppressive environment, while a Greek tragedy normally requires a sense of the out-of-doors and large areas to accommodate a chorus and principals. The setting for Greek tragedies, in contrast to most naturalistic plays, demands a size that is proportionate to their larger-than-life movement and gesture. Shakespeare normally requires various spatial illusions, from the close intimacy of the soliloquies to the larger scope of the battle scenes. The

Elizabethan stage apparently used the thrust stage to accommodate the former, where the proscenium stage must resort to three-dimensional enclosures or isolation through lighting.

Spatial size is most often dictated by the numbers of characters who must occupy it at the same time, by the suggestion of locale, and by the relationship desired by the director between the actor and the space around him. In *Macbeth*, a large space is necessary for the banquet scene because it must accommodate a large table, a separate area for the two thrones, and an entrance area where Macbeth may talk to the two murderers and be a reasonable distance from his guests. The scene requires from fourteen to twenty people. Such a scene would normally use as much width and depth as the stage allows. The heath scene (I, 3) requires fewer characters, but the locale should suggest the spaciousness of a countryside. But *Macbeth* abounds also in scenes that suggest the smaller spaces required for intimacy and for concentration on internal struggle. Such a scene is Act I, Scene 7, which takes place in a hall outside the banquet room. Realistically the hall could be as large as the vast halls of Scottish castles, but psychologically we would lose the sense of claustrophobia experienced by Macbeth when he is alone on stage, and the necessary emphasis on the psychological battle between the Macbeths, which follows. In some manner, the space of this scene must be narrowed. Sometimes a director must choose between two or more effects, each of which appears to be correct, but which are quite different. For example, if Lady Macbeth's sleepwalking scene is played in a large open space, her isolation is emphasized. If the director wishes, however, to stress her internal disintegration, her physical presence must dominate the stage and can only do so if the space around her is minimized. Physical proximity to the audience, of course, contributes to the effect.

The shape of the set is influenced by, among other things, its size. Maximum space is acquired by using a deep rectangle or curve, while a triangular shape will cut space down considerably. Except for the influence of locale on shape, however (such as the ship-house of Captain Shotover in *Heartbreak House*), shape is determined more by aesthetic than functional stress.

An extremely important functional aspect of the ground plan is the determination of the number of entrances and exits and their placement. In a box set, doors and arches are used for entrances; on the reconstructed Elizabethan stage, functional doors plus the openings created by inner stages are used; on an open stage where no wall units are used, entrances are made by simply moving into view, and exits are accomplished by the actor disappearing into wings or curtained areas. The principles for each kind of stage are the same, however, and the director must plan the entrances with precision. First he must determine the number of separate entrances for each locale. In a realistic play, the stage directions ordinarily make such requirements clear. In *Ghosts*, Ibsen tells us that there is a door on the left wall and two doors in the right wall in the room proper. In the conservatory, which is

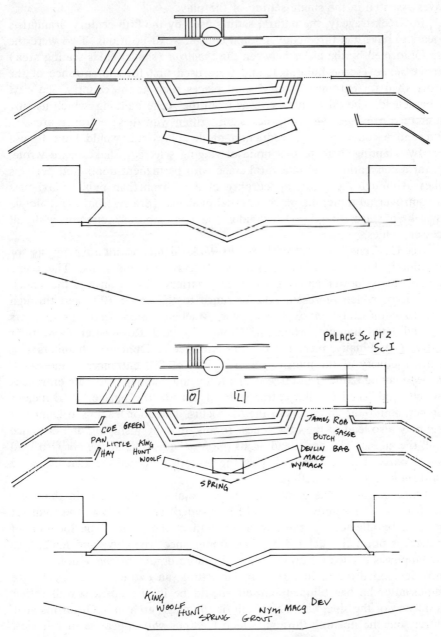

Ground plan for *Macbeth*, Act III, Scene 4. Royal Shakespeare Company, 1955, directed by Glen B. Shaw. Used by permission of the Royal Shakespeare Company, Stratford-upon-Avon.

upstage, another door is located in the right wall. Each one of these doors proves essential in the single setting of the play.

In Greek tragedy, the natural setting used by the fifth-century dramatists appears to have had three conventional entrance-exit positions. Two were the *paradoi* formed by the aisles between the *theatron* (semicircular seating area) and the *skene* (scene building), and were used first for the entrance of the chorus, then for entrances from distant places such as the country, the city, the battlefield. The third entrance was from the scene building, which usually represented a palace. The tragedies were written with these entrance areas in mind, and a contemporary production of the plays still would have to use them by adapting them to the mode of staging selected. Shakespeare wrote, too, for a conventional architectural stage with permanent doors and perhaps arches. Although the actual appearance of the Elizabethan public playhouse is a controversial topic, the plays' internal evidence (drawn from the dialogue rather than stage directions) provides the contemporary director with all necessary clues.

Act II, Scene 3 of *Macbeth*, for example, demands careful analysis for determining the number and positions of entrances and exits. The scene begins with the porter entering from his quarters (1) to answer the knock on the door, which represents the entrance to the castle (2), and through which Macduff and Lennox will appear. Macbeth enters from his quarters (3), and later Banquo, Malcolm, Donalbain, and Ross enter from their quarters (4). Finally, there must be an entrance to Duncan's chambers (5) for the discovery of the murder. A maximum of five entrances is indicated, but they may be reduced to three in the following manner: separate entrances *must* be established for the entrance from outside the palace, to Duncan's chamber, and to the chambers of the Macbeths. The door leading to Duncan's room may also lead to the other guest rooms, thereby justifying one entrance for all the guests. The door leading to the Macbeths' chamber may also lead to other parts of the castle, justifying the porter's entrance through the same door through which Macbeth enters.'

Entrances and exits create two other major considerations in the creation of a set: (1) where each should be located, and (2) how the total set plan is to be affected by plays with more than one locale. The location of entrances is normally dictated by their importance, visibility, and logic. The more emphasis needed for an entrance, the more dominant and visible a position is demanded for it. In a rectangular setting, an entrance such as that of Oedipus after he has blinded himself should be in the upstage wall rather than in one of the side walls. Not only is the stage area in such an instance stronger, but the opening through which Oedipus will appear is in full view of the audience, anticipating the emergence of the king as he gropes his way into the open air. In addition, as he enters the actor will be seen from the greatest advantage—in a full front position, fully revealed to the audience. If a diagonal setting is used, such an entrance would have to be located on one of the sides of the apex, which will create the most "open" position for the actor, and will focus attention by the diagonal line leading to the entrance area.

In *Hedda Gabler*, Ibsen wants the audience to be able to see through open doors into an adjoining room. This is important in Act II, when Hedda is attempting to manipulate Lovborg, while her husband and Judge Brock drink in the other room, and in Act IV, when it is vital to see Thea and Tesman diligently at work together while Brock tries to trap Hedda. Only by placing these doors in the upstage wall can the entire audience see what it is intended to see.

In other instances, characters may have to play a scene while focusing on or through a door or archway. In such cases, we must be able to see the actor as fully as possible while he relates to the offstage area. It is almost obligatory to place the offstage action on the side, preferably downstage. At the conclusion of Act I of *Ghosts*, Mrs. Alving and Pastor Manders hear Oswald and Regina flirting in the dining room, and we are provided with a tableau of Mrs. Alving's shocked response as she stares in the direction of the dining room and whispers "Ghosts." Obviously this is most effective if the entrance to the dining room is in one of the side walls. The play is about the impact of the past on Mrs. Alving, as affected by her decision to stay with her husband. If the dining room wall were placed upstage, the scene, as Mrs. Alving faces away from the audience, would emphasize the offstage action. With the door in a side wall, the offstage action remains important, but primarily in relation to its impact on the fully exposed Mrs. Alving.

Entrances and exits also should have logical associations. Entering actors are coming from somewhere and exiting actors are going somewhere. In drama this is more often explicit than not, and when an actor enters or exits the audience should be able to make some logical association between the direction in which he moves and where he is supposed to be coming or going. In a production of *Romeo and Juliet*, the director established four different directions for access to Friar Laurence's cell. Yet Shakespeare makes it perfectly clear that there are only two: one to the "study" and the other, represented by a door, to the outside. The identical locale is used three times in the play, and there is no reason to use more than two entrances. In the aforementioned production, however, in which no walls were used, characters entered and departed haphazardly from right, up right, left, and up left. Even with nonrealistic conventions, this sort of thing becomes confusing and contradicts the text, which requires the nurse in Act III, Scene 3 to keep pounding on the door for access, when other persons in the play had been moving freely in and out from other directions!

Act I, Scene 3 of *Macbeth* provides a basic situation for entrances and exits that is simple enough, yet demands a certain logic. The scene opens with the entrance of the witches, who are joined by Macbeth and Banquo. They will eventually leave, and the pair on stage will be joined by Ross and Angus.

At the end of the scene the four men exit together. The witches can, if the director wishes, appear or disappear by stage magic, but if he wants them to enter, clearly they should not enter from the same direction that Macbeth and Duncan do. Because Ross and Angus are coming from Forres in search of Macbeth who is coming from Fife toward Forres, the entrances of the two pairs of men should be from different areas—probably from opposite sides of the stage. The witches then might appear from up center and move downstage. Macbeth and Banquo enter from left stage—preferably upstage so that they may be seen in frontal positions as they comment on the witches. The witches vanish—perhaps through a trap door—whereupon Macbeth and Banquo move into the predominant area of the stage for their scene together. Ross and Angus should then appear from the right, where they are eventually joined by Banquo. Macbeth will be separated from them for his asides ("Look how our partner's rapt"), but will join the others for the exit to Forres, right stage, the area from which Ross and Angus appeared.

When there are two or more entrances in a realistic interior, logic most often makes it necessary to avoid putting all of them in the same wall. A room might have its only two doors in the same wall, but on stage this somehow appears unnatural. Besides, the director deprives himself and his actors of more interesting theatrical movement and use of stage space when all entrances and exits are made through one side of the stage only.

An additional problem is created in the placement of entrances and exits in a play with more than one locale. Chekhov's *Uncle Vanya* calls for three interior sets, each representing a different room in the same house. The director and designer should try to vary the placement of entrances to these areas so that they are not duplicated from locale to locale. Changing locales are supposed to suggest different environments and new associations. Duplicating entrance areas creates a sameness—even if everything else is different— and produces unvaried traffic patterns in stage movement. Shakespeare's plays, with their numerous locales, create similar problems, even when no doors or arches are used. There are just so many directions by which characters may come and go from scene to scene, but in the quick flowing action demanded by Shakespearean staging, some imagination must be used in working out the logic and variety of entrances and exits in the play's progression. At the end of the third scene of *Macbeth*, for example, it was suggested that Macbeth and Banquo depart with the nobles at right stage. If this is done, then the entrance of Duncan and his group at Forres in the next scene should not be made from right stage, but from up center or left stage. Macbeth may then reappear with the others from the area in which they had previously departed. The scene ends with the king and his company following Macbeth to the latter's castle at Inverness. Since stage right in this scene would represent the area to the battlefield and Fife, and the upstage area the palace entrance at Forres, left stage remains to suggest the direction to Inverness, where the next scene takes place. Lady Macbeth enters in the new locale as soon as the stage is cleared of the characters in the previous scene. She must therefore enter from upstage or stage right, where she will not collide with the exiting characters. Her entrance will establish the entrance to the castle, which is also used in the next scene. If up center is chosen, then she and Macbeth will exit through it at the end of Scene 5; she will reappear at the same place to greet the king in Scene 6 and they all will enter the castle through the same area at the end of the scene. In the meantime, Macbeth in Scene 5 and the king with his followers in Scene 6, all arriving from the same place, will enter left stage where they had exited in Scene 4. Finally, in the last scene of Act I, a hall within the castle is suggested. Servants with dishes for the banquet will pass from left to right, or vice versa, and establish the entrance to the banquet hall, from which the solitary Macbeth and later his wife will enter, resolve their differences, and return to the banquet hall.

Other aspects of the ground plan include the placement of such architectural structures as windows, platforms, stairs, and fireplaces. Exteriors might include set pieces suggesting the natural environment such as trees, slopes, or boulders. Similar principles as those applied to entrances and exits apply to each of these. They should serve some purpose in the setting, they should be placed on stage according to the relative dominance or weakness of their function, and they should be related to the setting and the action in a logical, coherent way. Windows that the entire audience must be able to see through should be placed upstage, while those that the actors (whose responses are emphasized) look through normally are placed in the side walls. Lighting may influence the location of a window. If the director wishes to have a beam of light strike an object or a character on stage, and feels that it must be realistically justified, the most effective source of light normally would be from the sides rather than from the rear of the set.

Platforms or levels are effective devices for solving problems of visibility and for emphasis, such as elevating dominant characters during crowd scenes. The texts of some plays demand platforms for important dramatic functions. Juliet's balcony, the multilevel interior of O'Neill's *Desire under the Elms*, the plinth for the hanging skeleton and gatling gun in Arden's *Serjeant Musgrave's Dance* are indispensible to the action and dramatic effectiveness of these plays. In plays not specifically requiring levels, the director and designer may seek justification to raise parts of the stage for added visibility or for dramatic effect. An example of such an addition for visibility occurred in a production of Chekhov's *The Sea Gull*. The setting for Act III is a dining room, and begins with an eating scene. There is a great deal of physical action in the scene, including Sorin's heart attack, two violently emotional scenes involving Arkadina—first with her son, then with her lover—climaxed by a chaotic departure scene. With a relatively small stage, the director decided that raising one area of the stage would not only create the potential for more variety in movement and composition, but would make it possible to divide the stage into planes, the elevated upstage area for the eating sequences, and

133

the downstage for luggage and pieces of furniture, in which the more intimate scenes might be enacted. This also opened the downstage area for the
traffic of the departure scene, making it possible for characters who were
standing upstage to be visible and involved while the downstage area was in
use.

Functionally, *Macbeth* does not actually *demand* the use of levels, but
Shakespeare suggests in one portion of the play that another level was
probably intended. In the murder scene (II, 2) Macbeth speaks of having
"descended," and in the next scene he shows Macduff the "door" to Duncan's
chambers. The suggestion that the door leads to an upper chamber creates
the possibility for the use of an upper level to contribute to the dramatic
effectiveness of the discovery of the murder. On an Elizabethan stage, one
door probably led to the exterior and would have been the door used by the
porter. Macduff and Lennox would enter through this door. The other door
would have led to Duncan's quarters above, and the exposed area above
might represent a hall between Duncan's quarters and those of Banquo,
Malcolm, and Donalbain. Lady Macbeth would appear, then later be assisted
off through the inner stage below. This makes it possible to build the chaos
and excitement of the discovery by using every entrance on stage and above,
causing the audience to witness the entire castle in uproar. Macduff, who
has discovered the body, would appear above shouting the alarum and calling
for bells from a strong central dominant position. Malcolm and Donalbain
can remain above where they have appeared from their bedrooms after the
others descended. Their isolation will make their asides more meaningful,
as well as suggest suspicion.

The director should have some ideas about where he would like levels
to be placed and the amount of space they should occupy on stage. Generally
speaking, platforms, unless they comprise the main acting area, should not
be placed downstage center. In such a position, they remove the most useful
and dominant parts of the stage from use in scenes not played on the platforms; they split the stage into three small areas, making one side useless
when the other is in use; finally, a raised area down center will make the
area above it depressed, perhaps screening it altogether and rendering it
useless as a playing area. Platforms are best placed upstage or at the sides
of the stage. When symmetry is desired in composition, and a level is needed,
the upstage center area is useful, but if an important scene is shared by a
speaker on a platform and another below, then the platform might well be
placed in a diagonal position up left or up right; otherwise the actor below
must upstage himself while addressing the actor on the platform. In a
proscenium production of *Oedipus Rex,* Oedipus must share scenes with
Teiresias and Creon, and occupy the palace platform at least part of the
time. Teiresias and Creon must have equal emphasis during much of these
scenes yet appear to be addressing their king. The best means of accom-
plishing this is by angling the staircase and platform on one side of the stage

so that characters below may remain in open positions as they relate to characters on the platform.

Fireplaces, when they are used for decorative purposes, may be placed in any of the walls of the setting. But when they become functional to the action, they must be located in the side walls, and when they become important the further they are placed downstage the better. Scenes of warmth and intimacy before a stove or a fireplace should be close to the audience. When Hedda burns the manuscript, it should not only be close to the audience, but the audience must be able to see her face as she burns Thea's "child." The light of the intensifying flames flickers on Hedda's face and perhaps throws grotesque shadows on the upstage walls of the room.

Properties.   Properties are objects appearing on stage that are not part of the architectural or natural structure of the setting. They may be furniture or "dressing" pieces such as clocks, vases, pictures, or other objects that contribute to sense of character or locale in a set. They may also be "hand props," objects carried on and offstage by the actors during the progress of the play. Properties come under the category of design because they must be consistent with the style and statement made by the setting. Sometimes, properties are especially designed for a play: a throne for Macbeth may be intended to suggest by its shape and texture "evil power," so that something more than an accurate period piece is necessary. Otherwise real pieces are selected from antique stores and other appropriate sources for their period accuracy, their size, texture, and color.

The arrangement of furniture on a stage becomes part of the ground plan. The director must base furniture arrangements on the selection, space, sight lines, and the relationship of furniture to the set and to other pieces. Selection, as is the case in the design of the set or in the determination of the "business" of the actors, normally will be based on the functional requirements of the play, such as the thrones and the table in the Banquo ghost scene in *Macbeth,* or on environmental demands such as furniture and accessories in a realistic play like *Hedda Gabler,* which must represent in detail a middle-class nineteenth century room. Pinter's *The Caretaker* calls for a crowded and cluttered effect, while Greek and Shakespearean tragedies often require little more than empty stages. Directors may be tempted to use more furniture and properties than actually are needed in Shakespeare to establish a sense of locale and to stimulate more interesting business and movement. This is often a mistake because the shifting of furniture for the number of locales in the average Elizabethan play would slow down the action and interrupt the play's rhythm and fluidity. On the other hand, realistic and naturalistic settings in plays with a single set, or with a few sets for longer scenes justify the inclusion of properties that will stimulate realistic movement and interesting business by the actors.

The size of the stage certainly will influence the amount of furniture to be used. On a large stage, for example, Hellman's *The Little Foxes* single set calls for an ostentatious living room with lots of expensive furniture, including a large piano. Many community theatres and universities do not enjoy the spaciousness of the theatre in which the play originally was produced. For them, the attempt to squeeze all the properties used in the Broadway production onto a small stage would create a clutter that is not appropriate to the play. The solution is to select pieces that represent the character of the room, and that will contribute most to the realistic action of the play.

Selection and space are related in another way. In most plays, there must be enough space left after the furniture has been placed for a free flow of movement. Unless, as in *The Caretaker* or *The Lower Depths,* a sense of confusion and crowdedness is necessary, props must be selected and arranged to permit easy movement and sufficient open space so that some actors can stand while others are seated, or so that, when necessary, several actors can circulate freely at the same time.

This principle has a bearing too on the organization of furniture pieces on stage. The director may allow for plenty of space in his arrangement of furniture, but the open spaces may be improperly placed. By placing most of the properties down stage, he minimizes the strongest planes at his disposal and forces much of the action to take place behind the furniture, which will block the lower parts of the actors' bodies. The reverse of this has equally bad consequences. With most of the furniture upstage, there is plenty of space in the emphatic areas of the stage, but the characters then appear to be playing in front of their furniture rather than within it, and the effect is that of a room which has been prepared for a party or a dance. In addition, all seated scenes would have to take place far upstage. Another mistake can result from placing furniture too close together. Normally space is needed for movement and composition, as well as naturalness, between and around pieces of furniture. By placing a sofa and an armchair too close to each other, a potential area for movement is eliminated. In most cases the actor should be able to stand or move between these objects, and it is more interesting and natural for him to have access to the sofa and chair from both sides. Furniture may, of course, be placed against the walls of a room, but some scenes require it to have space all around. The director may want to play a sofa scene with one character seated while another character stands above leaning over the sofa. A table may have to seat more people in an open position than one next to the wall will permit. The angle of a wall may create a poor position for a piece of furniture set against it. If a sofa is set against a wall that angles more than 45 degrees upstage and two actors sitting on it are required to converse, neither's face will be visible. The downstage actor must face three-fourths up, and at the same time he will cover the other actor from the audience on the same side of the theatre as the wall.

Normally, pieces of furniture will be arranged so that actors may use or relate to them and to each other. Tables and chairs most often should

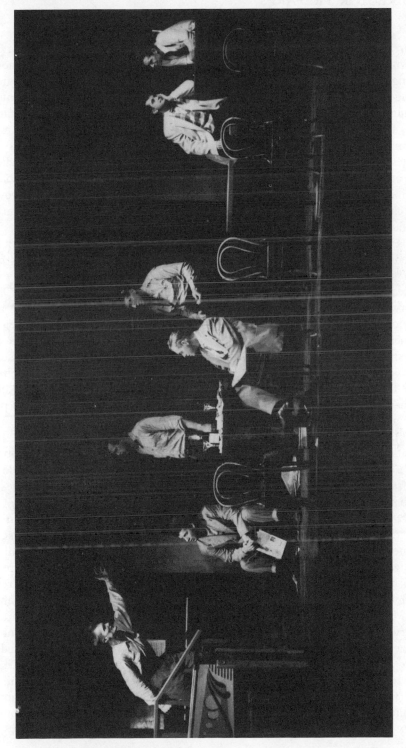

Furniture arrangement: conversational grouping. *The Time of Your Life* by William Saroyan. Set design by John Van Duzer, Humboldt State College.

be arranged to make it possible for characters to converse without having to twist or strain unnaturally. Furniture placed at the sides normally should be angled toward the center of the stage, while furniture in the central areas of the stage might, depending on the circumstances, be placed full front or be angled to favor the furniture at one side of the stage or the other. On a fairly large stage, space may be divided into two or three separate areas with furniture arranged in groups. In Saroyan's *The Time of Your Life,* a bar creates one possibility for grouping, tables and chairs distributed throughout the room form their own groupings, while the pinball machine adds another possibility. All of these props must be arranged in such a way, however, that characters in each area may naturally relate to characters in other areas without obscuring each other.

Emphatic properties—those used for important action or for extended periods of time—must be placed in emphatic areas of the stage. Juliet's bier must be in a prominent position for several reasons. Romeo must play his suicide scene near her body, as Juliet must play her final scene near his. Afterwards, their bodies become the focal point for the lamentation and reconciliation that ends the play. In *Twelfth Night* a stool or garden seat is frequently placed at or near center so that, after Malvolio discovers the forged letter (II, 5), he can sit, stand, move around, and even assume ridiculous postures in the strongest possible position. Secondary emphasis may then be created at one side of the stage, probably upstage of Malvolio, where the heads of Sir Toby and the other schemers may occasionally peer over a property or set piece that conceals them.

The placement of properties also should take proper visibility into consideration. A piece of furniture requiring emphasis, or having symbolic value should rarely be obscured by another object. We must be able to see from any part of the theatre Macbeth and Lady Macbeth's thrones in the banquet scene, as well as the chair that Banquo's ghost will occupy. An object may be in the strongest area on stage, but if it is concealed from the audience by another object its importance is diminished. Common sense dictates that the taller properties in a scene be placed against a wall or upstage of the major action, but often directors fail to notice that lamps or other objects placed on tables will get in the way of important scenes. Margery Pinchwife's letter in Wycherley's *The Country Wife* is written by candle light, but the candelabrum must be placed upstage on the desk if we are to observe the marvelous facial expressions that this lengthy scene requires. Neither should furniture be placed so that the faces of the actors seated in them are forced constantly to be turned away from the audience. Chairs used in center areas of the stage should normally be placed in open positions (full front or one-quarter), while chairs at the sides of the stage normally face in, in one-quarter to one-half positions. Exceptions will occur, of course, when the scene calls for deliberately obscuring seated characters.

138

The banquet scene in *Macbeth* provides an interesting example of how to determine furniture placement according to the principles above. There are many methods of staging this scene, but the following situations must be recognized so that the ground plan is appropriate:

1. The text clearly indicates that at least one entrance area is required, possibly two. Entrances include those of all of the participants in the banquet as the scene opens, of the servants who carry in the feast, of the first murderer, and some solution to the appearances and disappearances of the ghost. All of these might conceivably be made from one door or area, while the ghost disappearances may be achieved supernaturally—that is, appearing and disappearing into space or a trap door rather than through formal openings.

2. The text informs us about the furniture that is vital to the scene. The nobles are told by Macbeth to sit down according to rank, so there must be an adequate number of stools to accommodate them. Macbeth announces that he will mingle among his guests while his queen "keeps her state" remains on her throne. We may assume from this that thrones for the monarchs are on stage and are set apart from the dining table. Macbeth says in referring to the guests seated at the table, "Both sides are even. Here I'll sit i' the midst." If the table is positioned so that all of the guests sit upstage and at the sides, then the empty stool will be in the center. If the nobles occupy two sides of the length of the table, the empty stool should be placed at the foot of the table for visibility.

3. The thrones of Macbeth and Lady Macbeth must be placed together in a dominant position separate from the banquet table and stools. If the thrones are placed directly upstage of the table, they must be elevated.

4. The entrance of the first murderer must be a reasonable distance *away* from the banquet table so that Macbeth may converse without being overheard.

5. An open area away from the banquet table and the throne—perhaps between the throne and the murderer's entrance—should be available for the Macbeths' hushed discussion after he sees the ghost.

6. The banquet table must be large enough to seat all present plus the empty stool reserved for Macbeth. The empty stool *must* be in a position of prominence for the first appearance of Banquo's ghost.

Costumes and accessories. The functional or practical demands of costume and accessories are influenced by locale, season, emphasis, number of costumes, and the logic suggested by the situations of the play. Period often is an explicit practical consideration, but it will be discussed later as an aspect of interpretative design. (See illustrations pp. 140-141.)

Locale is important in determining costume decisions because people of different countries and climates dress in distinctive ways. Russian backgrounds call for furs, boots, and characteristic hats. Berets typify the Frenchman, sombreros the Mexican, kilts the Scotsman. Even though modern fashions are becoming more homogeneous, the uniforms of soldiers and policemen are

Property arrangements for *Macbeth* banquet scene as designed for two different productions shown on this and the facing page. Note placement and angles of furniture, and relationship between throne and banquet table. On p. 140 is a set design by Edward Carrick, Royal Shakespeare Company, 1949. Courtesy of The Central Press Photos Limited. Set design above by John Gielgud and Michael Northen, Royal Shakespeare Company, 1952. Both reproduced by permission of the Royal Shakespeare Company, Stratford-upon-Avon.

still quite distinctive for each country. The northern countries demand different dress than the southern countries because of climate differences. But one locale may call for a variety of dress if the play covers several seasons. In Chekhov's *The Sea Gull*, the first three scenes take place in the summer and the last scene takes place in late fall or winter since the wind is howling and "there are waves" on the lake. But the first scene is at twilight, when the characters might dress for the coolness of evening. The second scene calls for a lazy afternoon with a blazing sun, so the characters would be wearing cool clothing, perhaps lots of white. The third scene is indoors, but some of the characters are preparing for travel, and traveling clothes are called for. In the last scene, evening dress is required, and those coming inside from the wind and rain should have the appropriate protective clothing.

Effectively planned costuming contributes significantly to emphasis and subordination of character. In the early stages of costume design the designer and director should agree on the major figures in each scene of the play. Emphasis is most often achieved through contrast. Normally, bright colors will attract more attention than sober colors and quantities of striking materials will attract the eye from simplicity. But when sober or austere garb is seen isolated in the company of larger numbers of brightly or overdressed characters, the audience will pay more attention to the nonconforming apparel. A Hamlet all in black in Act I, Scene 2 will stand out in a court completely clothed in white or in multicolors with the absence of black. Lord Foppington in *The Relapse* should easily be spotted in a society marked by ostentatious dress by being costumed more outlandishly than anyone else. His colors should be more bizarre and the fashion of his dress an exaggeration of the established mode.

The number of costumes required often is more than the number of characters in the play. Decisions about costume changes should be made as soon as possible. Sometimes this is clearly indicated in the text as when Lady Macbeth orders her husband to "get on your nightgown" in Act II, Scene 2, and when Macbeth in the following scene suggests that he and the other characters on stage who have been awakened from their beds "briefly put on manly readiness,/And meet in the hall together." Even when no such explicit suggestions are made, directors may want to see certain characters change their costumes for symbolic purposes. Such justifications will be discussed later.

Costumes may contribute importantly to the plot of a play and then should be given special consideration. *An Italian Straw Hat* by Labiche is about a madcap search for the hat of the title, and when that hat is discovered it should have a special, unique quality. In *Twelfth Night,* Malvolio is tricked into wearing yellow stockings, cross-gartered, and in farces such as *A Comedy of Errors* two sets of twins identically dressed are responsible for the play's ridiculous complications. In such instances, costumes are of infinite value in suggesting identical appearances when the actors who are playing the roles actually may differ in many respects.

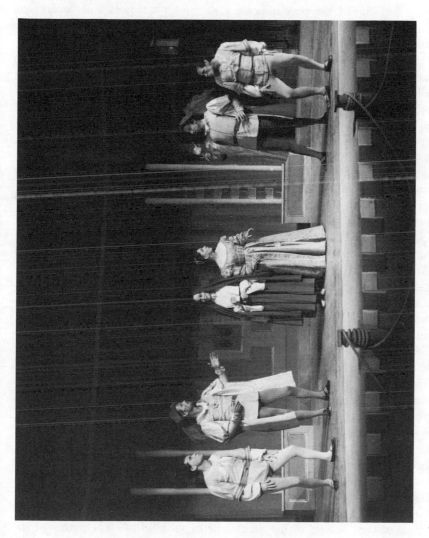

Creating twin identities by means of costume and makeup. Note that costumes of the two sets of twins, though similar, are somewhat varied. *Comedy of Errors* by William Shakespeare. Costume design by Herman George, University of California at Santa Barbara.

A brief summary of *Macbeth*'s costume requirements based on functional rather than interpretative considerations should clarify this criterion for costume planning. In Act I, Scene 3 Banquo informs us about the special quality of the witches, describing them as "So withered, and so wild in their attire,/That look not like the inhabitants of the earth." The battles at the beginning and end of the play indicate that most characters will be dressed for fighting. Rank will demand differentiation in soldierly dress, and those who have been fighting should show it by the condition of their costumes. The bleeding sergeant of Act I, Scene 2 should have a tattered, bloody, and grimy costume. In Act I, Scene 7 Macbeth has made the transition from soldier to host, which can be demonstrated by a change in costume. Sleep garb for most of the characters in the murder scene—including perhaps the porter—are clearly specified by the text. Characters entering from the exterior during the night of the murder might enter with cloaks. The exterior scene in Act II, Scene 4, when the Old Man and Ross discuss "this sore night," might be played with an illusion of cold wind and darkness, in which case the two men would tightly clutch their cloaks around them, as would Macduff who appears a little later. In Act III, Scene 1 Macbeth and his wife enter "as king and queen" suggesting a change of costume suitable to their new positions. Macbeth refers to a "fruitless crown" and "barren scepter," which he could be wearing as costume accessories. Later the sleepwalking queen is reduced to nightwear, and her husband reverts to his armor. In the final scene, opposing sides in the fighting must be distinguished by their colors or heraldic symbols.

Lighting. Electricity created a new aspect of theatre art, lighting design. In former times, artificial light from reflected candles or gas illumination led to some interest in lighting effects, but not until the kind of control that could be achieved by electricity was a lighting designer considered of great importance in theatrical productions. Now he is as important as, and in some special instances more important than, the designer of costumes and scenery, and is counted on to contribute to the expressive aspects of interpretation.

Specific details of lighting for a play normally await discussion until a ground plan has been established, decisions about set and costume colors have been determined, and the director's basic placement of actors has been thought out. However, certain functional and interpretative concepts may comprise the body of initial discussions about how the play is to be illuminated.

Functionally (and some of these points will overlap with the interpretative), time of day, season of the year, whether the setting will represent interiors, exteriors, or both, light sources, and special effects represent many of the justifications for illumination that must be considered.

Most of the functional characteristics just mentioned may be illustrated by tracing the lighting justifications in *Macbeth*, even though Shakespeare, because his plays were performed out of doors in daylight, relied on language to suggest season, climate, or time of day. The director may decide that he wants to use lighting purely for atmospheric and symbolic purposes in *Macbeth*. There is nothing wrong with this, but to demonstrate the director's and lighting designer's stimuli for illumination, the following more literal examples are given. It should be noted, however, that Shakespeare's atmospheric suggestions are frequently based on climate and time of day.

In Act I, Scene 1 the witches meet in an exterior during the day (they refer to meeting again "ere the set of sun"). They refer to the "fog and filthy air," and editors suggest thunder and lightning (special effects). Scene 2 is also an exterior daylight scene. (We have been informed in the previous scene that the sun will set "when the battle's lost and won.") Scene 3 takes place on the heath at sunset if the witches have kept their word, and Macbeth tells Banquo as they enter, "So foul and fair a day I have not seen." Scene 4 presents several options. It might be an interior or an exterior. Assuming that this is the same day of the battle, then the sun has set much earlier. Macbeth, at the end of the scene, asks the stars to "hide [their] fires" and urges that "light [not] see my black and deep desires." Scene 5 takes place during the day because the messenger announces that the king will arrive "tonight" and Lady Macbeth appeals for night to fall to conceal the violence she plans. The sixth scene suggests evening because Duncan's arrival was to have occurred at night. It is probably dusk since Duncan sees the castle, and Banquo refers to the sparrow's nest. Light sources might consist of moonlight, and torches carried by Duncan's attendants. In the final scene of the first act, the setting is clearly an interior later that night, and torches would appear to be the most justifiable source of illumination.

During the following two acts Shakespeare makes significant use of weather and time of day. In Act II, Scene 1, which may be an exterior courtyard, "The moon is down" and "There's husbandry in Heaven,/Their candles are all out." It is very dark and torches are the apparent source of light. In this scene Macbeth sees the dagger in the air. If the director believes that the audience should view it too, then a special effect is required: either a small spotlight on a hanging dagger, or a projection of the dagger itself. Scenes 2 and 3 continue into the middle of the night with torches suggesting whatever illumination is necessary. In Scene 4, the night is over: "By the clock 'tis day." But daylight unnaturally has not emerged: "And yet dark night strangles the traveling lamp," and "darkness does the face of earth entomb/When living light should kiss it."

The close analysis of lighting possibilities in the first two acts of *Macbeth* should suffice, but perhaps it would be helpful to include two other examples of a different nature. At least one scene in the play suggests a change of illumination as the scene progresses. In Act III, Scene 3, the first murderer observes that "The west yet glimmers with some streaks of day," but soon after Banquo calls for "a light," as does the second murderer a few lines on. Blackness then is suggested when the third murderer asks "Who did strike out the light?" making possible the confusion that covers Fleance's escape. Finally, special effects are a distinct possibility in the scenes dealing with the supernatural. Should Banquo's ghost receive special illumination—perhaps by using a follow spot? How are the apparitions in Act IV, Scene 1 to be lighted? Might projections be used here rather than live actors? These questions are also the concern of style and interpretation, which will be discussed later.

Music and Sound.   It was stated previously that music and sound have been part of theatre art since its Greek beginnings. The development of melodrama (the word combines *melody* and *drama*) emphasized the use of music and developed the concept of underscoring, or using music that did not require a realistic justification to heighten the emotional effects of certain scenes (a technique that later became an important motion picture device). Musical effects normally are atmospheric, so they are better discussed in the interpretative aspects of design. It must be noted here, however, that the use of music must be considered well in advance of production, especially if it is to be newly composed. The director must make himself aware of the actual musical demands of the play, and undertake the research necessary for finding the original music and the availability of recorded or live music for his production.

Functional sound effects and offstage noises, however, may be dealt with at this point. Realistic plays make it quite clear through stage directions and dialogue allusions when sound effects are to be used. Sound is most important, for example, in the plays of Chekhov, who, except for the dying harp notes in *The Cherry Orchard*, used realistic sound sources for atmosphere. In plays where no specific instructions are provided, however, the director must decide on the necessity and importance of sound as it may be implied by the text. Consequently, the use of sound effects will vary considerably in productions of Shakespeare's plays. Let us explore *Macbeth*'s possibilities in this respect. The text does not clearly state that the first witches' scene requires sound, yet the entire scene traditionally is played with a background of thunder and rain. This is perfectly justifiable, of course, but invariably the sound is so loud that we fail to understand a single word that the witches utter. The director's responsibility is to choose between clarity or splendid effects, or to insist that words and sound are timed so that meaning and effectiveness both are possible. "Alarums" or trumpet calls are common devices in the staging of Shakespeare. They herald the arrival of princes or kings; in the second scene of *Macbeth*, an alarum announces the arrival of the bleeding sergeant. In Scene 3, the third witch refers to "A drum, a drum!" which warns of Macbeth's arrival, and in Act III, Scene 3 the third murderer says, "Hark, I hear horses!" as Banquo and Fleance approach.

One of the more serious decisions in *Macbeth*, which is so much a play of atmosphere, is that concerning how much, if at all, to use the bird sounds alluded to in Act II ("I heard the owl scream and the crickets cry"). These scenes surely justify the inclusion of such sounds, but some directors will carry these effects to an extreme with a sound track of virtually uninterrupted bird and cricket sounds. The problem here is not that they might be distracting, but that silence and soundlessness, with the terrifying shocks of occasional bird shrieks interrupting a "one-half world" where "nature seems dead," are far more appropriate to the atmosphere of these scenes than constant noise.

Bells interrupting the peaceful silence of the night are important. In Act II, Scene 1 Macbeth orders his wife to strike the bell when his drink is ready. When it later rings, it becomes "a knell/That summons thee [Duncan] to Heaven or to Hell." The bell is also enormously effective in transferring the still night to a chaotic nightmare, and is demanded by the text when Macduff twice calls for it to awaken the rest of the castle. Here it should continue to ring as characters enter from various directions. The balance of the play includes other scenes with similar suggestions in the dialogue and in the implications of the action, but the major effects of the first two acts described above demonstrate sufficiently the director's concerns with sound.

INTERPRETATIVE DEMANDS

Recognizing functional requirements for a play's design requires little more than a careful reading of the play, some common sense, and careful attention to detail. While the process may appear tedious to some, not unlike the preparation of a laundry list, it is nonetheless essential that the director leave nothing to chance (or other people) if he does not want the more imaginative aspects of design aborted by a failure to heed the logical or practical necessities of the play.

There is little question, however, that what we have termed the "interpretative" demand of design is more challenging to the director and the designer. This area establishes the difference between competence and artistry. Here the director uses his analysis of the play; here he works with the designers to manifest theatrically the expression of the play's intent, of its rational and emotional potential.

Now the director must explore once more the areas of theatrical design (set, properties, costume, lighting, music, and sound), this time attempting to express the play's style, genre, and intent.

Style. In an earlier portion of this book, style was discussed at some length, with examples that anticipated our present concern. It would be helpful if the reader reviewed the ideas developed there before proceeding further (see pp. 32-35). Here we will be concerned with two of the major influences on a play's stylistic treatment: milieu and theatre conventions.

Milieu. The drama of the nineteenth and twentieth centuries normally has been conceived with the idea of representing specific periods of time, and with the assumption that settings, costumes, properties, and manners would be selected to theatrically mirror those periods. In *A Doll's House*, Ibsen was dealing realistically with a social problem of his own time, and visually the play recreates the environment of the last quarter of the nineteenth century. Modern dramas that are concerned with history—such as Bolt's *A Man for*

All Seasons or Brecht's *Galileo*—require that the milieus of these plays be accurately suggested by some or all of the theatrical conventions available. A theatrical expression of period, however, is not nor has not always been a requisite in the major plays of the world. If we are correct in our assumptions about the Greek theatre, for example, the acting area—consisting of the orchestra and a scene building of some kind—was a permanent environment for the enactment of ancient myths (*Heracleida*), historical dramas (*The Persians,* and contemporary plays (*The Clouds*). Costumes were conventionalized contemporary garb with the addition of mask, *onkos* (high headdress), and *cothurnai* (boots, possibly elevated). Shakespeare's theatre also used a permanent set for the plays of all the periods with which Elizabethan and Jacobean playwrights were concerned. Costumes, too, were primarily contemporary dress, with some occasional suggestion of the historical past. It is extremely doubtful, for example, that *Macbeth* originally was costumed for eleventh-century accuracy.

The problem that confronts the contemporary director is determining what period conventions to use for plays that deal with specific historical periods in an unhistorical manner. Should he ask his designers to suggest the period of the Trojan war (*c.* 1184 B.C.) for *The Trojan Women,* or to re-create the fifth century in which it was written, or to adapt it to modern times? Should *Antony and Cleopatra* suggest ancient Rome and Egypt, or the Renaissance?

There also is the question of whether to adjust the original periods of realistic plays written more than 25 years ago. *A Doll's House* today would not be significantly altered if it were set in 1890 rather than 1879, but would updating it to the 1970s because of its relevance to the women's liberation movement be more satisfying? Would *Strange Interlude* (1928) work as well in contemporary dress?

Let us deal first with the concept of updating a play's milieu to the present. Generally this is done so that the play's relevance will be made "clearer" and perhaps "more meaningful" to a modern audience. This concept must be challenged. It is, to begin with, inconceivable that any director would select a play that has no significant meaning for himself or for his audience. If the parallels are clear, what is the necessity of altering its original form, especially, as shall be noted later, when such alteration most often creates distortion and inconsistencies that work against the play? The parallels between the American involvement in Indochina and the situation in *Troilus and Cressida* are so strong that Shakespeare's extraordinary play now should enjoy the greatest revival in its history. Will the parallels be made *more* clear or effective by setting it in today's Viet Nam? Such a modification easily might suggest a lack of confidence in the audience's ability to grasp such significances for itself. Is it not unnecessarily laboring the point, emphasizing the director's cleverness in "discovering" relevance and his ability now to make it absolutely clear to his unsuspecting audience?

The relationship between the play's contextual concerns and its original form and structure must also be considered. A play by Ibsen, even though written within the past hundred years, has a certain formal quality and idiom in its language which dates it. In addition, its Scriban structure is no longer considered modern by today's audiences. Placing *A Doll's House* or *Ghosts*, both of which deal with ideas that still interest and concern us, in a late twentieth-century setting would, by the juxtaposition of a modern setting on a nonmodern language and structure, justify their being called "old-fashioned." In the same way, the language of Shakespeare works against our contemporary dress and life style. Placing the words of *Troilus and Cressida* in the mouths of contemporary soldiers who are called Achilles, Ajax, and Agamemnon, and hearing Ulysses "specialty of rule" (I, 3) speech coming from General Westmoreland will increase our response to the production in a way that has little to do with relevance.

Practical considerations must be dealt with as well. Characters in Shakespeare's plays often refer to properties and costumes that are clearly Elizabethan. Sometimes such references can be cut or changed, but often at the expense of language and imagery patterns. Try to adjust Macbeth's references to his armor (V, 3) without destroying the clothing imagery so important to the play (see pp. 166-170), or ask yourself if it is worth the sacrifice to eliminate the sexual imagery and the irony suggested by the Elizabethan sleeve that Troilus offers to Cressida (IV, 4).

A different problem emerges when the director must make a decision concerning the actual historical period of a play in an older drama whose conventions clearly ignored it, as Shakespeare's Roman plays did. When is it possible to justify finding a period other than the present for a play's milieu? In both instances the results are perhaps less offensive than attempts to modernize, because it is possible for the play's noncontemporary form to work in periods far removed from the present. Clearly it is simpler and in many ways more satisfying to design Elizabethan plays in the period in which they were written rather than the periods about which they were written. Language references to contemporary clothes and properties, and the baroque quality of the structure of these plays will be more consistent in late Elizabethan or Jacobean environs. Nevertheless, productions that use other periods of the past have worked and should not be dismissed.

What is most important, and what can be justified in such alterations in the time aspects of older plays, is that decisions be governed by the relationship between what Stark Young calls "the theatrical idea" and the theatrical setting, rather than what Michel St. Denis refers to as "this flippant approach" to a selection of period. A good example of this can be made with *Antony and Cleopatra*, where locale is important not for topographical reasons, but because Rome and Egypt represent the two separate ways of life between which Antony is torn. These two ways of life may be theatrically realized, or symbolized, by different sets, costumes, properties, and music (as well as manners) for each locale. The use of ancient Rome and Egypt with their disparate styles of dress and ornamentation is one way in which the symbolic differences may be suggested while at the same time conforming to period accuracy.

Macbeth might be designed for its historical milieu—the eleventh century—or for its Jacobean conception. If the director and designers wish to emphasize a more violent and primitive society, and believe that the play's supernatural beliefs today are more successfully associated with the Middle Ages, then medieval Scotland should work quite well. Costumes will be coarser and simpler; leather, fur, and heavy wools would form its basic textures; Romanesque arches or primitive post and lintel structures of stone or rough-hewn timber might be used, and food at the banquet would be eaten with the fingers rather than with utensils. Music would be selected to represent the composition and instrumentation of the Middle Ages. The most serious objection that comes to mind regarding a medieval *Macbeth* is the possibility that Lady Macbeth will resemble, as she often has, the wicked Queen in *Snow White*.

In the discussion of milieu, it should be understood that references to historical environments were not intended to emphasize realistic settings or exact period duplications of architecture, costumes, and properties. In the example of *Macbeth*, the *qualities* of a period that might be selected and suggested were stressed. *Macbeth* certainly needs no picture-frame box setting with realistic interiors and exteriors. But the director may want set pieces such as doors, arches, and ornamentation, as well as the sense of a time and place. Design styles of an actual period may then contribute to the decor of the production whether it is realistic or not.

Theatre Conventions. It was stated previously that a director should be familiar with the conventions for which the play was originally written. The importance of such knowledge is not to insist that every revival must be performed in an antiquarian way, but that such knowledge stimulate a recognition of the relationship between stage conventions and play structure. New conventions that replace the old will function well if they create a reality consistent with that of the text's language and structure. Greek stage conventions demanded that tragedies be written with size and grandeur, that character stress broad essences rather than psychological nuance, that language go beyond that of everyday speech, that a quality of ritual be present with a sense of direct audience contact, and that few attempts be made to relate characters to a realistic environment.

Elizabethan stage conventions influence the playwright to view the stage as the cosmos in which any part of the universe may be suggested at any time in the play. It makes possible rapid and fluid, even cinematic, transitions from one locale to another without the necessity of realistic scenic elements. "The Shakespearean play is a continuous stream of action, thought, and emotion,

Contemporizing the conventions of plays of the past. *Prometheus Bound* by Aeschylus. Design by Stanford University. Photo by Derek Hunt.

151

Contemporizing the conventions of plays of the past. *As You Like It* by William Shakespeare. Design by J. Svoboda, National Theatre at Prague. Courtesy of Art Centrum.

with psychic rather than topographical panoramas."[1] The stage itself, being a poetic metaphor, encourages poetry and metaphor in language. Its size and its relationship to the audience provoke both intimacy and scale, as well as direct audience contact.

These generalizations do not describe the specific details of stage convention. They emphasize the *effects* of style and the link between style in theatrical presentation and style in the text. Given these generalizations, the task of director and designer is to achieve them by any convenient modern or ancient conventions. There is no reason why modern lighting techniques, scene changing devices, scenery, platforms, elevators may not be exploited to theatrically realize the style suggested by the text.

A play is a piece of writing in which the idea has found a theatrical body for itself. The rightness of this theatrical body derives from the relations among its elements. But with the passage of time comes a change in certain elements; to produce the play again the relationship among them must be again discovered. To keep the play alive we must find always anew a body to express this idea. In sum we

Contemporizing the conventions of plays of the past. *Macbeth* by William Shakespeare. Design by J. Svoboda, National Theatre at Prague. Courtesy of Art Centrum.

must translate it into the medium of the moment; we must discover afresh for it the right mental and visual accents, or it will be dead, an empty mask that no longer contains the life that is there to be expressed.[2]

Macbeth can be performed on a relatively bare stage, on one with numerous platforms, on one with realistic, multipurpose set pieces such as arches, pillars, and galleries, or on a revolving stage with varying forms to suggest locale or atmosphere. A recent production of the play directed by Peter Hall at Stratford used no scenery or levels. Instead the raked stage and the back wall were covered by a blood red carpet. Entrances were made through the wings rather than through doors or arches. Lighting produced the atmosphere and combined with stage areas to suggest changing locales.

John Masefield, in *A Macbeth Production*, suggests a more realistic setting, but one that does not prevent the flow of action or make overly prosaic the poetic environment that the play demands. He calls for a thrust into the audience and a "backcloth," which may either be plain or a tapestry woven with Scottish emblems. Exterior scenes would be played before the cloth, which would be raised for interior scenes to reveal a permanent setting of a wall with doors and an upper landing with a wooden railing, which might be hung with shields.

Robert Edmond Jones' successful set for *Macbeth* is described by Stark Young, who called it

> the most creative and exciting staging of *Macbeth* or any Shake-speare play I have seen anywhere. There was a stage enclosed with a background of black—it was very likely velvet, for no light was caught there to break the complete darkness of it. Neither photographs nor drawings could give anything but the slightest suggestions of the gold frames, or sharp gold lines, or the forms like Gothic abstractions or however you would describe them, that, standing alone against the black, defined the scenes. Three huge tragic masks hung to the front above the action. Vast daggers of light poured down, crossed, pierced, flooded the scenes of the witches. The banquet hall with its gold and light and figures—above all, Lady Macbeth's robe, in which by a hidden combination of many shades an unheard-of intensity of red was achieved—defied any conveyance in words. Some of the effects were like those of early paintings where more than one incident or scene is visible at the same time. For example, in the sleepwalking scene you could see Lady Macbeth crossing from the left of the stage in her long white gown before you saw her enter through the form that made the doorway. The very intensity of this dramatic use of abstraction in this decor for *Macbeth* makes the effort to describe it merely futile.[3]

For a play whose theatrical form expresses nonobjective reality the most modern technological devices may be used with greater freedom than for realistic plays. Lighting, for example, may use colors and come from directions that do not have to be justified by the natural world. If movable sets and properties are used, they may be shifted in full view of the audience. With nonrealistic conventions established, actors dressed as servants or porters may bring in and later remove the banquet necessities in *Macbeth*. The director need not be concerned if the Birnam Wood episode does not look absolutely real. The designer may even stylize the branches. Sound and music may function atmospherically rather than suggesting real sources. Underscoring may be used without suggesting that an orchestra is playing in the other room or that the radio has been turned on. The supernatural elements such as the witches, ghosts, and apparitions in *Macbeth* can be done unpretentiously—with no effort to devise tricks and stage effects to make the supernatural appear realistic. The witches may enter and exit in a normal manner instead of by the distractions created when we try *really* to make them vanish into air.

For most plays of the past hundred years, however, objective reality is the required theatrical form, and in most instances, such requirements still

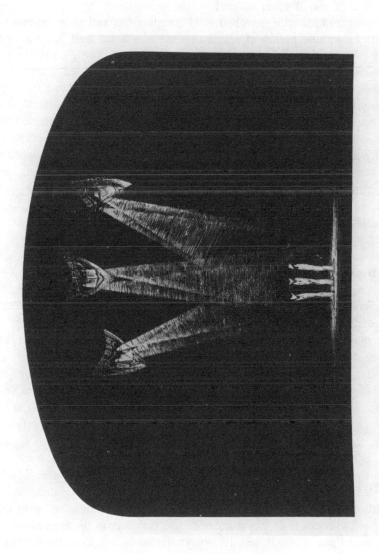

Set and lighting design for *Macbeth* by Robert Edward Jones. Copyright 1925 by Theatre Arts, Inc. Copyright © 1970 by Theatre Arts Books.

must be respected. It appears as we move into the last quarter of the twentieth century that realism and naturalism in the theatre have become styles of the past, but the great plays in these styles will be revived again and again. Chekhov, Strindberg, and Shaw will have something to say to succeeding generations. But the illusion of reality, the importance of the environment and its impact on character, psychological complexities and their intimate expression, the symbolic nature of *real* things such as a sea gull, the red velvet drapes in *Ghosts,* the real pistols on the real wall of *The Father*, and the foolish *nouveau* setting of *Arms and the Man* must be recreated if these plays are to make theatrical sense. The director of the future will have to investigate the conventions of the naturalistic theatre, in which environments must express the illusion of surface reality and the stage must be dressed with objects that exist primarily to make an area look "lived in." Light sources realistically must be justified. Sunlight, lamps, and other sources of light must be suggested, and the illumination must appear to emanate from their direction. Sound must similarly be justified by a realistic source such as the Jewish orchestra in the ballroom during the third act of *The Cherry Orchard.*

In realistic plays such techniques are not cumbersome. They are relevant to the play's theatrical ideas, which are often expressions of man's relationship to his environment, and which may be used to embody poetic as well as scientific truth.

Genre.   Again, the reader is urged to review the previous discussion of genre before studying its application to the design aspects of the play. The director's and designer's concern here is to determine how theatrical devices may contribute to the play's predominant mood, and how they may stimulate sobriety or laughter. Generally speaking, color and shape are among the most important considerations. Serious drama will most often require dark shades of rich, brilliant hues (rather than pastels) in the settings, costumes, and lighting, while the colors of comedy usually are lighter and brighter. The shape of a setting for serious drama depends on the effect desired. Classical tragedy tends to emphasize the vertical: it deals with kings and princes with whom we associate tall columns and high ceilings but, more important, with issues that stretch to the heavens. When oppressiveness or claustrophobia are suggested by texts such as *The Weavers* or *The Lower Depths,* the set should seem to press in from all sides. Comedy, because it is domestic, middle or lower class, stressing the ludicrous frailty of human nature rather than its aspirations, and more physical than spiritual, nearly always demands a horizontal setting.

For the same reasons, classic tragedy makes fewer material demands. It is reflective, more dependent on language than overt physical action, and consequently is best viewed in barer, simpler surroundings with a minimum of properties. Comedy, especially farce, is rambunctious, emphasizing physical incongruities, the failure of an environment to properly operate, or its tendency to confuse, frustrate, or get in the way. This requires more complicated sets,

Setting, properties, and costumes for serious drama. *The Crucible* by Arthur Miller. Set design by Richard Baschky. Costume design by Jack Byers, University cf California at Santa Barbara.

Setting, properties, and costumes for comic drama. *The Taming of the Shrew* by William Shakespeare. Set design by Richard Baschky, costume design by John Furman, University of California at Santa Barbara.

Costume design for farce drama. *The Comedy of Errors* by William Shakespeare. Costume design by Herman George, University of California at Santa Barbara.

properties, and costumes. There must be rugs to trip on, windows that will not open, numerous doors for split-second surprise entrances and exists, chairs that collapse, and costumes that break away or create comic incongruity by their size or their quality.

Lighting and sound also may contribute heavily to the predominant genre of a play. Both of these theatrical devices could almost singlehandedly create atmosphere. Given a bare stage, the color of lights, their intensities, and their distribution can create gloom or cheer, mysterious chiaroscuro or blinding incandescence. Music and sound can do as much. Few dramatists demand as extensive a use of lighting and sound as Chekhov. Each of his major plays contains changes of season and time of day. *The Sea Gull* opens at dusk and during the scene night arrives. A dog howls, and we hear the sounds of crickets and frogs. Music comes from across the water. The second scene is outdoors on a hot summer afternoon. The third act is an interior as is the fourth, but the latter takes place in winter, at night. The trees are rustling and the wind is howling in the chimney. Piano music is heard offstage, and the night watchman knocks. Candles are lighted, then blown out, and finally a shot is heard offstage. All of this contributes to naturalism, but more important is the symphony of atmosphere that undersores the play, reflecting and provoking the moods of the characters.

Few of Shakespeare's plays make as much of lighting and sound for atmospheric purposes as does *Macbeth*. Of course, Shakespeare does this with language and imagery (as has been indicated in the chapter on language), and Shakespeare's open-air theatre relied very little, if at all, on lighting effects. It would be inadvisable, however, in today's interior theatres not to respond to the language or atmosphere with visual and aural images. A. C. Bradley's appreciation of *Macbeth*'s atmosphere provides an excellent stimulus to the director and the designer in their preparation for a sound–light plan:

> Darkness, we may even say blackness, broods over this tragedy. It is remarkable that almost all the scenes which at once recur to memory take place either at night or in some dark spot. The vision of the dagger, the murder of Duncan, the murder of Banquo, the sleep-walking of Lady Macbeth, all come in night scenes. The Witches dance in the thick air of a storm, or "black and midnight hags," receive Macbeth in a cavern. The blackness of night is to the hero a thing of fear, even of horror; and that which he feels becomes the spirit of the play. The faint glimmerings of the western sky at twilight are here menacing: it is the hour when the traveller hastens to reach safety in his inn, and when Banquo rides homeward to meet his assassins; the hour when "light thickens," when "night's black agents to their prey do rouse," when the wolf begins to howl, and the owl scream, and withered murder steals forth to his work. . . .

When the next day should dawn, its light is "strangled," and "darkness does the face of earth entomb." In the whole drama the sun seems to shine only twice; first, in the beautiful but ironical passage where Duncan sees the swallows flitting round the castle of death; and, afterwards, when at the close the avenging army gathers to rid the earth of its shame. . . .

The atmosphere of *Macbeth*, however, is not that of unrelieved blackness. On the contrary, as compared with *King Lear* and its cold dim gloom, *Macbeth* leaves a decided impression of colour; it is really the impression of a black night broken by flashes of light and colour, sometimes vivid and even glaring. They are the lights and colours of the thunderstorm in the first scene; of the dagger hanging before Macbeth's eyes and glittering alone in the midnight air; of the torch borne by the servant when he and his lord come upon Banquo crossing the castle-court to his room; of the torch, again, which Fleance carried to light his father to death, and which was dashed out by one of the murderers; of the torches that flared in the hall on the face of the Ghost and the blanched cheeks of Macbeth; of the flames beneath the boiling caldron from which the apparitions in the cavern rose; of the taper which showed to the Doctor and Gentlewoman the wasted face and blank eyes of Lady Macbeth.[4]

Music often is used externally to prepare and sustain the appropriate mood of a performance. Directors often require that an overture be played while the audience arrives, or during the brief period between the dimming of the house lights and the raising of the curtain. Sometimes music is played during intermission, or the same effect is used for the beginning of each act. In such instances, the director will be concerned chiefly with establishing the proper mood, but he also must demand a consistency with the play's period and style. Selections from Lully and Rameau, for example, would work well for Molière's *The Misanthrope* or *The Learned Ladies*, but the same playwright's *Scapin* or *The Doctor in Spite of Himself* require music that is lighter and more earthy in style and atmosphere, such as ballads or folk songs.

Ideally, music should be composed for each play, because then the director may work with the composer as he does with the designers toward achieving a score that in every way meets the theatrical concerns of the text.

Intent. Plays are written ultimately to be expressed through theatrical images, both visual and aural. Every line of a text is created for some kind of physical expression, every object for its relationship to characters and ideas that achieve their deepest impact only when they are made materially manifest on the stage. Texts of plays are created to be amplified, energized, completed on the stage. The text is the source for expression, but the stage is its fulfillment. We know from the written page that goblets are used in the banquet scene from *Macbeth* but it took an actor's imagination to use one of them to illuminate Macbeth's response to Banquo's ghost, linking his action to the earlier "poisoned chalice" line. The excitement created by this stage business must have been enormous to have been singled out by Simon Forman in his recollection, and by Beaumont's parody in *The Knight of the Burning Pestle* (see pp. 109-110).

Everything seen on the stage is a symbol, for actors and objects represent something they really are not. The actor not only represents a fictional person, but dramatic character in itself symbolizes some aspect of the human condition. The scenery represents, but rarely actually is—even when most realistic —the actual place for an action. But stage symbolism also is created on another, more poetic level. The throne in *Macbeth* not only represents a royal chair, it may also symbolize Macbeth's ambition and Macbeth as usurper—sitting where he has unseated. Ibsen's wild duck is supposed actually to be a wild duck, but it also symbolizes living the "life lie," among other things.

Physical things and sounds also are employed metaphorically. Shaw's setting for *Heartbreak House* does not merely represent the interior and exterior of Captain Shotover's living quarters, nor does its boatlike construction and decor merely symbolize his naval career. More significantly it is a metaphor for the ship of state, which Shaw sees floundering apocalyptically in 1916: "And this ship we are all in? This soul's prison we call England?" (Hector in Act III). The examples from *The Wild Duck* and *Heartbreak House* reveal the use of poetic symbolism and metaphor as directly specified by the texts. Directors and designers, however, often use symbol or metaphor when the playwright has not described it. The clues are in the text: in the plot and super-objective, in the characters, in the language and in the unifying idea or intent of the playwright. It requires the theatrical imagination, however, to illuminate them with the relevant and tasteful manipulation of setting, properties, costumes, lights, and sound.

Intent: Scenery and Property Design. Ben Jonson in *Volpone* is concerned with how men, obsessed by greed, descend into bestiality. To emphasize this point he names characters metaphorically: Volpone (Fox), Corbaccio (Raven), Corvino (Crow), Mosca (Fly), and Voltore (Vulture). While this is an obvious clue for the costumer and makeup staff, it might also serve as a metaphorical stimulus for the scene designer. Volpone's apartment might be designed to suggest a cave, Corbaccio's a bird's nest, and Corvino's (who keeps his naive young wife locked up) a gilded cage. Not all plays provide such clear-cut clues, but many suggest or imply numerous possibilities. Perfectly realistic sets for *Antony and Cleopatra* might contribute symbolically to the differences between Egypt and Rome. But because the play's style allows the settings to be more abstract, nonrealistic ways may be found to achieve the same purpose. For example, simple cool-colored drapes versus hotter, sensuously patterned drapes might be used to symbolically suggest mind versus heart, or duty versus passion. In a recent production of the play at Stanford University, the central image for the director and the designer was the heart of Antony. The play's action emphasized not just the struggle *for* the heart of Antony, but Antony's internal struggle between the "Roman" and the "Egyptian." The set design represented the interior of a gigantic heart, which revolved to establish different locales.

Macbeth suggests an unusual assortment of possibilities. In our analysis, the unifying or main action proved to be "the struggle for the throne of Scotland." A set that emphasized Scotland, such as an ancient map, or some kind of national symbol might be designed. Or it might be possible to go further and attempt to symbolize "the progression of the moral dissolution of both Macbeth and Scotland because of a struggle for power to the eventual restoration of political and moral order." (See p. 62.) If we wish to key in on the words "dissolution" and "restoration," the map or symbol might be in some sort of disarray (torn, burnt, soiled) at the play's beginning, restored with Duncan's victory, despoiled with Macbeth's ascendancy and tyranny, and restored once more as his decapitated head is held high in the play's final scene. Or ideas may be developed from unifying patterns of language and thought. The text's concern with the natural and the unnatural represents such a strong unifying concept in its relationship to plot, character, and thought that it could form the basis of a symbolic setting. The designer might be asked to find a way of creating a physical sense of the unnatural, of "great perturbations in nature," or the recurring image of broken sleep—of nightmare. Expressionistic devices such as distorted walls and furniture, grotesquely twisted pillars and trees, might be used.

There are many ways in which the play's essential Christian concepts may be emphasized in sets and props. Duncan's and eventually Malcolm's attendants might carry large crosses, while Macbeth's attendants do not. G. Wilson Knight suggests in an "ideal" production of the play the permanent placement of a niche containing the figures of Madonna and child on one side of the stage, and an elevated golden throne on the other, both as a constant reminder of the play's religious–political–moral struggle and as a potential focus for associative action. The Madonna is brightened during the Duncan scenes and dimmed for Macbeth and the witches. Lady Macbeth challenges the Madonna (or she can scorn it) on "unsex me here." Macbeth moves to the Madonna on "pity like a naked newborn babe," and ends his soliloquy in prayer. Macbeth might refer to the Madonna, or if such a setting is not used, to his own cross, on "mine eternal jewel" thus clarifying the meaning of that expression to a contemporary audience. Peter Hall's Stratford production emphasized the play's religious theme by starting the play with a silhouette behind a scrim of two of the witches pouring blood through an inverted cross into the third witch, whom they were bringing to "life."

Blood is also a valid choice for the play's central image. Knight enlarges on Macbeth's line, "Will all great Neptune's ocean wash this blood/Clean from my hand? No, this my hand will rather/The multitudinous seas incarnadine,/Making the green one red" (II, 2) by suggesting that a green carpet be used at the play's beginning, to be replaced by a red one with the crimes, then become green again with the death of Lady Macbeth. Jan Kott's essay "Macbeth or Death-Infected" stresses the blood image: "*Macbeth* begins and ends with slaughter. There is more and more blood, everyone walks in it; it floods the stage. A production of *Macbeth* not evoking a picture of the world flooded with blood, would inevitably be false."[5] Perhaps this suggestion influenced Peter Hall's 1966 Stratford production, whose set was composed completely of a red carpet-covered floor and rear wall.

An important function of settings and properties, especially in the real-

Symbolic set progression for a production of *Macbeth*. Above is a distorted, expressionistic-type of setting for Macbeth's castle in Scotland. On page 165 is a symmetrical, "pure" setting for castle in England. Design by John Gielgud and Michael Northen, Royal Shakespeare Company, 1952. Both reproduced by permission of the Royal Shakespeare Company, Stratford-upon-Avon.

istic theatre, is to reveal and emphasize character. "The typical Mielziner setting," states an interview with the designer,

> is intended primarily not as an eye-filling spectacle but as array of clues, hints, symptoms, innuendoes, keys to personality. . . . For Lillian Hellman's "Another Part of the Forest," Mielziner started off by designing an interior decorator's dream, a beautifully furnished old Southern mansion, and then carefully disarranged and cluttered it, so as to suggest that the characters didn't quite belong there.[6]

Such methods, in principle, needn't be restricted to the modern realistic theatre, as John Masefield suggests in his set and property requirements for his ideal *Macbeth*. "Instead of making your castle grim and ghastly . . . make it the trim, bright attractive home of two remarkable Scots, both of royal blood. Let it have the brightness and manliness of a ship's deck. Let the shields hung on the railing and the staircase and the stair be smart and gaily painted." But following the murder, Masefield suggests, that the designer "let the display be a little less smart and more vulgar; let the decorations on the rails be less manly; . . . let there be an emphasis on the fact that the Macbeths are now King and Queen."[7]

Masefield suggests something else here that is also important: the idea of changes in setting to reflect the progression of plot, character, or theme. This approach was implied previously when it was suggested that a symbol such as a map might be altered throughout the play to coincide with Scotland's travails. Such variety need not intrude on the symbolic unity, or sustained motif, that a set is intended to provide. But the director should be wary of insisting on an inflexible set for the sake of unity. For example, if he chooses a permanent nightmare motif for *Macbeth*'s setting, he will encounter problems in Act I, Scene 6 in which Duncan describes the loveliness of the environment, at the same time disturbing the irony that contributes to the thematic concept of deceitful appearances. And in Act IV, Scene 3, with the sanctuary of the divine Edward as the locale, such distortion would be unsuitable. The emergence of the natural order in the final scene is likely to be contradicted by such a set. It is *not necessary* for directors to insist on a central image or metaphor for every play. Sometimes it is more appropriate and interesting to create a succession of impressions by changing sets and introducing new properties from scene to scene. Meanwhile, a statement of unity may be created primarily by the consistent style of each design, and by the meaningful relationship of the various images introduced on the stage. For example, suppose the director and the designer agree that the basic design is to be based on the concept that man's submission to evil plunges him into a hell on earth. Settings might then be organized so that all the witches' scenes would connote a supernatural hell (for here the devil himself is operating), and all scenes between Duncan's murder and the moving forest (except for the scene in England), will suggest hell on earth. The second scene of the play and the battle scenes at the end represent struggles to end hell on earth, while the two other Duncan scenes, the meeting of Macduff and Malcolm in England, and the final scene in the play would be contrasted by their purity to the inferno created by the rest of the play. Here the use of a variety of images, symbols, or metaphors in the design may create as interesting a theatrical and meaningful unity as a single, dominant image.

Intent: Costume Design. Costumes will, of course, be influenced by the symbolic and metaphorical stimuli suggested for the scene design and should complement the settings in color, texture, and design. Ultimately, however, the major contribution of costume is toward the delineation of character. Almost invariably, the first thing a costume designer wants to discuss is the nature of each character and how characters are related to one another. Costumes offer symbolic aids to characterization at two levels: the level of the particular (or surface) man, and the level of the inner man or the man as he represents the abstract qualities of life.

On the level of the particular, the designer needs to know the social, economic, national, and vocational (if relevant) conditions of each character as well as his behavior and idiosyncracies. In *Macbeth*, we are dealing with kings, noblemen, common soldiers, doctors, and servants, not to mention

MACBETH

Lady M. #1+

bound, wrapped,
imbalanced- topheavy
elegant in simplicity-
      severe

The Oriental Raglan cut-
      gusset

heavy-wgt. cotton burlap
      drapery

cobra/snake
image -

RDM.

Costume progression. Lady Macbeth before she becomes queen. Costume design by Robert Morgan, University of California, Santa Barbara.

LM #2+

Eliminate flap
over ear

hammered
copper plate
jewelry on
leather
backing

Costume progression. Lady Macbeth as queen. Costume design by
Robert Morgan, University of California, Santa Barbara.

Costume progression. Lady Macbeth's sleepwalking scene. Costume design by Robert Morgan, University of California, Santa Barbara.

witches (shall we place them in the "vocational" category?). The nobles are of different clans, and the English army joins the Scottish army in the final battle scenes of the last act. This aspect of dress has been noted previously when function was discussed. Such characteristics as elegance, sloppiness, coarseness, casualness, or affectation may be suggested by dress. Accessories such as gloves, rings, jewelry, cuff links, and hats provide characters with objects to which they might habitually relate to establish idiosyncratic patterns.

To symbolize the "inner" qualities of character, color is one of the most useful resources of costume. Cool colors can be used for calm, reasonable characters and hot colors for the more emotional or passionate ones, gay colors for the light-hearted characters and somber ones for the melancholy. In *Macbeth*, more may be accomplished with costume than the mere distinction of clans or of status. The purity of Duncan, who "Hath borne his faculties so meek; hath been/So clear in his great office," and his sons may be expressed by simple white or off-white garments. Malcolm in uniform at the end might wear Duncan's color. Shakespeare informs us of Macbeth's apparel and makes symbolic points with costume suggestions in the dialogue. Macbeth is first the armed warrior, who asks when he is told of his advancement, "Why do you dress me in borrowed robes?" Then (as Angus says) the usurper-king "does feel his title/Hang loose about him, like a giant's robe/Upon a dwarfish thief" (V, 2). Finally in Act V, Scene 3 Macbeth sheds his kingly garb for his armor once again, alluding at least four times in this very brief scene to his costume change. He ends Act V, Scene 5 with "At least we'll die with harness on our back." He will die, if he must, in his more natural and more suitable clothing.

Three fine essays concentrate on the importance of clothing imagery in *Macbeth* and how the costumes delineate character and theme. Caroline Spurgeon views the "ill-fitting" reference literally. Instead of the heroic and sublime character that Bradley sees, Miss Spurgeon interprets Macbeth as lacking "nobility of nature,"[8] and feels that references to ill-fitting garments suggest "the spectacle of a notably small man enveloped in a coat far too big for him."[9] Cleanth Brooks agrees that clothing is important as a symbolic means of interpretation, but objects to the nearly comic spectacle of clothes that *literally* do not fit. Macbeth is, rather, uncomfortable because he is aware that he has no right to kingly garb. Clothing, Brooks believes, is related to the broader issue of false appearances: "False face must hide what the false heart doth know" (I, 7); "we/Must lave our honors in these flattering streams,/And make our faces vizards to our hearts,/Disguising what they are" (III, 2).[10] The third essay, Alan S. Downer's "The Life of Our Design, emphasizes the poetic–dramatic importance of recognizing the writer's references to physical objects in his text. Downer enlarges on the clothing images in *Macbeth*, adding the significance of the dressing gown, which first disguises Macbeth's armor, and suggests that from this point he is "cowardly, melancholic, suspicious, and unhappy; the reverse of all the qualities that had made him the admired warrior of the early scenes."[11]

A similar progression may be suggested by the manner in which Lady Macbeth is costumed. To suggest a contrast, she might first be dressed nobly, but simply, with a minimum of adornment. When she appears first as queen (in III, 1), she could wear richer, more ostentatious clothing in addition to her new crown. She, unlike her more imaginative husband, wears her new robes quite comfortably. In her final scene, however, she is reduced to even less than her pre-royal simplicity as she appears in a drab, unadorned night-gown.[12]

The director and designer might place more value on a metaphorical representation of Macbeth's step-by-step descent to complete bestiality, culminating in Act IV, Scene 1 when he says "From this moment/The very first-lings of my heart shall be/The firstlings of my hand" and decides to murder Macduff's wife and babes. This need not be achieved in an obvious or heavy-handed manner. Instead, increasing use might be made of furs and skins, and perhaps a wilder, more disarranged manner of dress.

Intent: Lighting and Sound Design. Aside from their purely functional requirements, lighting and music contribute chiefly to atmosphere. However, each can be used imaginatively as symbol or metaphor. Color is probably the most frequently used device in lighting for these purposes. As with the use of color in costume, colored illumination can create a psychological or emotional warmth, from a comfortable glow to a passionate or fiery heat. Realistic plays may deliberately suggest different times of day for the action, or a particular kind of interior lighting to justify the emotional impact of certain colors. In a nonrealistic play, the director need not justify his use of color in light as a natural phenomenon. A scrim, cyclorama, or backdrop may be illuminated with colors that change according to the psychological or emotional action of the play. Sophocles' *Oedipus*, for example, might begin at dawn with the effect of semidarkness broken by streaks of cold light. This might slowly work into a full hot white light effect, which would contribute to the effect of plague and a parched environment. Teiresias' mysterious prophecies might be accompanied by a change of color, or by a weird play of light on his figure as he speaks, to suggest his supernatural powers. Lighting during Oedipus' narration of the three crossroads adventure could begin with a pink glow and, as his description of his fury mounts, intensify into a violent crimson. When the old shepherd arrives, the lights could begin to dim and, by the time the terrible truth is revealed, develop into a murky, shadowy overcast. Oedipus' final scene, in which both he and Thebes are purged, might be played in a softer, warmer—but not bright—color. It might be interesting, if possible, to play this scene with a rain effect to suggest the purgation of both Oedipus and the plague.

Expressionistic drama has made effective use of lighting and sound to externalize the mental and emotional states of the protagonist. The following stage directions from Elmer Rice's *The Adding Machine* externalize the development of Mr. Zero's hysterical rage, which culminates in the murder of his boss:

BOSS: I say I'm sorry to lose an employee who's been with me for so many years—
(Soft music is heard—the sound of the mechanical player of a distant merry-go-round. The part of the floor upon which the desk and stools are standing begins to revolve very slowly.)
But, of course, in an organization like this, efficiency must be the first consideration—
(The music becomes gradually louder and the revolutions more rapid.)
You will draw your salary for the full month. And I'll direct my secretary to give you a letter of recommendation—
ZERO: Wait a minute, boss. Let me get this right. You mean I'm canned?
BOSS: *(Barely making himself heard above the increasing volume of sound.)*
I'm sorry—no other alternative—greatly regret—old employee—efficiency—economy—business—*business*—Business—
(His voice is drowned by the music. The platform is revolving rapidly now. Zero and the Boss face each other. They are entirely motionless save for the Boss's jaws, which open and close incessantly. But the words are inaudible. The music swells and swells. To it is added every off-stage effect of the theatre: the wind, the waves, the galloping horses, the locomotive whistle, the sleigh bells, the automobile siren, the glass-crash. New Year's Eve, Election Night, Armistice Day, and the Mardi-Gras. The noise is deafening, maddening, unendurable. Suddenly it culminates in a terrific peal of thunder. For an instant there is a flash of red and then everything is plunged into blackness.) [13]

Sometimes perfectly realistic use of light and light sources may be an effective symbol. In *A Streetcar Named Desire*, for example, the naked light bulb is appropriate to the environment and to the taste of the Kowalskis. But Blanche's need to soften the light with a colored shade expresses her fear of the harshness of reality, and her tendencies to romanticize her existence.

We have observed previously how vital color is to *Macbeth*. Earlier suggestions concerning the relation of color and meaning can be applied to lighting. Red might be introduced in each of the witches' scenes—perhaps emanating from the cauldron. Later, when the murder plunges us into hell, the same red might be reintroduced. For example, the murder scene itself should probably be played in a dark atmosphere where black predominates, or where huge black shadows are cast by torches. Then with the entrance of the porter and his allusions to Hell-Gate, red light may emerge and intensify as, figuratively, all hell breaks loose with the discovery of the murdered king. Special lighting effects might be useful in the banquet scene whenever

Banquo's ghost appears. If the director wishes to emphasize the violence of Banquo's death, a red follow spot might be used, or if he wishes to create an other-world effect, a pale green color might prove effective. Macbeth's final meeting with the witches would reintroduce fiery reds and use other unnatural colors or unnatural means of illumination as the apparitions appear and fade away. Finally, in the play's last scene, colors and effects suggesting rebirth, cleansing, new hope, "the dawn of a new day" can be used as a contrast to the former alternation of the bloody and hellish reds with the blackness of night and unnatural day.

Symbolic effects may be emphasized by isolating objects with illumination. The symbolic Madonna and throne suggested by Knight are specially illuminated or dimmed at key moments to associate their special meaning with certain incidents or states of mind in the play. In the Peter Hall production, the opening Black Sabbath scene was illuminated only by lightning. Novel electrical devices such as the strobe or projections of the changing shapes of colored liquid have been used effectively. Wagner's *Gesamtkunstwerk*, the combined use of all of the arts in the theatre, must now be viewed as a continually expanding concept as advancements in science lead to the development of new art forms. Since Wagner's time, the projection of slides and film, as well as the use of the strobe have been incorporated into dramatic presentation, and a new phrase, "Total Theatre," has replaced Wagner's term.

Music contributes to meaning primarily in an associative way. Besides locale and time, music may also suggest ideas. We associate lullabies with children, there are familiar melodies that we connect with weddings, funerals, revolution, and religion. Musical instruments suggest associations: a single flute may be "lonely," a harmonica rustic and nostalgic, a harpsichord aristocratically elegant, bugles and drums military, electronic music unnatural, supernatural, or futuristic. Chekhov's "sound of a snapped string, dying away, mournful" in *The Cherry Orchard* first ominously and finally sadly represents the fading of an age and a way of life. The same playwright uses music ironically and, in *The Three Sisters,* as a kind of counterpoint when the final poignant moments, which are concerned with the tragic losses of each of the sisters, are underscored by the stirring martial music of the departing troops. In *Macbeth,* Shakespeare makes extraordinary use of music and sound. Music generally is either martial or royal, using drums and trumpets. Such effects do not merely "announce" arrivals, they contribute to the martial and "imperial" themes of the play. Shakespeare's sound effects, too, are not merely the recreation of a realistic environment; the sounds of night birds and beasts contribute to the nightmare qualities of the play—to the "perturbations in nature." We hear them in the terrible moments before the murder as ghastly warnings and later as part of the bestial inferno of Act IV, Scene 1. Additional music might be composed or extracted from existing sources to further enhance character and meaning. Discretion, of course,

173

always must be exercised in the use of music and sound. In *Macbeth* silences may be as terrifying and significant as sound. When music or sound is used, its placement and duration must be controlled, and it must support the action rather than distract or bring attention to itself. Unlike opera or musical comedy, introductory music should *briefly* prepare the audience for the immediate start of the play. The audience will not have come for a musical performance, and it will normally stop listening if a lengthy overture is played. Underscoring, or the use of music to accompany dialogue, can be dangerous. Too often this device is obvious, sentimental, and substitutes musical emotion for that of the actor.

NOTES

[1]G. Wilson Knight, *Principles of Shakespearean Production* (London: Penguin Books, 1949), p. 65.

[2]Stark Young, *The Theatre* (New York: Hill and Wang, 1958), p. 66.

[3]Stark Young, *Immortal Shadows* (New York: Charles Scribner's Sons, 1948), p. 100.

[4]A. C. Bradley, *Shakeaspearean Tragedy* (London: Macmillan, 1951), pp. 333–335.

[5]Jan Kott, *Shakespeare Our Contemporary,* trans. Boleslaw Taborski (New York: Anchor Books, 1966), p. 87.

[6]Alva Johnston, "Profiles: Aider and Abbettor," *New Yorker Magazine,* Oct. 30, 1948, pp. 28–43.

[7]John Masefield, *A Macbeth Production* (London: William Heinemann, 1945), pp. 23–24.

[8]Caroline Spurgeon, *Shakespeare's Imagery* (Boston: Beacon Press, 1958), p. 327.

[9]Spurgeon, p. 325.

[10]Cleanth Brooks, "The Naked Babe and the Cloak of Manliness," in *Approaches to Shakespeare*, Norman Rabkin, ed. (New York: McGraw Hill, 1964), pp. 66–89.

[11]Alan S. Downer, "The Life of Our Design," *The Hudson Review*, II: 2 (Summer 1949), pp. 242–263.

[12]In a 1972 film of *Macbeth* (directed by Roman Polanski) Lady Macbeth's sleepwalking scene is played in the nude.

[13]Elmer Rice, *The Adding Machine* (New York: Samuel French, 1929), pp. 28–30.

Preparation for Expression: Working with the Actors

The director should do a thorough job of analysis in developing character because of its importance in the search for a play's intentions and unity. This does not mean that the actor necessarily will be deprived of an independent interpretation of his role. In fact, as with the designers, the actor should be encouraged to find his character's objectives and characteristics, and to discover the relationship of his character to the other persons in the play. Unlike the director, the actor concentrates almost solely on the character he is to play, and his identity and thinking essentially is with that character. The director has an overview of the entire play and of all of its characters. During the rehearsal period the actor and the director attempt to find the most meaningful way to relate the parts to the whole.

While the director has been working with theory the actor's job is to create the living character—or the expressed character—on stage. Ideally, while the director shares with the actor the job of interpretation and of justifying actions, the actor is largely responsible for finding a physical and vocal form and manner for the character. Unlike other art forms that use humans as their subjects, characters in plays must be completed by agents other than the artist who invented them. The more profound the imagination and skill of the actor, the richer the stage creation, and the more interesting and exciting the entire play. The director should know this and should give the actor every opportunity to use his experience, imagination, and talent.

The actual contribution of the actor or director, however, in developing the expressive aspects of characterization is a matter of degree and varies considerably, depending on the individuals, the plays, and the conditions in which they are rehearsed. Successful directors have included both those who assume the responsibility for most of the gestures, movements, and sounds made by the actor, and those who practice *laissez-faire*. Personality is an important factor, and actors and directors approach their jobs in the manner that works best for them. The autocratic director may do a superb job of bringing a text to life and teach the most experienced actors a great deal about their roles. The methods of the *laissez-faire* director may achieve equally good results while it appears that he has done very little. Each man works best in his own way, but the success of each depends on working with responsive actors. Some experienced actors can work with any director, others want desperately to be told what is expected of them, while others want as little interference as possible. Actually both extremes of directing may be deceptive. With even the most explicitly demanding directors, the roles finally must be played by the actors. They must assimilate the director's suggestions and make them interesting and believable. Ultimately the character must belong to the actor. Only a foolish director insists on retaining business and movement that the actor is unable to adapt. The *laissez-faire* director, if he is good, is always in control but is never obvious about it. He suggests rather than dictates, and by indirect means guides the rehearsals of a play. Of course, he must become explicit if his procedures fail to bring out appropriate and imaginative responses.

Young and inexperienced actors usually require coaching from the director, and in this realm methods will vary according to the nature of the director and the responsiveness of the actor. Some prefer to stimulate responses through questions, allusions, images, and improvisations. Others demonstrate vocally and physically and hope that the actor can successfully imitate them or be stimulated into a similar, but more personal, means of expression. The nondirective technique may stimulate the actor's creativity to a greater extent, and certainly, if successful, will result in more integrated expressions. But even *laissez-faire* directors have to and should demonstrate when their preferred methods fail.

Sometimes, plays themselves make it necessary to use one technique or another. Highly stylized plays or ones whose conventions are unfamiliar to the actors require demonstrations by the director or by special coaching aides in voice and movement. Movement and masks in Greek tragedy and the Commedia dell'Arte demand special training, as does speaking the dramatic verse of Shakespeare, or correctly handling the fans, snuff, and canes of Restoration comedy. In plays where naturalness and a life-like illusion is necessary, actors must rely more on their own intuition, sense of truth, and lack of affectation in the development of physical and vocal expression.

Finally, the amount of rehearsal time may be a factor in determining how much guidance is necessary from the director. *Laissez-faire* methods and experimental approaches normally take more time than the more "controlled" directorial methods, especially with relatively inexperienced actors. When a play must be "whipped up" in a short period of time, the director must be prepared to get results quickly, and is more apt, under such conditions, to impose interpretation and the means of expression. Ideally, of course, the rehearsal period should meet the needs of the play and the desired method of the director, but more often than not, the length of rehearsal schedules in both the professional and amateur theatre is determined more by practical than by artistic considerations.

The relationship between the cast and the director is so complex and often so subtle that it would take an entire book to adequately explore it. The remarks above talked primarily about the roles of actor and director in their creative relationship and only in a very minor way about their psychological relationship. It is easy to say that actors and directors should respect one another personally and professionally and should be guided in their relationship by respect and by their mutual concern to achieve the best possible performance of the play. But, in acting, the personal traits and sensitive egos of the artists who are working closely together are involved; the instruments of expression are the actors' bodies, minds, and emotions; the pressures of time, strain, and uneven rates of development are prevalent; differences of opinion are inevitable: all these contribute to different problems for every cast with which a director works. Of course a director should possess a deep understanding of human nature and be able to recognize and respond to individual differences, but this quality alone will not insure effective results; some directorial geniuses succeed despite their abusiveness. The perfect combination of psychologist-artist is very rare, and perhaps directors should aspire to this. It is no doubt more realistic to recognize that we are involved in a craft that requires skill and artistry from a group of individuals who share a variety of human imperfections. Respect for the skills and tolerance for the foibles with the united objective of successfully realizing the text may be the most satisfactory and least disappointing attitude for actors and directors to share.

The following principles are offered as the common denominator for the director's responsibility to the actor, and should be workable for most directors, including those who may differ in their means of achieving them:

1. The director provides a stimulus or a direction, with a conception or possible conceptions for the play.

2. The director attempts to guide individual characterization so that it relates to the meaning and style of the entire play.

3. The director should help the actor explore, when necessary, the stimuli for the most truthful and correct expression of character.

4. The director acts as an audience during rehearsals, and informs the actor if he is using his voice and body with clarity and expressiveness to successfully communicate.

5. The director should make suggestions that simplify and economize movement and gesture. Usually the actors—especially the most imaginative ones—require help in selecting expressive details, and in eliminating irrelevant or random business.

6. The director is responsible for resolving differences of opinion between the actors on stage. It is advisable to make it clear that his judgment is based on what works best for the play. He should feel responsible for establishing a sense of the ensemble: the conviction that every role is important to the play and that the play is more important than any role.

The interpretative functions of the actor are developed in the processes of casting the play, rehearsal organization, the working out of movement, business, and composition, and finally in performance.

Casting the Play

If we accept the principle that the director is responsible for the cohesiveness of a play's performance, then we must agree that the director should select each member of the cast. This chapter is based on this principle of directorial responsibility, but it must be stated that the director is sometimes relieved of this duty. In the professional theatre, motion pictures, and television, casting agencies or a "casting director" may choose the actors. Sometimes, the producer will cast at least the star parts to assure box office success. In other instances, a financial backer may insist on the casting of his wife or daughter in return for his investment. In the amateur theatre, particularly in community theatre, a casting committee may be appointed to select the actors for a play. Often this is done to protect the director from the accusation of "playing favorites," but then the director must work with people who in his opinion have been miscast, or who prove to be incompetent. Of course, he is ultimately blamed for a play's failure, even when the choice of actors has been the major cause.

Theoretically, no one, with the possible exception of the playwright (who may have sound judgment about an actor's appearance, but not about his theatrical ability), is as qualified as the director to cast the ensemble. He is most familiar with the text, and his conceptions about the text are to be creatively developed. A cast should be selected to most fruitfully realize that conception, which has been derived in part by the director's study of character.

While it is unrealistic for the director to hold auditions with an absolute, photographic impression of each character in the play, he should be prepared to search for certain qualities. Most of these are based on what actors are able to suggest physically, vocally, and emotionally at an audition. The director's task is to discover the best combination of characteristics for each role, while maintaining an awareness of ensemble requirements, of relating the qualities of the actors to one another.

PHYSICAL REQUIREMENTS

Although actors are expected to have the skills to create the physical illusion of ages and postures not their own, there are some physical qualities that the actor cannot establish. Extremes in height and weight often cannot be successfully suggested by costumes or other devices. For example, there are many small actors who can act Macbeth. But if the director has determined that a large Macbeth is more consistent with the violently successful warrior who begins the play, and has visualized Macbeth as a hulking monster descending into bestiality, then he looks for the best big actor he can find. The actor chosen for Falstaff need not be obese; he may require additional padding to assume the hyperbolic proportions suggested by the text, but ideally, given equal acting ability, the more physically monumental the actor, the better.

Some aspects of the actor's shape should be anticipated. Rosalind and Viola must disguise themselves as men. Some very good actresses have been forced to struggle against the costumer's inability to conceal their large busts and hips. Directors should not feel constrained to request the exposure of knees and legs when he knows that they will be exposed during the course of the play. Skinny legs and knock knees may be inappropriate for Macbeth, but absolutely correct for Sir Andrew Aguecheek.

Besides height, weight, and shape, agility and control are important considerations in the physical requirements for some roles. An actor's size, voice, and even nose may suggest a perfect Cyrano, but you may have to start over if you find out later that he is incurably clumsy and uncoordinated. Ariel must be graceful and airy, Mirabel unself-consciously elegant and masculine, and Mame must do cartwheels. A farce such as *The Comedy of Errors* requires principals (essentially the two sets of twins) whose physical condition is vigorous enough for the speed of movement, nearly acrobatic business, and breath control required by the play. Stamina, too, is important for actors who must play demanding roles such as Lear, Peer Gynt, Rosalind, or Nora through intensive rehearsals and continuous performances. In casting such roles, it is not really out of line for the director to investigate the health and stamina of the actors under consideration.

VOCAL REQUIREMENTS

Before tryouts, the director should know which of the characters require extreme power, broad pitch range, and special qualities of voice and speech. Nearly all of Shakespeare's tragic heroes require great vocal strength. Othello's rages, Lear's challenges to nature on the heath, and Macbeth's fury as the battle scenes develop demand actors who can roar without labor and strain.

Nearly all major roles require variety, but some run the gamut more than others. Cleopatra's infinite variety must be vocally expressed as she alternates between tenderness and rage, commanding and cajoling, ecstasy and despair. Macbeth must be capable of shifting from the hushed terror of "Now o'er the one-half world" to the tormented self-debate of "If it were done when 'tis done" with his response to its varied images, to the calculating cruelty of the deliberate killer, to the manic "The Devil damn thee black, thou cream-faced loon!" to the monotonous despair of "Tomorrow and tomorrow and tomorrow."

Certain characters require a predominant pitch. In the opinion of the director, Othello may have to possess a low, deep, sonorous voice, and Viola or Rosalind, voices in a relatively low register for women so that their male disguises do not excessively strain credibility. Osric in *Hamlet* or the fops in Restoration comedy may be expected to maintain speech in an upper register. Sometimes, actors may be required who can characterize with gutteral, de-nasal, or aspirate qualities. In casting the weird sisters in *Macbeth,* actresses must be tested for the capacity to speak with unusual qualities and to voice unnatural sounds and shrieks.

Speech demands also must be anticipated. If dialects are necessary, the actors must be tested on their ability to reproduce the pronunciation, rhythms, and inflections of the specified dialect. If the play is a verse drama, the auditioning actor's ear for cadence and his potential for uttering words more descriptively and with more duration than in everyday speech should be tested. If the part calls for sophisticated verbal humor such as that of Congreve, Wilde, Coward, or Albee, the director must be certain that actors can speak with the lightness, subtlety, and innuendo that the language of those writers suggests.

Clarity and the ability to be heard are necessary from all speaking characters. The director must consider the acoustical condition of the theatre in which the play is to be performed and evaluate voices accordingly. In a large auditorium, control of speech pace is as important as volume, because clarity will depend on slower, more deliberate articulation. Directors should resist being won over by the perfect physical specimen for a role if the actor does not enunciate well or has poor speech patterns and habits.

EMOTIONAL REQUIREMENTS

The director should anticipate the degrees of emotional intensity for every character in the play, and seek ways during the audition period of testing the actors' capacity for emotional release. The director can ill afford the risk of a Medea, no matter how striking in appearance or powerful in voice, who is incapable of expressing the suffering, the wrath, and the ecstatic triumph through which Euripides' heroine ranges throughout the tragedy. The problem of successfully casting Macbeth is due chiefly to the difficult combination of intense sensibility, trepidation and fear, and the soldierly courage and unrestrained violence required to portray him.

Emotional demands are not always as obvious as the examples just cited. Sometimes it is more difficult to find actors who must express emotions in a subtle manner, or who can suggest powerful emotions lurking beneath the surface. The audience must be aware of Lady Macbeth's suppressed emotions as she struggles for the strength to suppress those of her husband. Not all actors and actresses are capable of suggesting the anxieties, fears, and desires that lurk under the surface of Harold Pinter's characters, and the director must be in a position to determine which actors possess such emotional potential.

ENSEMBLE REQUIREMENTS

It is not enough to concentrate on individual character requirements when preparing for auditions. The director must consider the collective appearance and sound of his cast to achieve variety and unity as well as meaning in the ensemble. Actually, if individual differences suggested by the text are observed, variety should take care of itself. But there are instances when the physical or vocal traits of characters may not be strongly distinguishable. In *Macbeth,* for example, Macbeth, Macduff, and Banquo are successful warrior-noblemen. They should give the impression of physical stature and strength, as well as breeding. No indication of age differences is provided. While the characters behave differently, and they may be distinguished from one another by costume, the director could individualize them more by differences of weight and shape (lean versus husky), hair (color, texture, length), and voice (normal pitch levels, timbre, resonators).

Essentially, unity and variety, as well as meaning, are accomplished by the process of matching and contrasting characters. The example just cited from *Macbeth* shows how both may be necessary at the same time. Less contrast is necessary for the minor soldiers, but a certain unity of size and strength should be achieved, not just because they are soldiers, but because they should be observed as a group rather than as distinct characters. Differences that are too striking will bring unnecessary attention and significance to the group or to its deviant members. In *Henry IV, Part Two,* however, extreme differences in the country recruits are desirable, because of the comic requirements of the text, which calls for a hodge-podge of unlikely-looking warriors.

Similarities in appearance may be required when characters are supposed to be members of the same family. Obvious examples occur in plays such as *Twelfth Night* and *Comedy of Errors,* which require twins. Of course, actual twins do not have to be found to play these roles, but care must be taken to minimize the difficulties of creating the illusion of identical twins. The actors chosen should resemble each other in height and build. Wigs, costume, makeup, and the actor's invention will take care of the rest. Duncan and his son, Malcolm, while differing widely in age, might be cast with some physical similarities, so that Malcolm's triumph at the end of *Macbeth* might suggest the spiritual rebirth or triumph of Duncan and all that he represents.

Emphatic contrasts often should be anticipated when characters are paired. Sometimes the text makes this clear as in the case of Helena and Hermia in *A Midsummer Night's Dream,* but in other instances variety requires it. Efforts should be made clearly to differentiate Viola and Olivia, Rosalind and Celia, Kate and Bianca, Vladimir and Estragon.

In more general terms, such demands as style, genre, and dialect must be seriously considered in selecting the ensemble. Ideally, the director seeks consistency in the cast's capacity to achieve the vocal and physical demands of a classical play. The magnitude and control for Greek tragedy, the ability to speak the verse of Shakespearean drama, the sophistication, lightness, and flair for Restoration comedy, should permeate the entire cast of the plays that represent these styles. Some excellent actors cannot successfully perform in certain styles, and their presence in a cast whose other members are stylistically proficient may prove embarrassing and distracting. This is one of the more serious problems in the American theatre, where tradition and the training of the actor for the classic theatre has been deficient.

The same problems occur with genre. Comic or tragic capabilities are not shared by all good actors, and the ability of the ensemble uniformly to create the appropriate atmosphere for genre is vital. Comedy also normally requires more contrast than tragedy. Even when not specifically suggested by the text, the effect of comic contrast becomes one of the objectives of the director. In Molière's *The Imaginary Invalid,* the Diafoiri, a father and son doctor team, may be sharply contrasted physically as fat and thin or extremely tall and short. (On the other hand, they may be cast and made up to look *exactly* alike except for the color of their hair and beards, which might be white for the father and dark for the son, or black for the father and blonde for the son.) Harpagon's servants in *The Miser* should be as physically diversified a ragged group as the director can find.

One of the major problems in casting is created by dialect, especially if most of the characters are members of the same geographical locale. An Irish dialect really is quite necessary for *The Playboy of the Western World,* and it is vital that dialect should be consistently spoken by the entire cast. Pronunciation, inflection, and rhythms must be the same, otherwise complete belief from the audience will be jeopardized, and inconsistencies will jar the audience from its involvement in the play.

There also are considerations in casting that have little to do with the appropriateness of the actor for the role. These include the actor's reputation and experience. In all levels of theatre, professional and amateur, are actors with exceptional talent but a poor attitude. Some directors will insist that immoderate temperament has no place in the collaborative nature of the theatre. They prefer the harmony of a dedicated and selfless group of individuals.

Others are willing to put up with the whims or excessive behavior of a star, and will risk the morale of a cast for the sake of a more dazzling performance. This is especially understandable for plays that strongly depend on a single role, such as *Cyrano de Bergerac, Oedipus the King,* or the musical comedy *Auntie Mame.*

The actor's experience often may be the deciding factor in casting the play. At auditions, a relative newcomer to the stage may give a very impressive reading. In the professional theatre, casting such a novice in an important role is a serious risk, because the director cannot be sure that the actor will be able to sustain a character, probe more deeply into a role or advance beyond the initial reading, and acquire the confidence necessary for success. On the other hand, a director often prefers to cast an unknown over a successful and popular actor, because he wants to avoid audience recognition of the actor and his personal style and mannerisms. The director may believe, too, that for certain roles the play would benefit from the kind of naturalness —even crudity—of an inexperienced performer.

Finally, it should be noted that casting possibilities will vary with the available talent and that in the amateur theatre much of what was suggested above must of necessity be compromised.

In educational theatre, the director on principle must assume a somewhat different perspective in casting than he might in the professional theatre. His purpose must continue to be that of interpreting the play as capably as possible, but in casting he must be willing to accept and work with whatever talent is available, and to recognize the importance of the development of the student actor. Obviously he will have to adjust his preconceived ideas of character requirements, and make the best of what is available. In some instances, he may be presented with just enough warm bodies to match the size of his cast. He must be prepared to cast young people in elderly roles, but this means that he must be even more astute in casting, because he must determine the potential ability of the actors to perform such tasks.

One of the arguments in educational theatre deals with the competitive principle that is prevalent in professional theatre. With a wide diversity in talent, should the educator be obliged over a period of time to give everyone a major role, regardless of potential or ability, so that such experience may be shared, or for therapeutic reasons? Much will depend, of course, on whether the school regards its program as one of professional training. If so, it may be argued that its acting classes will provide the experience of performing major roles in scenes, while the student must be educated in the reality of competition when major productions are cast. In less professionally-minded schools, however, it is also argued that casting people who are incompetent or unsuited for their parts can only make them more self-conscious and miserable, and put a strain on the entire ensemble. Is it therapeutic to create a situation that increases the individual's awareness of his inadequacies? Much will depend of course on the expressed purposes of the experience, and on the attitude of the director and the staff.

Another problem shared by directors in casting amateur productions is that of attempting to cast a play with individuals whose abilities and experiences are widely varied. If the play is one in which a single character must dominate, the best available actor probably would be cast—provided he was reasonably suited to the role. On the other hand, it is often advantageous to distribute strength among the cast, even when it means weakening a major role. An obvious example can be made with *Othello*. Suppose a director is confronted with two capable actors: one is superior to the other in his ability to play Othello, but his Iago would be equally as good. The other actor could do a competent, if not superior Othello, but would be unsatisfactory as Iago. If the director's concern is with the play rather than with a star performance, he will sacrifice a splendid Othello for a well-balanced team.

Finally, we must deal with the problem of tentative casting and double-casting. In the professional theatre, unless the actor has a no-cut contract, all roles are tentative for a certain period of time. If the director believes that he has made a mistake, he may dismiss the actor concerned and replace him. This is a rather severe attitude in amateur, especially educational theatre, where there are no contracts, no salaries, and a lesser regard (it is hoped) for the box office. It might correctly be regarded as a result of his own casting incompetence or carelessness when a director has a change of heart or mind, and the consequences are unfair and cruel to the student-actor involved. Unless the actor is uncooperative or proves to have some problem that seriously impairs his ability to act (such as the inability to memorize lines), the director should, after *conscientious* casting, determine to stick with his original choices.

Double-casting is justified when actors are abundant and the director wants to give as many of them as possible an opportunity to perform. It also is used when the director wants the security of having understudies. Another advantage is the experience gained by a cast that must learn to adapt to the varying interpretations and techniques of different actors. But double-casting sometimes creates additional problems, particularly as it affects rehearsal time. Depending on the size of the role, if each actor is given equal time to rehearse and develop the character, then rehearsal time may be doubled. If such time is limited, then the director has the option of giving each actor equal, but insufficient, time to grow and relate to the ensemble, or to allow one actor a majority of rehearsals, while the other is relegated to understudy status.

TRYOUT PROCEDURES

While the objective of all tryouts is to select a cast that fits the criteria described in the previous sections, procedures will vary according to the preference of the director, or institution, and the number of actors who are interested in getting roles. On some occasions tryouts for a play are not publicly announced but are by invitation only. In such circumstances, the competition is kept to a minimum, and actors usually are interviewed or auditioned privately. On other occasions, considerable precasting may have been arranged privately by the director, or through a casting agency. More common, however, is the open competitive tryout, where a fairly large turnout may be expected. This is the type of tryout with which we will be concerned.

Casting is too important a procedure to be rushed, and each actor who appears at tryouts should be given the opportunity to demonstrate his ability and appropriateness to enact one of the characters in the play. Yet time is usually limited, and in many—perhaps most—cases, the tryout period is less than one week. This means that procedures must be well organized and efficient, and that the director must be enormously perceptive. Such perception, of course, will depend on the adequacy of his preparation and his familiarity with the characters in the play, but nearly every experienced director will agree that intuition often plays a role at tryouts. He also must be decisive. It is too easy to procrastinate and spend more time than necessary in reading and rereading actors.

Perhaps the most efficient way of conducting unrestricted tryouts is the method of screening and callbacks.

Screening. The objective of the screening process is to narrow down the list of candidates for roles as quickly as possible. This may appear to be mercenary, as well as contradictory to the caution in casting advised previously. But it really does not take much time for the director to recognize actors who are unquestionably wrong or inadequate for his play. At a screening tryout, instead of laboring for long periods of equal time with each candidate, he will eliminate some actors and retain others for a later and more strenuous tryout on the basis of the following:

A. Acting potential
   1. Can the actor be heard and understood?
   2. Does his voice have stage energy?
   3. Does he appear physically poised, or does his manner suggest a complete lack of stage presence?
   4. Even when he meets the first three standards, does his reading or audition suggest inadequacy, maturity and skill well below the standards of the ensemble, or annoying affectations that are unsuitable to the play?
B. Appropriateness
   1. Does the actor appear to suit the requirements of any of the characters in the play?
   2. If not, does he suggest a different and perhaps more interesting concept for a certain role than that anticipated by the director?

If the director is uncertain about any of the above, he should provide the actor with a further opportunity to prove himself. In addition, it is possible that an actor may appear strongly appropriate for a particular role, yet not seem to possess the acting standards that the director seeks. In some instances, that actor might be worth further exploration. He may come closer to the director's concept than anyone else, in which case the director should try to determine the actor's capacity to take direction and mature with intensive rehearsal.

Materials for such tryouts vary. Perhaps the most dependable kind of presentation is the prepared audition, where the actor is expected to memorize and perform a speech or a scene to the best of his ability. The selection may be from the play that is being cast or, if scripts are unavailable, from another play of a similar style and genre. Sometimes when directors are selecting a repertory company, they stipulate that several selections be prepared to demonstrate the actor's skill in both classical and modern roles, as well as in comic or serious ones.

The value of the prepared audition is that it normally will best reveal the actor's maturity and interpretative abilities. Such presentations need not be perfect. The astute director will recognize talent potential and appropriateness during an imperfect audition by sometimes subtle signs. Such auditions are not preferred by some directors because of the slickness with which they often are presented. Sometimes they reduce spontaneity, or are deceptive, representing the limit of the actor's potential. Another reason for rejecting the prepared audition occurs primarily in educational and amateur theatre, when it is desired that as many people as possible be encouraged to try out. A large number will not feel qualified or will not have the time for a prepared audition.

The alternative to the prepared audition is to ask the candidates to read selected scenes from the play. Since the director's purpose is to eliminate actors who cannot possibly be considered and to see again those who indicate some promise, the selections should be simple and brief. As it is too soon to know which actors are best suited to particular roles, the same scenes may be read by everyone. For example, for *Macbeth* everyone might be presented with the scene between Macbeth and Lady Macbeth in Act I, Scene 7, from her entrance to the end of the scene—or sooner. The director should not expect a performance, but from what he sees and hears should be able to determine the qualifications of the actors and actresses to return for more intensive tests. He should indicate in his notes the role or possible roles for which each reader might be considered. He must not neglect, during his observations, the most minor characters, including walk-ons or spear-carriers.

Callbacks. The number of callbacks will depend on the number of actors the director is interested in, and the speed with which he is able to make decisions. The latter depends not merely on the director, but on the actors who are available. Sometimes, even at large tryouts, it is apparent almost immediately that certain actors are the most suitable choices for the major roles, while at other times, it may be agonizingly difficult to discriminate.

If the number of persons called back is large, the director may have to use the first callback to further eliminate before getting down to the job of making final choices. This process of elimination, however, requires more stringent scrutiny of the actors. Here the director must work more directly and more flexibly with them, as he attempts to find the roles for which each actor is most suited. If the play is *Macbeth*, he may have four or five men who show promise for the leading role, and an equal number of women, perhaps, for Lady Macbeth. There might be two or three possibilities for each of the character roles such as Duncan or the Old Man, and perhaps a dozen for the younger males such as Malcolm, Donalbain, and Young Siward. Now the director reads each of the actors in different scenes, and as they become more familiar with these scenes, he may test their vocal, physical, and emotional skills. He may provide improvisations to appraise the spontaneity and imagination of the actors. He might, for example, ask the candidates for Macbeth and Lady Macbeth to improvise a contemporary scene in which a wife tries to persuade her hesitant husband to quit his job. The director may, if he finds it necessary, actually direct small scenes to determine the actor's ability to respond to directing, or to bring out through suggestion more profound readings of certain scenes. At the same time, the director should be aware of matching and contrasting possibilities as he pairs actors who read different scenes from the play.

If second or third callbacks are necessary, they need not include all candidates who remain. By then, the director probably will have made decisions concerning many of the roles in the play, but will still be uncertain about some of the others. Perhaps he is torn between two excellent Macbeths, and still must select his weird sisters from six or seven fine women. His choice of Lady Macbeth may depend on his final decision on Macbeth.

The director must not leave minor roles or walk-ons to chance. Careless casting of smaller roles often may lead to disastrous results. In *Macbeth*, an unconvincing group of murderers, small as their parts are, will weaken the play. Lady Macduff appears in only one scene, and is not as important as Lady Macbeth, but the director will regret it deeply if he has not fully satisfied himself at tryouts that the actress he selects has the appropriate strength for the role. The director must remember that servants, attendants, and soldiers usually appear on stage together, and that casting leftover actors of incongruous sizes and shapes may create undesired, even startling, stage effects. The director will be assured of a more successful production if he considers *every* role important.

AUDITION FORM

PRODUCTION: _____

NAME: _____AGE: _____

LOCAL ADDRESS: _____

PERMANENT ADDRESS: _____

PHONE: _____
          (If none, how can you be reached?)

SEX: _____HEIGHT: _____WEIGHT: _____HAIR COLOR: _____

Please see page two to indicate past experience, and to fill out class and/or work schedule.

Please note any commitments that might conflict with night or weekend rehearsals:

_____

_____

I understand that I will be cast in the best interests of the production, and agree to accept whatever casting I receive.

_____
(Signature)

Callbacks will be posted_____.

Director's Comments

_____
(Please do not write below this line.)

PAST EXPERIENCE: (Character, Play, Where, When) _____

_____

_____

_____

_____

Can you dance ____, sing ____, play a musical instrument?

(specify) _____

SCHEDULE
SUNDAY MONDAY TUESDAY WEDNESDAY THURSDAY FRIDAY SATURDAY

8
9
10
11
12
1
2
3
4
5
6
7
8
9
10

Tryouts comprise a difficult period for actors and the director. The time required from actors is valuable, and the experience for each of them is fraught with tensions. Efficiency is necessary, but an assembly-line atmosphere is not desirable (though difficult to avoid if the screening tryout draws several hundred candidates). The following principles may help the director create a proper atmosphere for tryouts:

1. Have all materials such as scripts and audition application forms ready (see pp. 188-189).

2. Explain as much as possible of your procedure to the group. If candidates arrive irregularly, then such explanations should be mimeographed and distributed with the application forms.

3. Try to put the actors at ease. Humor will not destroy efficiency. If they appear to be overly tense, reassure them and let them begin again.

4. Be fair. Provide everyone with an equal opportunity to demonstrate his talent.

5. Be relatively unobtrusive. Some directors seem to find it necessary to use tryouts as a performance for themselves.

6. Do not expect readings or auditions to be on the level of a performance. The director's task is to recognize *potential*. He will be disappointed if he expects perfection at this point. Some very good actors are poor auditioners. The director's task is to look for signs of appropriateness and skills, then, by further probing, reassure himself that certain actors will prove to be the correct choices.

7. Give yourself some leeway by not limiting yourself to one choice for any role. You may have to resort to second or third choices later, especially if tryouts are being held for more than one play.

8. Be careful and thorough. Hasty casting may hurt you. Even though casting is always a risk, every effort should be made to minimize the possibility of miscasting.

Rehearsal Procedures: Organization and Techniques

In one respect, directing a play is like constructing a building. The contractor agrees to have it ready for inspection or occupation by a certain date, and during the period of construction a schedule is arranged according to a logical and necessary building plan. The foundation must be completed before the walls can be erected, while the roof must await the completion of the wall structure. In the same way, the director knows that he must have the play ready for an audience by opening night. He knows that he must establish an order of goals, each of which is built on the others and timed so that the accomplishment of each goal does not delay or undermine the completion of further goals necessary for a secure opening. Technical rehearsals, for example, cannot be cluttered with line study, the creation of new business, or lengthy discussions about characterization.

Of course a play is constructed with human beings rather than with building materials, and the final result of a play cannot be planned or engineered with the absolute anticipation of architectural drawings, but a discipline that makes the fullest use of rehearsal time will assure a reasonable progression toward a fully integrated performance by opening night.

No director should attempt to impose exactly the same kind of rehearsal schedule on every play, even though his total time period (as is usually the case in quarter and semester systems in the university) may be similar for each production. Every play poses different problems such as number of characters, length, difficulties of style or characterization, suitable rehearsal methods, and the experience of the cast. While these variables will dictate the number of hours and days per week for rehearsals, and the timing of objectives such as the memorization of lines, some principles are valid for the rehearsals of nearly every play whose opening date is established. These include an understanding of the timing of goals, the importance of repetition, and the most efficient use of each actor's time.

During the rehearsal period, the director's work with the actor will include the working out of blocking (movement) patterns, composition, line readings and memorization, characterization, personal business, technical and dress rehearsals. For obvious reasons, the technical and dress rehearsals comprise the final periods of rehearsal before the opening. The order of the other objectives, however, is relative to the problems mentioned above.

Generally speaking, concentrated work on characterization and personal business (including the use of properties) will not be emphasized in the early weeks of rehearsal. This does not mean that the actor should put these objectives out of his mind. Movement, composition, and characterization should not be thought of as isolated from one another. However, it often is simpler or more logical to *emphasize* certain of these purposes before the others. Fully understanding a character, getting the "feel" of him, and relating smaller actions to the whole is a slow process of development for the actor, and the director must not expect a full-blown characterization in the first week of rehearsal. If he insists on such a development too soon, the result will either be a stock characterization, or one that he imposes on the actor.

The common convention for early rehearsals includes one or more read-throughs of the play and discussion. Some directors place great emphasis on this procedure, and may spend a week or more with it before the actors step on the stage. There are several reasons for this. Actors will become more familiar with their parts before demands for expression begin. They will be able to think of the significance of words and ideas before being concerned about where to stand or move. The director can familiarize the actor with his views of the play and the direction he believes the actors might take in developing their roles. With the entire company present, each of its members will be participating in and listening to the entire play, rather than to their own scenes. The director or the designers may describe the sets and costumes, and the rationale for their development. The director may indicate whatever cuts he may have made in the text, as well as provide the proper pronunciation and meaning of unusual words or phrases. As the director listens to the readings of his cast, he may perceive their possible weaknesses and strengths in voice and phrasing.

While most directors seem to agree that such conferences are valuable, some regard more than one or two as excessive. Too much theorizing, they suggest, is a waste of time. The actors are not as familiar with the play as the director, and his ideas may have merely the most superficial meaning for the listeners at this point. Besides, the language of stage direction is action, and some directors believe that the sooner they communicate to the actors through physical action the better. Such activity is specified and detailed, while lengthy discussions produce little more than abstract generalizations. The purpose of the director's analysis, they believe, is not to lecture the actors, but to discover the foundation and the stimulus for stage action.

Ordinarily the next step is to develop general blocking patterns. "General" because they must be subject to later adjustments and developments as the actor begins to discover character justifications for movement. Early blocking normally is based on the logical action suggested by the text and controlled by the ground plan. Directors differ in their methods of achieving such a plan. Some prefer to work it out in advance, while others want it to come from the actors themselves, when the actors are sufficiently experienced, imaginative, and willing. Sometimes blocking patterns emerge from improvisations with the actors. Instead of saying, "During the next few rehearsals, we will block the play," the director may suggest a series of improvisations without the use of the text, which can stimulate the actors to explore the spatial aspects of the set and of each other, and to find basic actions that parallel those of the play. This procedure is, of course, more time-consuming but, given actors who are responsive to this technique, the results may be more imaginative and more intrinsically meaningful to them.

Composition, or a consistently meaningful stage picture, is often pre-planned and developed simultaneously with the blocking rehearsals. Often composition will take care of itself if movement patterns are valid, but usually there are moments when the director wishes to create a tableau or a deliberate statement by the arrangement of actors on stage. Principles of composition will be dealt with in the next chapter; here we are concerned with the question of its development during rehearsals. Although it is unavoidably a part of the blocking procedure—sometimes influencing the blocking itself—the director should at all times be concerned with creating the most significant stage pictures. Invariably, final compositional adjustments are made when the full set is in place, when the size and shape of space is more exact, and when stairs and platforms are installed.

When should the actor be expected to know his lines? Some directors would answer unhesitatingly, "As soon as possible," while others do not believe in setting a deadline at all. While it may be desirable for many actors to learn the lines "naturally" as they grow into the characters, and to accept the rationale that learning lines should be the result of familiarity rather than rote, the procedure of letting all actors set their own pace may lead to disaster. Rehearsals are devoted not merely to the separate development of each role in the play, but to the development of character relationships and the scene-by-scene action of the play. It is true that actors will develop at different rates, but if these rates are widely divergent, delays in character interplay, tempo, timing, and rhythm will prove to be insufferable. It is not frustrating for just the director. Actors who are ready to develop their emotional scenes, or to develop the invention and pace of farce scenes cannot proceed when the other actors in the scene are still struggling with their lines. It seems fairly obvious that the sooner the actor relinquishes his script, the sooner he will be able to think in subtext and thoughts rather than in lines and to relate to other characters, to the environment, and to objects more deeply and truthfully.

It is human for actors, especially inexperienced ones, to delay line-learning when the director does not establish deadlines for line rehearsals without scripts. At the same time, the director should be reasonable about such deadlines. In a six-week rehearsal period (not including technical and dress rehearsals) of a normal full-length play, it is not unreasonable to expect lines to be "cold" by the middle of the fourth week. The director may divide the play into three parts and insist that the first third be ready by the beginning of the second week, the next third a week later, and the final third a week after that. He thereby sets a reasonable pace for the actor to follow, and prevents the actor from putting off line study until the fourth week.

While line rehearsals may be tedious, they are necessary and, at the same time, may prove useful in other ways. For whatever reason, even the most conscientious actors find line rehearsals a struggle, especially on the first try. The director must patiently wait out the struggle and permit the actor to become secure. This is not the time for the director to press characterization, new business, or timing. He may interrupt when the actor is having difficulty with a particular line, and help him by relating the line to a thought or an image. Otherwise, this period is a good time for the director objectively to view the progress of the play to this point, and to determine what aspects of production will require most of his attention in the next few days. He may use these rehearsals as a stimulus for thinking about new business and characterization. It is a good idea to use at least two consecutive rehearsals for lines. By the second attempt, the actors are usually more settled, and the repetition will contribute to a better retention of lines. If the actors appear to have mastered lines by the second of these rehearsals, the director may feel free to work with them on something else, such as timing lines with movement, or improving line readings.

With the basic movement pattern and lines learned, ensuing rehearsals may concentrate on intensifying all aspects of character development, including personal business and timing. The last rehearsals before the technical rehearsal will be devoted to polishing the play, establishing its continuity and rhythm, and concentrating on scenes that need more work.

Rehearsal organization must consider the amount of time necessary for each rehearsal objective, and when and how often to rehearse the separate parts of the play. Using a six-week schedule, and assuming that the entire play must be learned by the middle of the fourth week, it is clear that the first three weeks must be used for blocking and line rehearsals for the first two-thirds of the play. There are two important principles to consider here. First, no part of the play should be neglected or put off until it is too late. Neither should a part of the play be rehearsed, then ignored for three weeks. Some directors will stress the first two acts of a play for five weeks, then use the last week to throw Act III together. Others will block Act I in the first few days, then neglect it for two weeks, by which time the cast will have forgotten the details of blocking. A more even development will be assured if the director takes about a week to block his first two acts, then allows a couple of days for line rehearsals of the first act. He may then spend a few days to block Act III, then return to Act II for a line rehearsal. He may then review lines and blocking for Act I, use another rehearsal to review the blocking of Act III, then schedule a line rehearsal of Act III. In this way, actors will have the stimulus of blocking for line learning, and will have spent an equal amount of time, with a relatively equal amount of development, on the entire play.

The second principle stresses the value of repetition. Every development during rehearsals should be repeated until the company is sure of itself and confident of retaining what has been accomplished. Several days might be spent in developing intricate movement and business for a scene, but if these are not "set" by repetition, they may be forgotten by the next time the scene is rehearsed. Not only is valuable time lost, but the progression of objectives is delayed.

Another type of rehearsal objective is the runthrough, during which the cast will rehearse an entire act or the whole play without interruption. Without runthroughs, a cast will not achieve a sense of continuity or the security of having performed the entire play without interruption before dress rehearsal. After all, rehearsal is essentially a process of dissection, during which each part of the play is explored as fully as possible. Eventually however, these parts must be synthesized into a fluid whole, with a sense of rises and falls, deliberate rhythms, and a natural flow from one scene to the next. For these reasons, the director cannot have too many runthroughs. He should, however, space them out so that they occur after each of the major objectives of the rehearsal period: after blocking each act, after blocking the entire play, after lines have been learned, and after character and business rehearsals. One or two complete runthroughs just before technical rehearsals should provide the security necessary for the interruptions that will occur during technical rehearsal, and make easier the actor's adjustment to the addition of a complete set, new properties, and costumes. Runthrough sessions should be followed by the director's notes, which correct errors and omissions or make new suggestions for characterization and business.

The technical rehearsal should be preceded by as much preparation as possible by the technical staff in focusing the lights, preparing sound effects, shifting scenery, and using the curtain. Ideally, a pretechnical period without actors should be arranged. At this time the director would check lighting focus and intensities, sound levels, and so forth. He would clarify light and sound cues and their duration. Such a procedure normally assures a smooth technical rehearsal and avoids situations where the actor is forced to wait for hours while lights are adjusted, cues are repeated, and shifts are organized. At the technical rehearsal the director is concerned with coordination. Just as the actor is spared undue fatigue and waiting by the pretechnical rehearsal, the technical crews must be spared the extra time the director might insist on taking to work with the actors.

Two dress rehearsals are usually considered necessary. They should be uninterrupted runthroughs, but during the first, adjustments caused by the initial use of makeup and costumes, plus a normal number of technical misunderstandings, will occur. It is best to give both cast and crew the experience of a runthrough here and to correct errors afterward. The final dress, of course, should approximate an actual performance, perhaps with a few invited guests in attendance.

Some plays require special kinds of rehearsal organization. Musical comedy rehearsals must be divided into individual sessions devoted to dancing, singing, and staging. Shakespeare's tragedies and histories require combat rehearsals, where the actors are taught to use the swords and weapons of the period, and battle action is worked out. And sometimes separate chorus rehearsals are required in Greek tragedy.

The rehearsal schedule should take the actor's time into careful consideration. An organized schedule, worked out in advance, informs the actor about what is expected of him and when it is expected. The director should try to avoid scheduling the actor at rehearsals where his presence is not required. This is especially true of the nonprofessional actor. In the university, some directors forget that student actors are carrying the burden of a full load of courses, and in community theatre, that the actors have full-time jobs and families. The director in both instances has a right to expect as conscientious an effort as possible from the actor, but he is obliged to create a schedule that fully justifies the use of the actor's time. This can be accomplished by indicating which acts or scenes are being rehearsed each day, and which actors are needed. In *Macbeth*, for example, the director need not require the presence of the soldiers and attendants in Act I on each occasion that Act I is rehearsed. In Act II, since the Old Man does not appear until the very last scene, the director may indicate a particular hour for the actor to arrive, rather than insist on his presence for the entire rehearsal. The director can be as considerate of the actors who appear only in the early part of a scene by releasing them when he knows that they are no longer needed.

For similar reasons, the director should consider the amount of time he should demand of the actors at each rehearsal. Even in the professional theatre where director and actors are expected to work full time, the director should be aware of saturation periods, when extending a rehearsal will accomplish very little. Well-timed days off may result in fresher and more cheerful actors. In the university, the director must have a longer rehearsal period because he cannot, with the exception of week-ends or technical rehearsals, work student actors for more than three hours per day. A free day during the week and one or both week-end days will enable the student actor to remain a good student, and also will afford him time to work on his role independently.

Finally, the time spent during rehearsal should be fully exploited for the progress of the play. Rehearsal can be fun, and a certain amount of joking and relaxation should be encouraged, but never allowed to be carried to extremes. The director cannot afford to keep actors standing around while he chats with visitors, and he must avoid careless rehearsals, where his objectives are uncertain, or where he becomes unnecessarily repetitious. The actor should be made aware of the necessity and value of each moment of each rehearsal. He may not always agree, but he usually will cooperate unless it is apparent that the objectives are arbitrary.

Directing the Ensemble

THE PROMPT BOOK

With a suitable ground plan and the casting of the play, the director is ready to proceed with his rehearsals. Before rehearsals begin, however, most directors will have started a prompt book which, when completed, will be a thorough record of the visual progression of the play, and, except for the spoken words of the actor, of the audible effects that have been used. Where directors differ in its use is in its preparation *before* rehearsals begin. Max Reinhardt used a *regiebuch,* which outlined in detail the physical action of the play before rehearsals. At the other extreme is the director who, while he has studied the play as profoundly as he should, prefers to find the action with the actors during the rehearsal period. This difference in approach is a matter of personal preference, but the flexible director may allow the nature of the play to guide his decision. For example, the large casts, the staging complexities, and the relative unfamiliarity of many actors with a Shakespearean play may dictate that the director plan much of the composition and blocking in advance. But for a play by Harold Pinter, in which there is normally a single realistic set, and in which it is so important to encourage the actors to discover a subtext and an inner life for the external ambiguities of Pinter's characters, only the most minimal plans for composition and movement probably should be considered.

Few successful directors leave everything to chance. Entrances and exits, placing the important props and set pieces, and other details of the ground plan normally are thought through in advance. This means that a degree of movement is already "built in" when rehearsals begin since the actors automatically will be confronted with the direction in which they will come and go. Specific textual requirements such as the necessary use of windows, desks, and lamps will force the actor to move wherever the director and designer have placed these objects. In some scenes the director will know that the space in front of a door must be cleared for an entrance, or that the physical relationship between the actors must be very exact, which forces him to think about these problems of composition in advance. Consequently, even when the director prefers not to plan every movement, his prompt book may specify some of the visual necessities that have been mentioned. As the physical action develops or changes during rehearsal, the stage manager or a script holder will record the details in stage shorthand. The director may draw little sketches of compositional effects of which he wishes to be reminded, and later, light and sound cues will be added to complete the prompt book.

The form of the prompt book varies (see pages 200-203), but whatever the form, it must be possible to write in stage directions and clearly relate such directions to the actual line, word, or pause during which the action occurs. For this reason, each page of the script is sometimes mounted on a larger sheet of heavy weight paper, whose margins may be used for notes. Another common method is to place a blank page of paper opposite each page of the script, and to write and sketch on the blank paper. Perhaps the neatest and most efficient method of incorporating stage directions is by using one column or margin for blocking or movement, and another for personal business. Each direction might be given a number or an alphabetical letter that corresponds to the same symbol written in the text on the word or line at which the action is to be performed. Other parts of the page may be used for rough sketches of composition. This is especially valuable when there are many characters on stage, and the director, if he is trying to work out such complicated scenes in advance, needs to be aware of the arrangement of characters from moment to moment as he diagrams the visual progression of the scene. Some directors will prefer to work out such details with the actors themselves, but it is wise to accurately record the results, or else a few actors with short memories may make it necessary to work out an entire sequence over again, wasting valuable rehearsal time.

No matter how a director plans his prompt book, no matter what form it takes, no matter if he uses one or not, every visual moment—which is to say virtually *every* moment on stage—must be justified. Stage pictures must not be created merely to be pretty and uncluttered; movement and stage business cannot be permitted merely to prevent the performance from being static. It is true that an attractive pictorial effect may be needed, that the composition should never be cluttered without a purpose, and that the action should never be permitted to bore the audience, but these ends must be achieved in ways that are justified by characters' conscious and subconscious objectives. A popular story that is intended to ridicule some of the excesses of the so-called method actor tells of such an actor responding to a director's instruction that he move from place A to place B. The actor asks for a reason, to which the business-like director responds, "Because you're being paid for it!" But unless the justification is ridiculously obvious, as it might be when Macbeth leaves the banquet table in Act II, Scene 4 to talk to the first murderer, the actor must understand the director's purpose if he is to

D/S table is moved out.

· Discovered on in B.O. MISS COURTENAY sitting. LADY M sitting. Everyone else standing. Purdom & Angus putting small bench down.

GRAHAM   ANYES
HARDY   DARE   STEWART
MONEY   DONALBAIN   GAY
HERITAGE GAY   CURTIS
DUNBAR
CAITHNESS
SEYTON
CLARKE
FOX   COURTENAY
MACBETH [LADY M]
ANGUS
PURDOM
HANSARD
LENNOX   ROSS   MENTEITH

(1) SEYTON calls "Silence"

(2) MACBETH comes down R stairs to LENNOX + ROSS — LC.   STEWART enters U.L with lamp for the C. table. Gay to top tables Purdom X R.C.

(3) Loud Shout

GRAHAM
DONALBAIN
BATEMAN   SLATER
ANYES DARE   HARDY
HANSARD X
HERITAGE GAY
CLARK
FOX [LADY M] COURTENAY
MONEY CURTIS
CAITHNESS   DUNBAR
MENTEITH   PURDOM
ANGUS   HARDWICK   X STEWART
ROSS
SEYTON
LENNOX

(4) CAITHNESS jumps up to toast LADY M. Purdom X to seat. All cheer

(5) 1st MURDERER enters up R pit steps

(6) SEYTON X to MACBETH, who X DR to MURDERER. SEYTON X to tables to wash up. GAY is handing round dishes to both tables.

(6A) Long cynical laugh from Purdom 'HANSARD'

Prompt book, example A. *Macbeth,* Act III, Scene 4 (redrawn). Royal Shakespeare Company, 1949, directed by Anthony Quayle. Used with

Hall in the palace.

*A banquet prepared. Enter Macbeth, Lady Macbeth,
Ross, Lennox, Lords, and Attendants.*

Macb. You know your own degrees; sit down: at first
And last a hearty welcome.

Lords. Thanks to your majesty.

Macb. Ourself will mingle with society
And play the humble host.
Our hostess keeps her state, but in best time
We will require her welcome.

Lady M. Pronounce it for me, sir, to all our friends,
For my heart speaks they are welcome.

Enter First Murderer to the door.

Macb. See, they encounter thee with their hearts'
thanks.
Both sides are even: here I'll sit i' the midst: 10
Be large in mirth; anon we'll drink a measure

The table round. *[Approaching the door]* There's
blood upon thy face.

Mur. 'Tis Banquo's then.

Macb. 'Tis better thee without than he within.
Is he dispatch'd?

Mur. My lord, his throat is cut; that I did for him.

Macb. Thou art the best o' the cut-throats: yet he's
good
That did the like for Fleance: if thou didst it,
Thou art the nonpareil.

Mur. Most royal sir,
Fleance is 'scaped.   20

Macb. *[Aside]* Then comes my fit again: I had else
been perfect,
Whole as the marble, founded as the rock,
As broad and general as the casing air:
But now I am cabin'd, cribb'd, confined, bound in
To saucy doubts and fears.—But Banquo's safe?

Mur. Ay, my good lord: safe in a ditch he bides,
With twenty trenched gashes on his head;
The least a death to nature.

Macb. Thanks for that.
[Aside] There the grown serpent lies; the worm
that's fled
Hath nature that in time will venom breed,   30

(1) Olivier a step L

(2) Leigh to below OP Pros   Olivier a step 2 R

(3) Olivier a little 2 R US

(4) She runs to him   (at C)

(5) She turns away

(6) He looks back at her

(7) He turns away and moves DS to bottom step
    She follows stands on top step at his R

(8) She moves US a little

(9) He turns to her taking her arm

(10) He crosses on bottom step 2 OP
        corner of step

Prompt book, example B. *Macbeth,* Act I, Scene 7 (redrawn). Royal
Shakespeare Company, 1955, directed by Glen B. Shaw. Used with

Will plead like angels, trumpet-tongu'd against
The deep damnation of his taking-off;
And pity, like a naked new-born babe,
Striding the blast, or heaven's cherubin, hors'd
Upon the sightless couriers of the air,
Shall blow the horrid deed in every eye,
That tears shall drown the wind. (1) I have no spur
To prick the sides of my intent, but only
Vaulting ambition, which o'erleaps itself,
And falls on the other.

Enter Lady Macbeth
(2) How now? what news?

L.M. He has almost supp'd: why have you left the
chamber?

Mac. Hath he ask'd for me?

L.M.   Know you not he has?

Mac. We will proceed no further in this business: 4
He hath honour'd me of late, and I have bought
Golden opinions from all sorts of people,
Which would be worn now in their newest gloss,
Not cast aside so soon.

L.M.   Was the hope drunk,
Wherein you dress'd yourself? hath it slept since?
And wakes it now to look so green, and pale,
At what it did so freely? 5 From this time,

Such I account thy love. 6 Art thou afeard
To be the same in thine own act and valour
As thou art in desire? Wouldst thou have that
Which thou esteem'st the ornament of life,
And live a coward in thine own esteem?
Letting 'I dare not' wait upon 'I would,'
Like the poor cat i' the adage.

Mac.   Prithee peace: 7
I dare do all that may become a man,
Who dares do more, is none.

L.M.   What beast was 't then
That made you break this enterprize to me?
When you durst do it, then you were a man;
And, to be more than what you were, you would
Be so much more the man. Nor time, nor place,
Did then adhere, and yet you would make both:
They have made themselves, and that their fitness
now
Does unmake you. 8 I have given suck, and know
How tender 'tis to love the babe that milks me: 9
I would, while it was smiling in my face,
Have pluck'd my nipple from his boneless gums,
And dash'd the brains out, had I so sworn
As you have done to this.

Mac.   10 If we should fail?

permission of the Royal Shakespeare Company, Stratford-upon-Avon.

203

execute the movement with any sense or believability. The director should always be ready to explain his justification for movement or business, simply because there is no reason for him to conceal his purposes or for him to contrive inexplicable actions to foist on uncomfortable actors.

Controlling the visual expression of the actor and the ensemble is achieved in three ways: through movement, through personal business, and through composition. The stimulus and rationale for whatever is developed in each of these areas comes from our close analysis of the text, especially from the architectonic unit. There we learn *what* each part of the play is intended to express; with this knowledge, the problem of the actor and director is to determine *how* to express, most tellingly and economically, what they believe and understand. Of course, the correct movement or business can occur intuitively or accidentally, but whatever is "invented" must be in accord with the significant purpose of the moment. The purpose of inventing movement, business, and composition is to illuminate rather than to obscure, to serve the text rather than egos and fancies.

MOVEMENT AND ITS JUSTIFICATIONS

Stage movement, or "blocking" refers to the execution of "crosses," when the actor moves from one place on the stage to another. Often, directions for such movement are directly suggested by the dialogue. "Round about the cauldron go" (IV, 1) informs the actresses playing the witches how their ritual is to be performed, and when Banquo says to Ross and Angus, "Cousins, a word, I pray you" (I, 3), he is intended to move toward them and away from Macbeth. In the texts of contemporary plays italicized stage directions are provided to aid the reader in visualizing stage action. Directors and actors should consider them only when they make sense or prove to be the only possible or superior direction for movement. One of the reasons for this is that sometimes such texts are inaccurate, sometimes the stage directions can be improved, and often they were developed for a stage and a ground plan that may differ significantly from the one currently being used. The reason that one *must* follow the leads in the dialogue is because there must be a logical consistency between language, which clearly specifies an action, and the action itself (unless a deliberate comic incongruity is desired). Playwrights generally do not suggest such actions, however, without a reason, and the director must discover the reason. But much movement in every play may be stimulated by less explicit stage directions. Generally speaking, the character will move because he wants to move, or because he must move. In some instances he may be ordered by another character to move or be pushed into another space. Most often, however, crosses are based on the necessity created by characters' desires and objectives. Sometimes the motivation is purely functional; at other times, it will be psychological or emotional. **Functional Justification.**   This kind of justification is often the easiest to recognize, and in many instances is unavoidable. Entrances and exits often occur for purely functional reasons; a character may be looking for someone, or he may have been sent for. When Macbeth and Banquo enter for the first time in Act I, Scene 3 they are on their way to Duncan's camp. At the end of the scene, their desire is to continue on their way. In the banquet scene, Macbeth is playing the host. He moves to a chair at the table rather than to his throne when he announces, "Here I'll sit i' the midst"; then, on seeing the first murderer at the door, he must cross to the door to speak confidentially to him. Later Macbeth must move to the table to pick up a goblet, or a servant must bring one to him on "Give me some wine, fill full." In a realistic play, the maid's crosses in an expository scene are necessitated by her duties; a character crosses to the window to open or close it, or to a desk to write a note. But behind even these functional crosses, there often lurk psychological and emotional stimuli.

Psychological and Emotional Justification. Except for the crisis it contains, Act I, Scene 7 could easily be omitted from *Macbeth*. But without this scene, the character of Macbeth, the relations between Macbeth and his wife, and the moral argument of the play would seriously be weakened and diluted. A scene that contributes so importantly to the play's design (not to mention its potential as effective theatre) must be given careful analysis and execution. It also provides an excellent source for demonstrating the present concern with movement and, later, with personal business.

A simple ground plan for this scene, whose locale is uncertain except that it takes place in a room inside the castle might include the following: two doors, one from which the servants enter with torches, food, and dishes, and another that leads into the banquet chamber; to demonstrate, a single prop—a throne—will suggest that this room is functioning as Duncan's throne room while he is a guest in the Macbeth's castle. The room then may be divided into two parts: upstage from right to left is a gallery formed by a platform divided from the downstage area by a series of pillars or arches. The door to the kitchen is on the right of the platform, and the door to the banquet chamber on its left. The throne is at center stage a few feet in front of the gallery. (It would be advisable for the reader to review other references made to this scene, especially those on pp. 56-58.)

The scene begins with servants crossing from right to left on the platform (1 in Figure 1). They disappear into the banquet chamber (from which the sound of voices is heard when the door is opened). After a pause, Macbeth enters at left from the banquet chamber. He is distressed. It has become impossible for him to remain in the same room with the gracious guest whom he plans to murder. His entrance purpose is to escape the suffocating situation at the banquet, to clear his mind, and to settle his doubts about the planned murder. Macbeth probably will close the door quickly to separate him from the festivities and shut off the voices of the participants. Before he speaks, he will have to pull himself together. The actor now has two options: he might move immediately to the throne, forgetting at the moment its function,

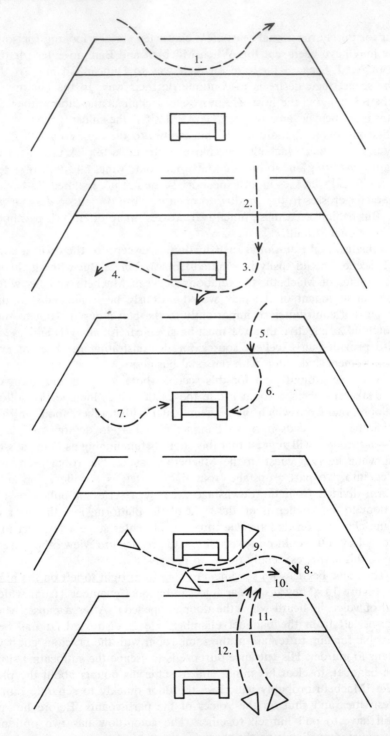

Figure 1. Movement: Justification.

and sit in it, lean back, eyes closed, and sigh as he collects himself. Later, when he thinks of Duncan and of his responsibility to the rightful king, "Who should against his murder shut the door,/Not bear the knife myself," he might associate his sitting on the throne with his irresponsible plans, and wrench himself away from the chair. Another possibility is to save the association of the throne with Duncan by not approaching it until "He's here in double trust," and not sit in the chair at all. The first suggestion, the move to the throne to sit is emotionally justified while at the same time representing an "unintentioned" symbolic action that the audience is intended to recognize. The second method (2 in Figure 1) is a consciously psychological one, as Macbeth allows the throne to be the stimulus to his first direct reference to Duncan.

Once the association is made, the throne may become the object to which Macbeth and, later, Lady Macbeth are attracted or repelled. Let us assume now that Macbeth is standing beside the throne on "Besides, this Duncan/Hath borne his faculties so meek," but continues to refer to it as he acknowledges the king's qualities, and how they weaken Macbeth's plan. But as his imagination of the consequences of the murder becomes more vivid and horrifying, he will have to alter the focus of his attention. He must now look up on "angels, trumpet-tongued" and allow the images to pull him forward, away from the throne and toward the audience (3). One reason for the move forward is admittedly for effect: as his speech becomes stronger and more violent, his stage action can be strengthened by his movement into a stronger position. This creates, too, an effect similar to the film close-up, when a greater emphasis is to be placed on the mental and emotional processes of the actor. But none of these effects is going to work unless the actor playing Macbeth can justify the character's impulse to move forward.

After the vision of violent divine retribution is over, Macbeth realizes that the bubble has been punctured. "I have no spur/To prick the sides of my intent" is a discouraged admission that his proposed deed is not justifiable, and may justify a move to a different area. For example, when he reaches the climactic image that completes his vision, he is at center stage in front of the throne, staring upward and out. Now, before he speaks, he shuts his eyes, lowers his head, and shakes it as he realizes his futility. This compels him to move away discouragedly as he utters the last line in the soliloquy (4).

Now Lady Macbeth appears from up left; the noise from the open door catches Macbeth's attention. He will hold his ground on "How now, what news?" because a cross to Lady Macbeth would only suggest that Macbeth really is interested in what is going on in the other room. Macbeth does not expect that anything of great importance has happened, and his question is no doubt rhetorical; he needs the time and courage to consider how he will tell Lady Macbeth *his* news. Lady Macbeth closes the door. This is a private matter, and suspecting why Macbeth has left the chamber, she knows that she will have to have it out with him. After shutting the door, she will take a few steps downstage (·5), not wanting to be too near the door to be heard in the next room.

Later, in our study of composition, we will discover that the distance between characters, and the variation of such distances in a scene will express a great deal about the psychic relationship between characters. In this scene, movement is affected by such spatial–psychic necessity. The two characters begin the scene at odds with one another. They are on opposite sides. Macbeth has made up his mind and wants no argument. "We will proceed no further in this business" is a pretty firm statement. Lady Macbeth must change his mind, but she must do it in a calculated, not impulsive or emotional manner. She chooses, too, to use scorn as a weapon, so while she will descend on him, she will keep her distance until the right moment. The scene progresses to and concludes with reconciliation, by which time the spatial gap should be closed.

Macbeth may take a step or two toward Lady Macbeth (who is upstage on a level with the throne, but several feet away from it) on "We will proceed no further," but the throne must remain between them. Lady Macbeth responds with her scornful lines about drunkenness, and on "From this time/ Such I account thy love," Macbeth should turn quickly toward her with amazement. After all they have meant to each other? She picks up on his reaction and makes her next line an explanation, when she equates his desire for her with his desire for the throne. On "Woulds't thou have that/Which thou esteems't the ornament of life" she moves to the up left side of the throne (6), using it to illustrate her meaning.

Macbeth is upset at her accusations of cowardice, and angrily tells her to hold her tongue. He moves to her (7), but only as far as the opposite side of the throne on "Prithee, peace." He asserts himself and his definition of man directly to her, "I dare do all that may become a man," then moves across and away from her on a diagonal to down left (8), as though wishing to end the argument with "Who dares do more is none." Lady Macbeth wastes no time in responding, and the strength of her reply "What *beast* was't, then,/ That made you break this enterprise to me?" might propel her forward but away from Macbeth in a curved movement so that she is slightly right of the throne in a plane above his (9).

Lady Macbeth's final, and ultimately triumphant, ploy comes with her reference to "the babe." She should pause just before this, then take a step or two closer to better impress him with the speech to follow. Then, quietly, "I have given suck . . . ." When she is finished, Macbeth has weakened, but not surrendered. He turns to her and, affected, stares for a moment, then asks "If we should fail?" Lady Macbeth knows she has the upper hand, and will now spur him on rather than defy him. "We fail!" she says, then moves closer to him (10) as she urges "But screw your courage to the sticking-place,/And we'll not fail." When she finishes, Macbeth is won over—not merely to their plan, but to a new admiration for his wife. Grasping her by the arms (the gap is now completely closed), he says, "Bring forth men children only,/For thy undaunted mettle should compose/Nothing but males." They might embrace at this point, then as Macbeth becomes concerned with the business of the night, he pulls away and asks for one further bit of assurance, which she provides. He tells her he is completely assured, moves to the chamber door, and stretches out his arm for her (11). She moves to him and puts her hand upon his extended forearm (12). With both in an open position, Macbeth reminds his wife, put perhaps himself more, that "False face must hide what the false heart doth know." He opens the door, and they return smiling together.

In the scene just described there are, except for entrances and exits, no functional justifications for movement. Nor are there explicit stage directions suggested by the text. "Bring forth men children only" is the only line that clearly insists on a specific action. Yet, the progression of the scene, the thoughts of the characters, and the relationship between them, when scrutinized in depth, inspire numerous motivations for stage movement with a variety of possibilities of execution.

Technical Justification. It is often necessary to get an actor into a particular position for reasons that are not logically motivated. For example, in the scene just described the director must be certain that Lady Macbeth's entrance at up left is not covered by Macbeth. When it was suggested that he cross to down right stage on his line before her entrance, one of the reasons was a purely technical one: if he crossed down left, he would have obscured her entrance, if he did not cross at all, the meaningful compositional effect created by their separation across the room and by the strength of the diagonal line that gives Lady Macbeth a dominant position would have been lost. There invariably will be moments in the blocking of every play when such and such a character *must* be in such and such a place. The director's task then, is to find a functional, psychological, or emotional justification for getting the character where he wants him to be. In the scene described above, Macbeth moves from center to right ostensibly because of the dejection to which his visions have brought him; it must never appear that he merely is clearing the way for Lady Macbeth's entrance.

Execution. It requires more than a clear motivation to make a stage cross meaningful. If the cross is not *executed* with a sense of purpose, it will appear to be arbitrary. If a director tells an actor to "pace across the room because you are worried," mere physical movement from one side of the stage to the other will be meaningless unless the actor's manner of pacing communicates the reason for the action. The pacing of a man who is waiting to learn whether his wife will live or die is different than that of a man who is about to become a father. How each man feels about the event—does the man detest his wife? does the expectant father want the child?—will influence the manner in which each paces about the room. The execution of a cross acquires meaning with its direction, its length, its speed, and its timing.

A DIRECTOR PREPARES

Direction. Most often, when an actor believes he has a need to move, he will link it with a direction. If Macbeth enters in Act I, Scene 7 desiring to sit and calm his nerves, he will move to the only chair in the room—the throne. When he exits at the end of the scene, he must pass through the up left door to return to the banquet chamber. Lady Macbeth, wanting to emphasize "the ornament of life," moves to the throne and gestures toward it. The two characters move toward one another partly on the basis of attraction, or to evoke a response from the other. But direction is not always based on the necessity to approach an object or a person. When Macbeth wants to move away from the visions that dissuade him from his purpose, or later from the tauntings of his wife, he will not necessarily move toward something, but *away from* what he wishes to avoid. In such instances, the guiding forces may be more technically influenced, as was the case when Macbeth's movement just before his wife's entrance placed him across the room and downstage of her. Later when he moves away from her on "Who dares do more is none," his direction down left needs no additional justification—he simply wants to avoid further argument. But the director wants to continue the scene with Lady Macbeth as the aggressor, and he wants his audience to observe Macbeth's face at the same time that it sees Lady Macbeth's, so he directs Macbeth down left facing full front while Lady Macbeth works upstage and to his right.

The direction of a cross also involves the shape of the movement as the actor approaches his objective. Different experiences, sometimes very subtle, are suggested by whether a cross is straight or curved. A direct line suggests, literally, a "direct" approach. Confrontation, straightforwardness, urgency normally are best expressed by a straight line movement, whereas uncertainty, tenderness, or sly manipulation are aided in part by the softer, curved approach. Is it possible for Lady Macbeth to move in a curve if her attitude is urgent, perhaps severe, when she asks "Why have you left the chamber?" Of course her posture and vocal manner will contribute strongly to her attitude, but given the same delivery the shape of her cross will modify its meaning.

The direction of a cross may also influence its strength. This was illustrated when, in the blocking of Act 7, Macbeth moved forward as the impact of his visions grew more violent and more vivid. The more open the actor when he moves, the more emphatic and strong the movement. When Macbeth moves straight toward us on "And pity, like a naked, newborn babe" he becomes larger, we see his face more clearly, and we must look directly at the fullness of his facial and physical expression. If he were to move diagonally, or horizontally, we would see less of his face and body, and would be more aware of the area of the stage in whose direction he is moving. The movement of the actor from a weaker to a stronger area of the stage (that is, upstage to downstage, right or left to center) will give his words and action greater significance than a movement from a strong to a weaker area (downstage to upstage, center to right or left) principally because of *how much* the audience can see of the actor's expression.

Length. From the simplest point of view, the length of a cross is the distance that must be covered by the actor in moving toward a goal on stage. When the motive for reaching a particular place on stage is functional the length of the cross is not always problematic. After Macbeth is persuaded at the end of Act I, Scene 7, his cross to the door is clearly justified, and the distance that he must walk to get there, unless it is excessively long, probably would appear rational. But if he is completely at the other side of a 40-foot stage, the duration of time given to the cross must be justified. Obviously, he cannot run. Even a rapid cross will consume an inordinate amount of time. He could move slowly as though he is pondering, but he has made up his mind already, and slowing down the tempo at this point would destroy the rhythm and build of the scene. In this instance, the director would be obliged to anticipate the cross to the exit, and have Macbeth closer to the door by the time he must move to it. Inordinately lengthy crosses may be broken up to appear more logical. For example, if, on Macbeth's entrance the throne was on the opposite side of the stage rather than at center, and Macbeth's state of mind is such that he would not move rapidly to it, and the director feels that a long slow uninterrupted cross to it would create too long a pause, then Macbeth would have to work toward the throne as he speaks. After entering, Macbeth might move in the gallery area upstage to a pillar about one quarter across the width of the stage, where he stops and says his first line (1 in Figure 2). This might be followed by a brief pause; than as Macbeth contemplates, he might move forward as he says, "If the assassination," stopping at center stage on "success" (2). Then before "He's here in double trust" he sees the throne, and using it as his stimulus for the thought that follows, moves toward it on the line (3). On a large stage, crosses generally will be longer than on a small stage. The distance between objects will be greater, and the appearance of naturalness in the length of movements will be in proportion to the size of the stage.

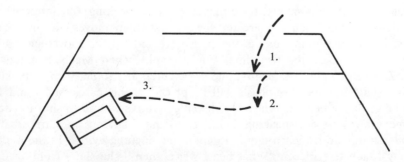

Figure 2. Movement: Breaking up the long cross.

When movement is a result of emotion or internal necessity, then the length of the cross must be justified by the size of the emotion or the duration of the mental process that provoked the cross. If Macbeth begins to move on "If the assassination," his justification for stopping could be a punctuation in thought. By "success" he has completed a thought, and the next phrase, "that but this blow," merely amplifies the first, and consequently could be uttered without further movement. The length of the cross then, will have been determined by the time it takes to complete the thought.

Speed. How fast or slow a character moves depends on his character and state of mind or emotion. If Macbeth is to be reflective on his entrance in Act I, Scene 7, then he will move slowly; if, on the other hand he is interpreted as agitated and moves during the early lines of his soliloquy, he might pace rapidly about the stage, matching his movement to the quickness of his speech. When Lady Macbeth pauses and moves a few steps toward her husband before "I have given suck," her cross will be slow and deliberate because she is calculating the move to set up the impact of her ensuing lines. But when she moves toward him on "But screw your courage," she knows that he has taken the bait and wastes no time in moving in to make the catch. Speed, like length, will be affected by the size of the stage. The longer the distance of a cross, the more time it will consume. To prevent the tempo of a play performed on a large stage from becoming monotonously slow, crosses must be executed more rapidly. It is the actor's job to create the illusion that he is not always hurrying to get from one position to another, and taking longer strides is usually the technique used to cope with the problem.

Timing. Timing is important for emphasis and clarity, and is achieved by the relation between speech and movement. The actor has several options: he may walk, then speak; he may speak, then walk; he may speak and walk at the same time; he may move, then begin to speak as he continues, or he may begin a speech standing still, then begin to move as he is speaking; he may complete a cross while his speech continues, or he may continue to move after he has finished speaking. Each of these variations produces different meanings, and failure to control timing frequently leads to confusion.

Obviously if a character stands perfectly still and speaks, we will concentrate on what he is saying. If he moves without speaking, our interest is in what he is doing. When a character speaks first, then moves, the move becomes doubly important, unless the pause created by the movement is intended to emphasize the next line. For example, when Macbeth enters in Scene 7, if he quickly says his first line as he enters the room, then stops himself and shuts the door, emphasis will be placed on his carelessness and the importance of not being overheard. If he enters and is careful to shut the door and move away before speaking, it makes us more anxious to learn what is troubling him, and we listen more closely to his opening words. In the middle of Lady Macbeth's speech "What beast was't, then," she shifts from accusations of Macbeth's weakness to an illustration of her strength. If the speech were to be uttered without interruption, several points would be lost. First, the importance that she places on a promise would be lost. Second, the awesomeness of her illustration would be diminished. Finally, we would miss the fact that it is Lady Macbeth's self-example that succeeds.

When the actor walks and talks at the same time, our eyes and ears both are occupied, and the visual and audible emphasis is shared. If Lady Macbeth were to continue to move as she spoke of the "babe that milks me," the images created by her speech would be diminished; they would have to be shared by her strong visual action on stage. Later, if she moves to him as she says, "But screw your courage to the sticking-place," both the movement and the line support the idea of quickly exploiting the success of her maneuver.

Starting a cross in the middle of a sentence without a break in speech may, on occasion, be justified, but is normally bad practice, because the line of thought started by a speech will be interrupted, even lost, as the attention of the audience is shifted to the movement. Movement that starts and stops during a single speech should begin and end with punctuation, which is intended to clarify shifts in thought and emphasis. Earlier it was suggested that Macbeth move forward as he begins to envision the images of cosmic justice. In timing his movement, he must first imagine above and in front of him, "pity, like a naked, newborn babe," and move as he *begins* the line, not on "naked," or "newborn," or "babe." He must stop his cross on "babe," or "blest," and remain in one position until "drown the wind." He moves as he is drawn to the vision, but then the vision must take over, and the terrified intensity of his imagination must be emphasized.

Continuing to move after a speech has been completed can be justified only infrequently. Normally, the conclusion of one character's speech is the cue for another to begin. If the first character continues to move, he will continue to hold the attention of the audience, who probably will lose the first few words spoken by the second character. The most common justification for continued movement occurs when the beginning of the other character's speech is intended to stop the first character. For example, suppose Macbeth moves away from Lady Macbeth after "Who dares do more is none." The purpose here is to suggest that the subject is closed, and Macbeth is ready to leave the room. Lady Macbeth's first words in the following speech must be used to stop him. "What beast," she might hiss, then pause until he stops moving, when she will complete her speech without further distraction.

Amount. Despite the fact that it might be part of the patterns of style and genre, there are no formulas for the amount of movement in plays; each play contains its own frequency of need for movement. A production of a play is "static" only when the director has not fully realized its possibilities for meaningful movement. Some plays like those of Pinter are intended visually to be relatively static, and the imposition of movement to "improve" the play often succeeds only in distraction and confusion. Some directors place an excessive emphasis on visualization at the expense of language and ideas.

They know the play quite well, take its words for granted, and keep adding movement and business during rehearsals to make the performance more "interesting." They lose their trust in the power of words to move us, and the result is a play that is so busy, its ideas go down the drain. Even plays that encourage lots of inventive movement can be overdone in this respect. An excess of unrelieved movement will lead to monotony, and the most brilliant and clever inventions will be unappreciated.

Style. Plays written in particular periods with certain conventions in mind may be characterized by qualities or patterns of movement. Greek tragedy, for example, requires less frequent, slower, and more calculated movement than Elizabethan tragedy. The action of the former is manifested for the most part in rhetoric and debate. This is not to say that characters in such plays as *Antigone* or *Hippolytus* just "make speeches," only that their conflicts take the form of argumentation, where gesture and speech are provoked more than vigorous and frequent stage movement. There are many more comings and goings in Elizabethan drama, more characters on stage to relate with one another, more onstage violence, and an exuberance of speech that suggests a greater amount of movement and flamboyance.

Naturalism provides even greater possibilities for justifying a great amount of movement on the stage. With its emphasis on the material reality of the environment, and the particulars of common behavior, it becomes virtually impossible *not* to justify an abundance of stage crosses. The actors have real doors, windows, fireplaces, tables, chairs, staircases, cigarettes, food, lamps, telephones, and knickknacks to which they may effectively relate in scene after scene.

The shape of movement also may be influenced by style. The elegance and sophistication of Restoration courtly behavior suggests a pattern of curved movement in the plays of that period. The distorted and nightmarish action of an expressionistic play is best suggested by a profusion of angular movement.

Finally the influence of meter on the manner of movement should be recognized. Characters will move differently when speaking verse than they will in prose drama. Verse is more obviously patterned and regular, while prose assumes the more random effect of everyday speech. A good way to illustrate this is to ask an actor to move while speaking Macbeth's "Tomorrow and tomorrow and tomorrow" (V, 5), then to move again while paraphrasing the same thoughts in prose.

Genre. As a rule, comedy will encourage more movement and a more rapid tempo of movement than tragedy. It has been said that farce must move rapidly so that the audience has no time to recognize its improbabilities. The farces of Feydeau and Labiche become, in their climactic moments, insanely frenetic with movement and business. Action melodrama, too, normally requires a great deal of physical action (the movie or TV western is a good example), while serious plays whose ideas and characterization are more fully developed encourage less physical action.

The director must be careful, too, not to confuse farce and high comedy. Farce is physical, while high comedy is intellectual. Too much movement will obscure the wit of Congreve and Shaw; too little will remove the fun from Feydeau. In farce, it is often necessary to appear to be going against the principles of logic and justification of movement. One of comedy's chief devices is incongruity, where action is ludicrous because it appears *not* to be justified or expected. One cause for laughter in the Porter scene in *Macbeth* is based on the Porter's failure to move where function demands. His reason for being on stage is to answer the knocking at the door. There is a clear-cut distance and direction from his entrance location to the door, and he starts in the right direction, but seemingly takes forever to arrive at his destination. Each time he acknowledges a demanding knock, he may start to the door ("Knock, knock, knock! Who's there?"), but each time he stops and, perhaps moving *away* from the door, proceeds to address characters he imagines may be knocking at the gate of Hell.

Despite generalizations about style and genre, the director remains bound to the rule of justification. Movement, its amount, and its manner must be justified by the logic and necessities of the text.

PERSONAL BUSINESS

Individual actions such as facial expression, posture, gesture, and relating to objects and other characters comprise "personal business." Ideally, a large proportion of such action should emanate from the actor as he begins to assimilate or identify with the character. The director, of course, will contribute ideas regarding such detail, especially in regard to business that relates symbolically to the play's meaning. Much of what has been said about movement applies to business, so to avoid repetition, brief references will be made to previous remarks that already have amplified certain principles. As with movement, the first principle in the selection of personal business is justification, and the discovery of such justification is derived essentially from the same direct or implied textual sources plus some others, which will be added in the following discussion.

Functional Justification. As with movement there normally will be some business that is based on the normal functions of the characters. *Macbeth* requires actors to open and shut doors, eat and drink, dress, and handle objects such as rings and swords. In realistic plays (see p. 221 f.), business usually is suggested in the stage directions to create the illusion of everyday life rather than to forward the plot or to emphasize the psychic state of the character. Such action is based on the relation between character and environment, and pre-Darwinian drama, while not stressing similar concerns, nevertheless often directs the actors to acknowledge environmental details. The heat of the day, in Act III, Scene 1 of *Romeo and Juliet,* is one of the factors contributing to the hot tempers which initiate the play's turning point. The actors are responsible for creating the illusion of heat, and will have to resort to realistic details such as mopping brows, loosening or even removing jackets, and fanning themselves. In *Macbeth*, much of the play takes place in darkness, and business will have to be created to strengthen the illusion. Torches will be used for recognition. In Act II, Scene 1 for example, we are told that "the moon is down" and that heaven's "candles are all out." Banquo will hold his torch to Macbeth's face to identify him, and throughout these scenes, characters may have to feel their way against walls, or take cautious steps as they move. The torch is struck out in the Banquo murder scene, and the business created for the struggle should be influenced by the confusion caused by "total" blackness.

Shakespeare even specifies explicit "ceremonial" business for the witches in Act IV, Scene 1, when he has them toss such delectable objects as a toad, fillet of snake, a newt's eye, a frog's toe, bat wool, a dog's tongue, and so forth into their cauldron. Even when the language or stage directions of a play fail to provide the actor with such clues, the actor and director must be aware at all times of the potential value of relating character to environment. When a character enters a room that he has not seen before, he should express his unfamiliarity with it if possible. Certainly he should avoid creating the impression that he knows just where everything will be. When relevant, the director always should remind the actors of locale, time of day, and season of the year.

Psychological and Emotional Justification.   As with movement, the bulk of personal business will be motivated by the internal workings of character. "Look how our partner's rapt" (I, 3), "Your face my thane is as a book" (I, 5), "Sleek o'er your rugged looks" (III, 2), "What is 't that moves your highness?" (III, 4), "You look angerly" (III, 5), and "Thy crown does sear mine eyeballs" (IV, 1) are a few of the directions Shakespeare provides Macbeth for facial expression, muscular tension, and gesture that reflect his inner states. But for every one of these aids from the playwright, there are a score of others which the actor and director must find for themselves from their interpretation of the character, and from the development of a subtext. In our character analysis, Macbeth's desires, his responses to obstacles, his attitudes toward other characters, and his psychological progression throughout the play were explored in some detail. All of this provides the actor with the materials for nourishing personal business. Macbeth is a brave warrior (physical strength, self-assured posture, gestures, and facial expression), a man of sensitive imagination who responds transparently to obstacles created by his imagination as well as to those that take him by surprise (facial and physical expressions that openly register fears, doubts, guilt), a man whose immersion in blood hardens his resistance to imagination and conscience and shapes him into a bestial tyrant (grosser posture, hardening of features, more physical force and violence).

But this progression requires that in each unit in which Macbeth appears, finer and more specific details, like brush strokes in a painting, be applied to contribute toward our comprehension of the character and his growth. Turning once again to Act I, Scene 7, let us observe how our understanding of this scene evolves into stage business. Macbeth's entrance must express his tortured state of mind. He has been sitting in a crowded banquet chamber honoring his royal guest, a kindly, benevolent man who has just rewarded Macbeth with a new title. Toasts have been made to the king, then to Macbeth for his valor and splendid hospitality. Macbeth, already tormented by his doubts concerning the murder of the king, has become embarrassed by the cordiality of the crowd and has strained to mask his anxieties and his appearance, which uncontrollably reflects his true feelings. He knows he should not leave, but he has reached a point of near-suffocation, and unless he leaves the chamber he will undoubtedly give himself away. When he closes the door, then, he must overcome his hot discomfort and try to clear his thoughts. Different actors will find different ways of achieving these objectives. Macbeth might try immediately to breathe deeply and unclasp his collar to find relief. He might move to one of the stone pillars and cool his perspiring forehead against it.

His first seven lines are lines of wishful thinking. His facial expression and tone of voice should express the sense of a desperate "if only . . . ." But he realizes the futility of such hopes and he might shake his head when he recognizes the impossibility of escaping divine justice. When he refers to Duncan's qualities, he might express disappointment as he speaks of Duncan's perfect character, for it deprives Macbeth of his justification for regicide. He looks up and begins to visualize the forces of divine retribution that will be marshaled against him, and responds wide-eyed, perhaps with his arms in the air as he protects himself from the violence of a last judgment. After "tears shall drown the wind," he might put his hands to his face to wipe out the vividness of his vision, then drop them in despair as he concludes that his cause is rotten.

In the subsequent part of the scene between Macbeth and Lady Macbeth, several decisions must be made regarding their relationship as the action progresses. How guilty does Macbeth feel toward his wife, who has supported the plan? How firm will he be when he tells her that they must put an end to their ambition? There can be little disagreement about Lady Macbeth's methods of persuasion (see p. 73). She surely uses contempt, but the actress must be careful not to suggest that she is a shrew; there must be none of the fishwife in her challenge to her husband. When she uses herself as an example of honor, she will probably touch her breast softly on "I have given suck," and on the word "plucked" tear her hand away, and forcefully gesture downward on "dashed the brains out."

There normally is a deep bond of affection between them, so when Macbeth praises her courage, he may embrace her and she respond with equal fervor. It is probably a good idea for the director to emphasize their closeness in the early part of the play, because one of the sacrifices that their conspiracy will bring about is their marital bliss. In Act III, Scene 2 each of them comments on his new condition. Lady Macbeth says, "Naught's had, all's spent,/Where our desire is got without content." Later, Macbeth says, "Better be with the dead,/Whom we, to gain our peace, have sent to peace,/ Than on the torture of the mind to lie/In restless ecstasy." She has commented on the fact that he has isolated himself more and will no longer confide in her. They still are affectionate. He calls her "love," and "dearest chuck," and asks her to be "jocund," while she is earnestly concerned over his unhappiness. But this is a melancholy affection, and marks the beginning of his growing independence of her. If he touches her at all now, he does not do it with the surrender and passion of the past. Preparation for this change could be made earlier in Act III, Scene 1 with a special piece of business. Macbeth and Lady Macbeth, now crowned, are passing through a room together when they spy Banquo. After Banquo leaves, Macbeth urges his retinue to do as it pleases until the banquet, and requests that he be left alone. Normally Lady Macbeth would remain with him, or he would go off with her. Just before the announcement that he wishes to be alone, the nobles and attendants begin to exit, but Lady Macbeth might move to her husband expecting to remain with him. The announcement which follows, "To make society/The sweeter welcome, we will keep ourself/Till suppertime alone," is then said aloud as if to the others, but Macbeth pauses briefly before "alone" and directs that one word to her. Her expression then momentarily would be troubled, and she might start to raise her arm in protest, but she would control her impulse and leave with her attendants. She might pause at the exit and look back questioningly before departing.

Symbolic Business.   While all business should be based on characters' needs and desires, business also may be selected with a higher purpose: to symbolize by repeated action or actions the statements that the play is making about character or a world view. Much of the poetry of acting and the theatre takes place when a vivid series of visual effects deepens our awareness of human experience. A suggestion that exemplifies this in a general way is the communication to the audience of Macbeth's descent from man to beast by progressively changing personal business and costume. Here are a few further examples of how objects, or the body of the actor himself, may clarify and emphasize meaning and experience.

Macbeth is a play with deeply religious values, and several of its patterns emphasize those values. Its view of man's nature is Christian, as are its political concerns (see pp. 88-90). An important property that may link the two is the cross. Duncan is a saintly king, as is Edward, and as will be

Malcolm. Macbeth at first has strong religious convictions, as his references to "the life to come," "deep damnation," "all that may become a man," "my eternal jewel," "wherefore could I not say 'Amen'?" indicate. The cross, and the sign of the cross can be used not merely to create a constant visual reminder of the metaphysical importance of the play, but to stimulate character associations and responses. A large cross may be carried in Duncan's retinue, and may be used as part of the ceremony in naming Malcolm as heir to the throne. In the last scene, when everyone kneels on "Hail, King of Scotland!" the only upright forms will be Malcolm, the cross behind and over him, and some distance away, the grisly head of Macbeth. During the scene in England between Malcolm and Macduff, a sculptured cross might be placed in the room—a reminder of the saintly Edward. It will become more organic if Malcolm moves to it on his line, "But God above/Deal between thee and me!" and swears to his purity on it.

No cross should appear in Macbeth's court once he has won the throne. Crowns, jewels, and gorgeous clothes, yes, but he has forsaken his soul. This point can be made even clearer if Macbeth wears a cross in the earlier scenes and touches it when he speaks of jumping "the life to come," a line whose significance may otherwise be lost on today's audience. Later, in Act III, Scene 1 when he is king, instead of the cross let him wear a jeweled pendant. When he comes to the line "and mine eternal jewel," let him automatically reach for the cross he wore formerly, then, not recognizing the touch, look down and see the substitute and say, "Given to the common enemy of man."

Hands are repeatedly referred to in this play: Macbeth in Act II, Scene 2 refers to his "hangman's hands," and Lady Macbeth tells him to "wash this filthy witness from your hand"; Macbeth wonders "will all great Neptune's ocean wash this blood/Clean from my hand?" and Lady Macbeth returning from her replacement of the bloody daggers, says, "My hands are of your color." Later, the bloody hands that bothered her husband return to torment her in her illness, and she tries to wipe out the "damned spot." Each reference to bloody hands demands personal business. Macbeth holds his hands away from himself; Lady Macbeth in her somnambulistic state tries to wash away the imagined stains—"Look how she rubs her hands." A particularly brilliant addition of business that took the bloody hands symbol a step further was used by director Peter Hall in his Royal Shakespeare Company production of *Macbeth*. When Lady Macbeth returned from her mission to restore the daggers, she kept her hands behind her as she approached Macbeth. Then she reached for his hands, laced her fingers to his, and raised their blood-mingled hands upward between them, then said, "My hands are of your color." She is doing here what she did in Act I, Scene 7, when she used her woman's valor to shame Macbeth out of his despondency. But now the clasped hands strikingly inform us of the new inextricable bond uniting them, which will replace the happier, more natural bond of matrimony.

Character Business.   It is difficult to separate whatever a character does physically from his psychological or emotional inclinations, but it is necessary here to distinguish between such inclinations and the fixed, or habitual mannerisms of character. Richard III for instance is permanently deformed, and the actor must determine the areas of deformity and their degree, and consistently assume them throughout the play. Sometimes, as is the case with Ricard III, the playwright has made physique an integral part of the character. Gayeff, in Chekhov's *The Cherry Orchard*, while not given specific physical features, is given certain physical habits such as pantomiming the action of a billiard cue: "Carom to the right into the corner pocket. I cut into the side pocket!"[1]

Such details, however, occur infrequently in texts, and in most cases, the director and actor must develop an external image from clues regarding age, status, occupation, and personality traits. Macbeth is middle-aged, strong, and an intelligent and well-bred nobleman. Lady Macbeth is, perhaps, in her middle thirties, a well-bred noblewoman, who imposes on herself a will of iron. Her posture will be perfectly straight, and her gestures will be carefully controlled. As was the case with Gayeff, actors and directors may wish to find some fixed habit of gesture or business for characters, to more sharply individualize them. Somerset Maugham's Arnold in *The Circle* might constantly be touching or adjusting pieces of furniture and bric-a-brac to emphasize his obsession with décor. Chain smoking, ring-fingering, ear lobe pulling, sniffling, scratching, and belching are a few of the mannerisms that exemplify external characterization. Analogy is another stimulus for physical characterization. Basing character on animals or objects may shape the posture, movement, gesture, and vocal utterances of character. Macbeth as a warrior hero might use the movement of a tiger in its more dignified moments, but the tiger becomes a beast of prey following Duncan's death.

Emphasis.   There are many ways in which personal business is used to stress a word or an idea. An example of this was described earlier when it was suggested that Macbeth pause, then direct "alone" to Lady Macbeth in Act III, Scene 1. Pointing to or touching an object on a specific word or phrase, as in the previously cited examples of the cross and the pendant, will stress either the object or an idea associated with the object. Emotional emphasis may be created by such actions as pounding the fist on a table, stomping the foot, throwing down a goblet, or kicking a chair on a particular word or phrase.

Any movement on the stage brings attention to itself. A gesture, or an action that creates a sound, is a device by which characters can control the shifting attention of the audience. This is especially necessary in a scene in which there are a number of persons on the stage, such as the banquet scene, or the murder discovery in *Macbeth*. As attention shifts quickly from one person or group to another, movements must be made to clarify the identity of the speaker to the audience. When one character's reactions are important while another character is speaking or moving, the reactor must momentarily force the attention away from the more active character. We have seen an example of this in the section on movement when in Act I, Scene 7 Macbeth responds to Lady Macbeth's "Such I account thy love" (p. 208).

Execution.   Many of the principles of executing stage movement apply to personal business. Emphasis as the result of timing the relationship between the word, the movement, and the pause is the same for business as it was for movement.

Visibility is an important consideration in the execution of personal business. There is little point in purposefully developing a gesture, a facial expression, or the handling of an object if the audience is unable to perceive it. First of all, such business must not be covered by other actors, by the actor himself, or by objects between himself and the audience. Secondly, the business must be sufficiently large and precise for the audience to clearly determine its purpose.

Actors also must be cautioned never to employ distracting personal business when the focus of the audience should be elsewhere. Overreactions or the use of broad, fussy business by nonemphatic characters on stage confuse the audience by obscuring the more important thoughts or actions taking place elsewhere. The distracting actor also hurts himself when he employs an important piece of business at the wrong moment. He may, for a short time, catch the audience eye, but the audience, if a strong action is taking place elsewhere, will not be able to give either action its full attention. Actors are not always aware of such problems, and the control of attention on the stage is one of the necessary functions of the director.

Style.   Some comment has been made already concerning the varying influence of realistic and nonrealistic drama on business. Classical and Elizabethan tragedy are more austere than contemporary realistic drama because they were created for a relatively bare stage, whose conventions made little claim to a photographic reproduction of particular environments. The actor can rely very little on furniture and the normal accessories of everyday life for the creation of personal business. Characterization in the older plays emphasized more the psychological and spiritual essences of character than particular external traits. Naturalism attempts to reproduce the numerous details of recognizable daily life. Euripides' Medea and Williams' Blanche have a great deal in common. They are women who have been rejected by men, who find themselves in alienated environments, and who suffer neurotically as a result. In both instances, their motivations are psychologically clear and probable. But the actress playing Medea has only her own body to express herself; she may gesture, tear her hair, grovel or claw, but she cannot, as can Blanche, smoke cigarettes, drink liquor, cover naked light bulbs, or change her clothes and makeup for different occasions. In a naturalistic play, the director must find as many ways as possible to create an environment that will provoke the common bits of business of our daily lives, while in a

Personal business. Influence of Restoration style upon gesture and posture. *The Country Wife* by William Wycherly. UCSB.

nonrealistic play, he selects only those few details of setting and properties that are necessary for plot and character, and minimizes the material possibilities for personal business.

Style as influenced by period conventions and manners is an important factor for personal business. The director will discover distinctive modes of behavior both in daily life and in the ceremony and rituals of a particular historical period. In *Macbeth*, he must familiarize the actors with how and when to bow or curtsy, salute, or exchange other forms of meeting and greeting. He must make suggestions for the handling of costumes, swords, shields, and scepters. He must make certain that the actors wear their costumes naturally, and that they know how to handle their costumes when they stand, sit, or walk. In periods such as the French seventeenth century or the English Restoration, the director must familiarize himself with the code of manners of the time, so that he may accurately recreate not only the customs of behavior, but the manner in which they were executed.

Genre. Here the same principles that were applied to movement may be applied to personal business. One additional comment should be made about the creation of business for comedy, especially farce. The texts for farce should perhaps be viewed more like scenarios than "finished" plays. Of course no play is finished until it is staged, and all plays go beyond the words in the text in the creation of business, but in farce, the writer gives us much more leeway. This is one of the reasons that *Comedy of Errors* or a farce by Molière is never fully satisfying when read. What is so funny about stage directions that merely specify a chase, or a beating, or a trick? It might be said that in farce, stage business is *the* major concern of the director. He must invent ways to make the chase, the beating, or the trick interesting and amusing.

The porter in *Macbeth* is intended to be a comic, if grotesque, character. He obviously is drunk, and the comedy in the text emerges from his delay in answering the door, his satirical references to farmers, equivocaters, and tailors, and his explanation of the effects of drink on sexual performance. But to play his scene without the elaboration of personal comic business would make it very dull indeed, especially because some of the satirical allusions may not be understood by today's audience. His drunken and perhaps drowsy condition will make him bleary-eyed, staggering, and uncertain of his direction. On each knock, he might start toward the door, then as he visualizes the imagined arrivals, he might move in the opposite direction. His costume would be sloppy and awry, and perhaps he only has his trousers and jacket half on. "A comedian playing a drunkard trying to dress can be very funny."[2] His business might be more complicated by his carrying a torch. When finally he does try to open the door, he might have some difficulty with the bolt, or fitting a key into the hole. His manner of illustrating how drink "provokes and unprovokes" lechery can be very funny, especially if it is done awkwardly, and finally a loud belch as he concludes his lecture can provoke a disgusted

Personal business: farce. *The Comedy of Errors* by William Shakespeare.
UCSB. Note comic use of setting as well as exaggerated personal business.

response from the others at the smell accompanying it, and justify Macduff's
comment, "I believe drink gave thee the lie last night."

The director of farce must use his greater freedom to invent responsibly.
The same principles of justification must be his guide to invention and selec-

tion. Comic business is never funny for its own sake, and is always funnier when it achieves the kind of illumination that is the object of good business in any play. Donald Sindon's Malvolio in a recent production of *Twelfth Night* incorporated a familiar piece of business, but its appropriateness and execution made it fresh and penetrating. He is asked to return a ring to Viola, who is disguised as Cesario. He catches up with her, but has put the ring on his own finger in the meantime. When the moment arrives to give up the ring, he cannot get it off. The business was germane as well as funny for several reasons. First, it would be typical of Malvolio's vanity to try the ring on. Second, Malvolio's pompousness is thoroughly deflated as he awkwardly struggles with the ring and tries at the same time not to lose his dignity. Finally, Sindon executed the business perfectly.

In a later scene, a sundial was placed in the garden to make a bit of comic character business possible. Malvolio notices the sundial as he passes it, and decides to check his watch. After, comparing the two timepieces, he looks at the sun, shakes his head and adjusts the sundial. The sun is more likely to err than Malvolio!

COMPOSITION

Composition is the physical arrangement of actors on stage. Such arrangement never should be arbitrary, but should be controlled to make character relationships visually meaningful and visible.

Meaningful Character Relationships. When two or more characters are on the stage, their spatial arrangement and body positions will directly influence the meaning of the lines they address to one another. "I love you" spoken by two characters separated by the width of the stage implies quite a different idea than if the two are embracing. The same expression will create one response if the characters are facing one another, another if they are back to back or side by side, and another if one character addresses the back of the other.

It was previously pointed out that Lady Macbeth and Macbeth should maintain some space between themselves in Act I, Scene 7 until the moment of their reconciliation. Body position also contributed to their relationship. Lady Macbeth is the aggressor. In a sense she is pursuing Macbeth. She is the dominant character, accusing and berating Macbeth who is forced to the defensive. Therefore, she is always upstage of him, always facing him, while he, except for a brief moment when he tells her that they "will proceed no further in this business," usually faces away from his wife. He can only fully face her and share the same plane when he believes that he is worthy once again of her respect.

Now let us change the compositional pattern of this scene to illustrate how character and character relationships are influenced. Suppose Macbeth crossed directly to Lady Macbeth on "We will proceed no further in this business" to a shared position, where the characters are face-to-face. The result is immediate confrontation, and a Macbeth who has made up his mind and is not at all apprehensive about how his wife will react. Now, suppose Lady Macbeth, after an immediate retort, crossed away on "From this time such I account thy love," and played the rest of the speech downstage, facing away from Macbeth. The new arrangement makes her even more scornful because she suggests by her position that she does not want to look at him. Her methods become more indirect—she will make him come to her; he must earn the right to return to her countenance.

Physical relationships become more complex with more characters on stage, when character groupings must be arranged for significant pictorial statements. One of the clearest and most obvious compositional effects is justified when there is clear-cut opposition between two groups. When order is restored after Prince Escalus arrives in the first scene of *Romeo and Juliet*, the stage picture must suggest the opposition and division of the Montagues and Capulets and the position of Escalus as their judge. So the two families will be grouped at opposite sides of the stage, while Escalus stands above and between them.

Act I, Scene 4 in *Macbeth* offers a group scene that is more complex and challenging to the director's pictorial imagination. The scene begins with an empty stage. There is a flourish, and Duncan enters from up right preceded by standard bearers and followed by attendants, then by Malcolm, Donalbain, and Lennox. Duncan speaks first addressing Malcolm, and must stop at right of center stage leaving the left area clear for the later entrance of Macbeth and Banquo. At this point, the characters are arranged as in Figure 3.

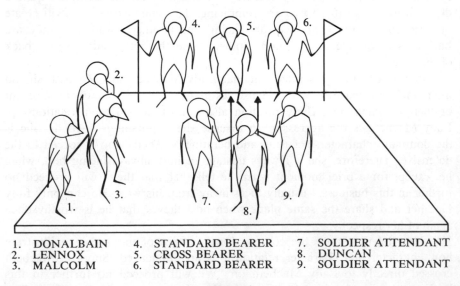

1. DONALBAIN	4. STANDARD BEARER	7. SOLDIER ATTENDANT
2. LENNOX	5. CROSS BEARER	8. DUNCAN
3. MALCOLM	6. STANDARD BEARER	9. SOLDIER ATTENDANT

Figure 3.

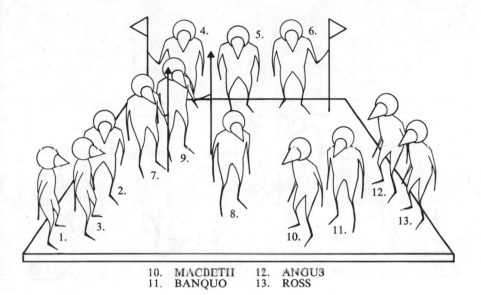

| 10. MACDETH | 12. ANGUS |
| 11. BANQUO | 13. ROSS |

Figure 4.

Macbeth and Banquo, followed by Ross and Angus, enter from down left and kneel immediately. Duncan welcomes Macbeth by crossing to him and raising him up, creating the picture in Figure 4. The attendants move to a less dominant position as Duncan crosses to Macbeth. The king permits himself this intimacy because of his gratitude to Macbeth. He raises Macbeth, they embrace, and Duncan addresses him. The placement of the attendants and the direction of Malcolm's attention to the reunion prevents Malcolm from being isolated, and prevents any suggestion of disapproval or alienation by Malcolm and his group.

After Macbeth has responded, and Duncan completes his retort, the king moves to the still-kneeling Banquo. Macbeth crosses to Malcolm and his group and is warmly greeted in pantomime as Duncan embraces Banquo and addresses him. Macbeth, Malcolm, Donalbain, and Lennox will turn back and respectfully observe the king's welcome to Banquo (Figure 5). Now there are two groups, the closely intimate one at right stage, and the more formal but tender group at left center. The direct attention from the group at right and the link to the group at left formed by the attendants prevents a sense of division or opposition.

Duncan wipes his tears after "drops of sorrow," and moves back to center to make his announcement regarding the succession. After naming Malcolm, he motions to him, and Malcolm crosses to his father and kneels, as Lennox and Donalbain move slightly upstage, isolating Macbeth (Figure 6). This is a vital, telling moment, and the composition must tell two stories.

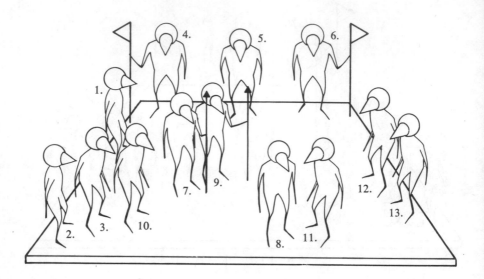

Figure 5.

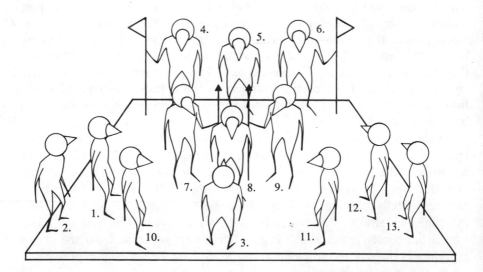

Figure 6.

First, the arrangement of characters is symmetrical, which suggests a ritual ceremony; second, all eyes are on the ceremony, except those of Macbeth and Banquo, who face each other. An interesting possibility might be for

everyone to kneel at the same time as Malcolm except Duncan and his servants, but for Banquo and Macbeth to hold their upright positions, looking at
one another, until Banquo remembers to kneel. Macbeth then takes this cue
to kneel himself. The composition tells us that Macbeth and Banquo are a
part of the ceremony and at the same time removed from it; without movement, one "action" becomes superimposed on another.

The ceremony ends with "But signs of nobleness, like stars, shall shine/
On all deservers," at which time Duncan looks at Macbeth, who looks up at
Duncan, then to Banquo, who already is glancing at him. Duncan touches
Malcolm's head, and as Malcolm rises, Duncan moves to Banquo at left
center, addressing Macbeth as he does so; the others move toward Malcolm
to congratulate him (Figure 7). Macbeth now is isolated. Banquo is at Duncan's side. After Macbeth's response to Duncan regarding his departure to
prepare his household for Duncan's arrival, Duncan turns to Banquo, and
Macbeth takes a few steps right and soliloquizes. Now there are three separate groups on stage. Up center Malcolm is predominant, the "Prince of Cum-
berland" to which Macbeth refers in the first line of his aside, surrounded by
devoted friends and relatives. Down left is Duncan, the object of Macbeth's
"black and deep desires," speaking affectionately to the loyal Banquo. Macbeth is full front. There is nothing to link him with the others. He stands
alone, brooding, while the others are warmly chatting. The total picture tells
its story, and symbolically anticipates the play's future development.

Emphasis.   Another important aspect of the use of composition to achieve

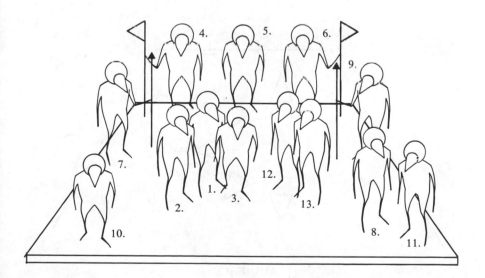

Figure 7.

meaning concerns the manipulation of characters so that their physical positions express their dominant or subordinate relationships in terms of psychological strength or emphasis. The director's task is to show the audience clearly where to look, and to whom it must pay the strongest attention at any given moment. This aspect of composition may be achieved by body position, stage position, stage level, focus, contrast, or a combination of these forms.

Body Position. It was stated previously that the more open the face and body of the actor, the more attention and greater strength he would achieve. It follows that the less we see of the more expressive parts of the body, the less interesting the character, so that a character's strength will increase or diminish according to his position in relation to the audience. Figure 8 illustrates relative strength or weakness as a result of body position. Each position is named according to its relation to the audience: #1 is full-front, #2 is one-quarter, #3 is profile, #4 is three-quarter, #5 is full-back.

All other things being equal, when two or more characters are on the stage, the one with the strongest body position will receive most emphasis, so that strength may result from the *relative* positions of the characters. In Figure 9 the circled symbols are the emphatic ones. When two characters share a position they have equal emphasis.

Stage Position. Stage space is divided into planes and areas. Horizontally, the division is into planes, with those closest to the audience called "downstage," those furthest from the audience "upstage," and between the two "center stage" (Figure 10). Vertically, the stage normally is divided into three parts; right, left and center, according to the actor's position as he faces

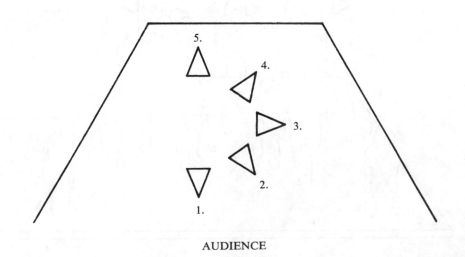

AUDIENCE

Figure 8.

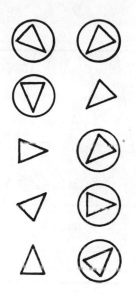

Figure 9.

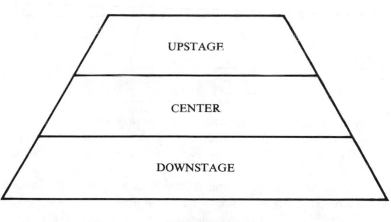

AUDIENCE

Figure 10.

the audience (Figure 11). "Areas" are created by the spaces resulting from the intersection of the horizontal and vertical divisions. As a result, there may be an almost infinite number of areas, but for the sake of clarity, directors usually refer to nine (Figure 12).

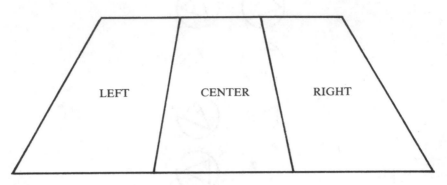

Figure 11.

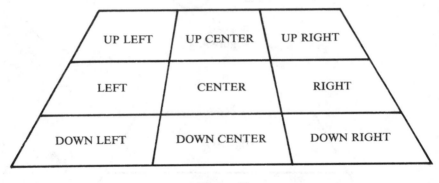

Figure 12.

As with body position, stage areas are stronger or weaker according to their proximity to the audience and to the greater visibility the area allows the actor. To this must be added the factor that, everything else being equal, the center of a framed area will be the most predominant. The strongest planes, then, are those closest to the audience, as are the areas closest to the center. Relative strength of areas is shown in Figure 13. Down right and down left actually are in stronger planes than center, but the latter allows greater visibility, and is close enough to the audience to retain strength. Making the right stage areas stronger than the left is based on our culture's habit of reading from left to right. The audience probably will be inclined when viewing the stage to notice center first, then look from left to right.

Level. Normally, the higher the position of the character, the more strength he will gain. The tallest man in a room will stand out more than others. We also associate height with social superiority: God hovers over us all; kings sit above their subjects on elevated thrones; judges sit at a bench above all other persons in the courtroom. Differences in height may be achieved when someone is sitting on the floor or a chair while another stands. If both persons are sitting, one of the chairs may be higher than the other, or one person may achieve more height by sitting on the *arm* of a chair rather than the seat. Staircases and platforms create greater possibilities for variations in height.

Focus. The body positions or actions of characters on stage can influence the direction of audience attention, and emphasize other characters or objects. When one or more characters position their bodies so that they face another character, they are creating a direct focus on him (Figure 14).

The most common compositional arrangement of three or more characters on stage is called "triangulation." Individual characters or groups are arranged to form three sides of a triangle, with the greatest emphasis placed on the person or group occupying its apex. The emphasis may easily and quickly shift from one corner of the triangle to the other when any two

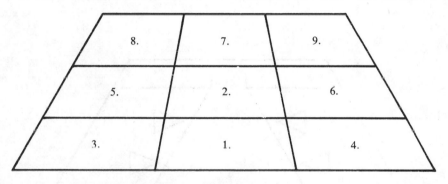

Figure 13.

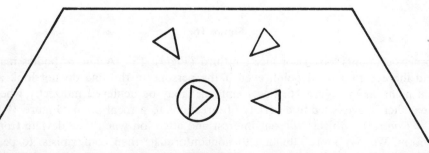

Figure 14.

233

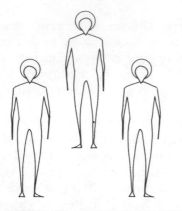 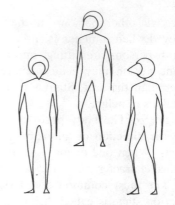

1. EMPHASIS ACHIEVED BY APEX
    OR STAGE AREA

2. EMPHASIS ACHIEVED BY
    DIRECT VISUAL FOCUS

Figure 15.

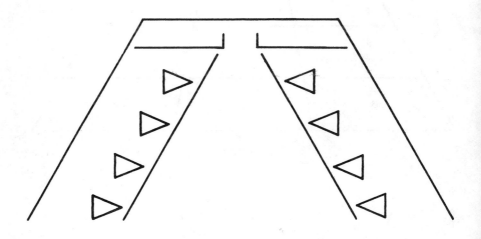

Figure 16.

corner occupants look at or face the third (Figure 15). A line of bodies may lead the eye to a focal point, even if the persons in the line do not look at that point, as in Figure 16. Focal emphasis may be achieved indirectly when the audience eye is led in a variety of directions to a focal point (Figure 17).

Contrast. Objects win our interest and attention when they deviate from a norm. We pay more attention to nonconformists than conformists, to persons with unusual physiques, to a particular color when it is the only different

234

color in a room, to someone standing on his head when everyone else is standing on their feet. Characters on stage may be physically arranged to achieve contrasts that similarly will attract attention, regardless of the previously mentioned methods of achieving emphasis. With three or more persons

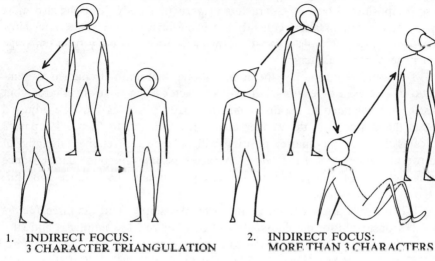

1. INDIRECT FOCUS:
   3 CHARACTER TRIANGULATION

2. INDIRECT FOCUS:
   MORE THAN 3 CHARACTERS

Figure 17.

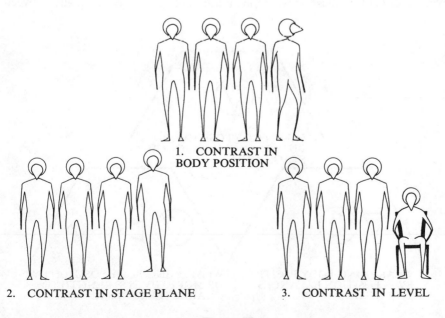

1. CONTRAST IN
   BODY POSITION

2. CONTRAST IN STAGE PLANE

3. CONTRAST IN LEVEL

Figure 18.

on stage, if all but one share the same body position, stage area, level, or isolation from a group, the remaining character will be emphatic (Figure 18).

Combined Forms. For purposes of explanation, body position, stage position, and level were separated from one another. But in the normal compositional situation, the director is faced with manipulating emphasis when he is working simultaneously with at least two and sometimes all three of these compositional factors. Characters in particular body positions also must occupy area positions and frequently are using levels at the same time. How then does the director emphasize a character in a weaker body position, stage area, or level than another?

The solution is to adjust the compositional factors to strengthen the emphatic character. For example, if one character is in a stronger area, but must be subordinated to another character, body positions must be adjusted so that the character in the weaker area will dominate. In Figure 19, part 2 indicates that the one-quarter position will balance the relative strengths of the two characters, but if the center character assumes his one-quarter stance facing right (Figure 20), then he is adding focus and the balance will shift to the right stage character.

When levels are used, the same principles apply, and all three factors must be considered for emphasis adjustment (Figure 21). Emphasis and subordination, then, are relative to the total stage picture.

Shared Emphasis. Illustrated above were several instances of shared emphasis when compositional factors resulted in a balance of strength. Whenever the director wishes to divide the attention of the audience equally between

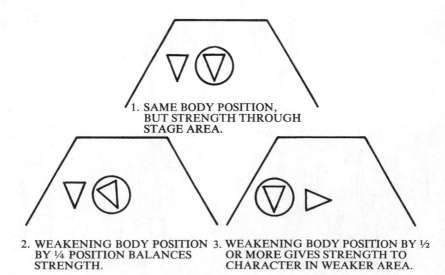

1. SAME BODY POSITION, BUT STRENGTH THROUGH STAGE AREA.

2. WEAKENING BODY POSITION BY ¼ POSITION BALANCES STRENGTH.

3. WEAKENING BODY POSITION BY ½ OR MORE GIVES STRENGTH TO CHARACTER IN WEAKER AREA.

Figure 19.

Figure 20.

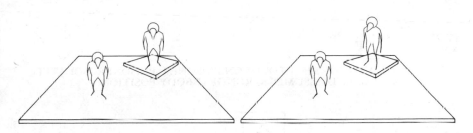

1. PLATFORM IN WEAKEST STAGE AREA, BUT WITH EQUAL BODY POSITION, HEIGHT WILL DOMINATE.

2. FOCUS, PLANE, AND BODY POSITION WILL DIRECT STRENGTH TO PERSON ON WEAKER LEVEL.

Figure 21.

characters in two different areas of the stage, he will try and achieve such a balance. When two kings or two challengers meet at opposite sides of the stage, or two pairs of lovers of equal importance are reunited, the body positions, planes, levels, and focus must be balanced.

Secondary Emphasis. Sometimes the director may wish to emphasize two characters, but wants one to be stronger than the other without losing the

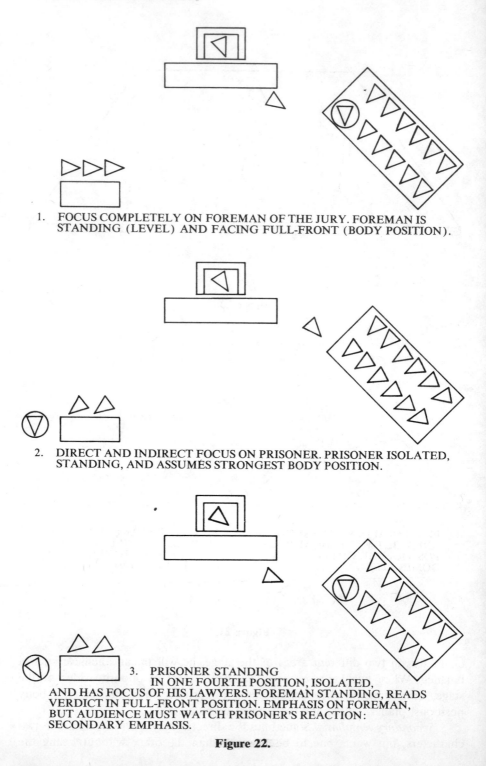

1. FOCUS COMPLETELY ON FOREMAN OF THE JURY. FOREMAN IS STANDING (LEVEL) AND FACING FULL-FRONT (BODY POSITION).

2. DIRECT AND INDIRECT FOCUS ON PRISONER. PRISONER ISOLATED, STANDING, AND ASSUMES STRONGEST BODY POSITION.

3. PRISONER STANDING IN ONE FOURTH POSITION, ISOLATED, AND HAS FOCUS OF HIS LAWYERS. FOREMAN STANDING, READS VERDICT IN FULL-FRONT POSITION. EMPHASIS ON FOREMAN, BUT AUDIENCE MUST WATCH PRISONER'S REACTION: SECONDARY EMPHASIS.

Figure 22.

attention entirely of the audience toward the other. One of his methods might be to isolate each of the characters from a group, so that both achieve more importance than the group. Then he adjusts the body position, stage area, or level of the isolated characters so that one is slightly stronger than the other. In a situation where a verdict is being read, for example, the director may wish to (1) emphasize the delivery of the verdict, (2) emphasize the reaction of the waiting prisoner, or (3) emphasize the prisoner without loss of interest and suspense about the verdict (Figure 22).

Another method of achieving secondary emphasis is by giving a character some sort of compositional emphasis while another character is speaking. Depending on the compositional arrangement, either character may achieve primary emphasis. In Act I, Scene 3 of *Macbeth*, Banquo converses with Ross and Angus apart from Macbeth. During most of this scene Macbeth should receive the emphasis. He may be put further downstage than the

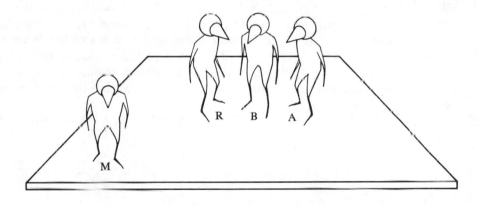

Figure 23.

others so that he is in a stronger plane. He will be in a fairly open position to deliver his asides. He also will be isolated. However, when attention reverts to Banquo, it is clear that Shakespeare wants to keep some attention on Macbeth. It is Macbeth to whom Banquo refers when he says, "Look how our partner's rapt." Macbeth remains isolated, and because he will speak again very shortly, he will probably remain in the open position. In such an instance, we will look toward the group when Banquo speaks, but as we continue to listen to Banquo, our eyes will return and rest on Macbeth (Figure 23).
Visibility. Composition is not merely a matter of telling the audience where to look; it also must be controlled so that every member of the audience will be able to see the significant action. An important function of the director is to check the sight lines (all of the angles of vision) from the auditorium.

239

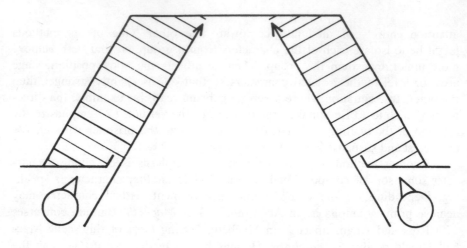

Figure 24.

It was stated previously that the scene designer is responsible for making visible important parts of the set; it is the director's responsibility that the actors be seen in the open area created by the design. For example, there may be upstage corners in a box set that are not visible to audience members who are seated at the extreme right or left of the house (Figure 24). A person seated in the balcony may have his view of a character standing on a level or a balcony upstage obstructed if the proscenium is too low and the platform too high (as in Figure 25).

When the entire stage is visible, a common fault is to allow properties

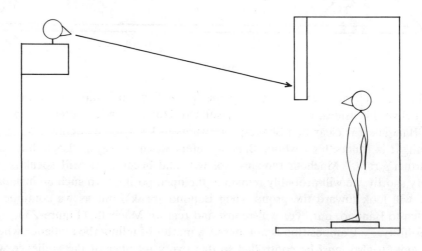

Figure 25.

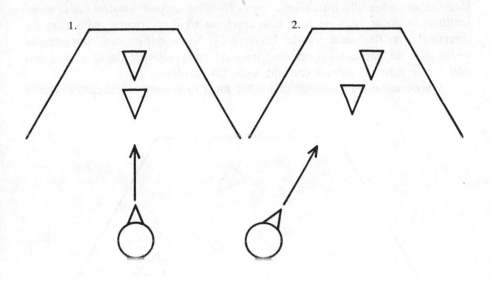

Figure 26.

and sometimes the actors themselves to cover important business or to destroy emphasis. A lamp on a table downstage may obscure the face or a gesture of a character standing upstage from a certain segment of the audience. Actors downstage may block the view of emphatic characters who are located up-

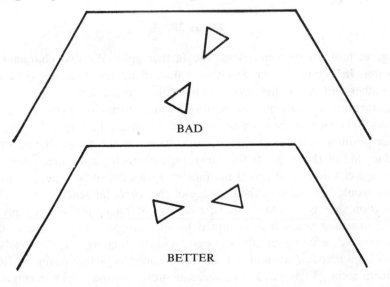

BAD

BETTER

Figure 27.

stage in the ways illustrated in Figure 26. The second illustration is more inclined to occur because it is less apparent to the director, who may be directing from the center of the house only. Some houses are considerably wider than the proscenium opening, making compositional depth almost impossible to achieve without creating sight line problems.

On occasion a downstage character must face another character who is

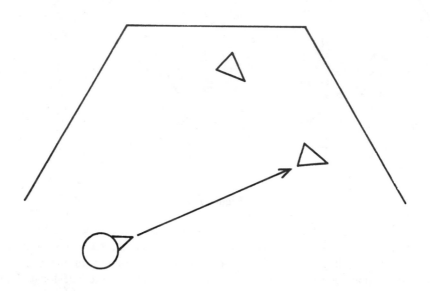

Figure 28.

upstage of him. In such instances, the farther apart the two characters are the better. In Figure 27, the first shows how characters may not only cover one another, but cover themselves as a result of placement.

Sometimes the one-quarter position, which normally is one of strength, becomes weakened at the extreme edges of the stage. In Figure 28, the one-quarter position becomes a three-quarter position for the audience on the opposite side of the stage. If the downstage character must face away from an upstage character and reveal his face or speak for some time, a full-front position would be necessary for the sake of the *whole* audience.

Action that is visible to the director from an empty auditorium may become obscured when it is occupied by an audience. For example, if the house is raked, which is usually the case, and the stage is low, the heads and torsos of the first few rows of the audience may completely cover an important death scene (Figure 29). The director must anticipate such eventualities, and in the example above will require a raised stage, or the playing of the death scene further upstage.

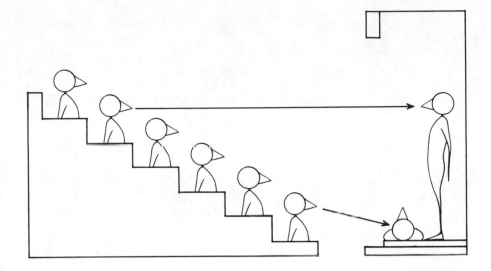

Figure 29

Director and designer must be just as careful about *preventing* visibility when necessary. Often the purpose of flats, drapes, or wings is to mask off-stage objects, technicians, and actors awaiting their cues. The most common mistakes in masking (Figure 30) are related to the extreme sides of the audience, from which one can see further into the wings (1), to the members of the first few rows, who can often see the areas above the stage and behind the proscenium where battens holding lights and scenery are hanging (2), and finally to the people in the balcony who may be able to see over the tops of flats (3).

Style.   Composition is influenced by the naturalness or artifice of the play's conventions. In realistic plays, characters generally speak to one another rather than to the audience; the one-quarter and profile positions when several characters are on stage conversing are prevalent. In classical dramas, with their soliloquies, asides, and the openness encouraged by amphitheatres or thrust stages, the full-front position tends to be more frequently used. Because real life groups tend to arrange themselves informally, composition in realistic plays will normally appear nonsymmetrical, the result of an apparently natural arrangement of characters. In presentational drama, where ritual and courtly ceremony are needed, or artificial comedy such as that of the Restoration or Wilde's *The Importance of Being Earnest,* symmetrical groupings occur with greater frequency (see Figure 6; the naming of Malcolm as heir).

Genre.   Serious and comic statements may be made by compositional ar-

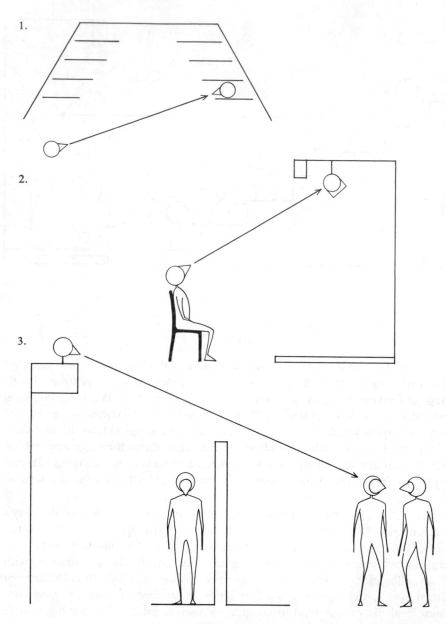

Figure 30.

rangements on the stage. Comic drama often relies on undignified stage positions and incongruous groupings, while serious drama must carefully avoid them. When a character in a serious play bends over to pick something up, the less posterior he reveals the better. Comic grouping occurs when there is a discrepancy between the ideal and the real. For example, an ideal corps

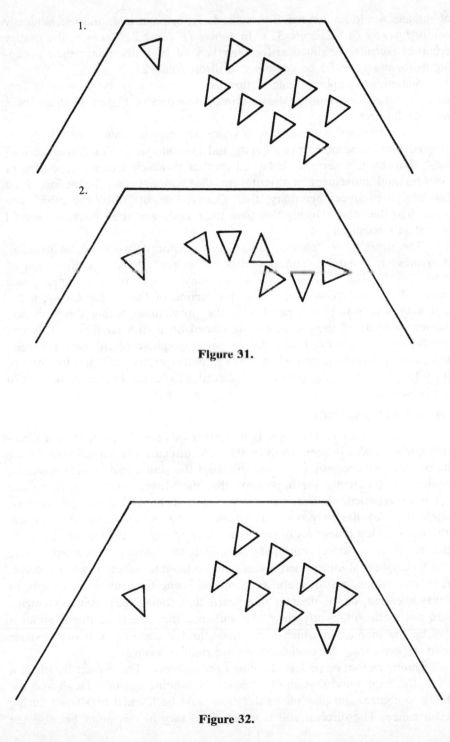

Figure 31.

Figure 32.

of soldiers would be composed in an orderly, symmetrical, and mechanically controlled way (1 in Figure 31). In *Henry IV, Part 2*, however, the motley group of recruits are ridiculed for their lack of such discipline: their grouping deliberately should be random and disordered (2).

Sometimes emphasis gained through contrast may be developed into comic contrast, as would be the case in the top part of Figure 32 if one man was out of order.

Sometimes the unnaturalness of symmetry may become comically incongruous. The tea scene between Cecily and Gwendolyn in *The Importance of Being Earnest* is a perfectly balanced conflict in which a comic repetition of business and movement contributes to the symmetry of the action. First Gwendolyn produces her diary, then Cecily; one sits, then the other; one rises, then the other. During this time their body and area positions should be perfectly balanced.

The straight, or "chorus," line on stage normally should be avoided. It creates an unnatural flatness and works against the depth dimension of most settings. But breaking such a rule may contribute to an appropriate comic effect. In a recent professional production of *Design for Living*, a 16-foot long sofa was placed parallel to the proscenium facing the audience. At one point all of the characters are seated on it in a straight line, forced into full-front positions. This produced an atmosphere of enforced formality and comic discomfort, and when two characters argued at opposite ends of the sofa, the seated characters were forced to observe the exchange like a tennis match.

THE PERFORMANCE

"My job is done. The show is in your hands now" has become a director's cliché. There is some truth in this; the director will be helpless during the performance because he cannot interrupt the action and correct mistakes. Neither can he change the impression that the viewers of each performance will have experienced. But it is erroneous to believe that his job is done unless the play has only one performance. First, although the director has attempted during rehearsals to be an audience of one, and to anticipate audience response, a perfect objectivity is difficult to maintain. In comedy, there may be laughter at unexpected places, and no laughter where it was expected. In serious drama, a suspenseful or climactic scene may not work exactly as it was intended, or the director may learn that some interpretative elements were not made sufficiently clear. An audience may teach us things about a play by the manner in which it responds, and it certainly will demonstrate by its response what directorial devices are right or wrong.

Timing cannot be perfected without an audience. The correct length of a pause, the tempo and rhythm of a scene, the waiting out of a laugh and the ability to control and play off its duration must be learned or altered during performance. The director still is vitally necessary at this point because the actors are unable to see or hear themselves, and often will not be able to solve their performance problems. Some directors say that they cannot watch the performances of plays they have directed. They prefer to pace nervously in the wings or in the lobby. This is unfortunate because they incorrectly assume that they have nothing more to learn or to do.

Even after a director and his cast have made their adjustments successfully, it is a mistake to completely ignore the rest of the play's run. Live drama is not a filmed performance. Actors may become stale and mechanical, or they may begin to lose their effectiveness without realizing why and try to improve by experimenting. Sometimes they try to improve even when things are going well, but the danger of such "improvements" is that they sometimes do not work, or they clutter up the action, or they confuse the timing and rhythm of a scene. The director should keep his eye on the play so that he may come to the rescue when necessary. He may make suggestions that help the actor keep his performance fresh and energetic; he may show the actor why an "improvement" is unworkable, or how it may be made to work without upsetting the balance of a scene. He still is needed.

NOTES

[1]Anton Chekhov, *The Cherry Orchard* in *Best Plays by Chekhov,* trans. Stark Young (New York: Modern Library, 1956), Act I.

[2]John Masefield, *A Macbeth Production* (London: William Heinemann, 1945), p. 43.

BIBLIOGRAPHY

Albright, Hardie, *Stage Direction in Transition* (Encino, Calif.: Dickenson, 1972).

Appia, Adolphe, *The Work of Living Art,* trans. by H. D. Albright (Miami, Fla.: University of Miami Press, 1960).

Bartholomeusz, Dennis, *Macbeth and the Players* (Cambridge: University Press, 1969).

Beckerman, Bernard, *Shakespeare at the Globe* (New York: Macmillan, 1962).

Boulez, Pierre, "Pelleas Reflected." Introduction to the Libretto of Debussey's *Pelleas and Melisande* (New York, Columbia Records).

Bradley, A. C., *Shakespearean Tragedy* (London: Macmillan, 1951).

Brook, Peter, *The Empty Space* (London: MacGibbon and Kee, 1969).

Brooks, Cleanth. "The Naked Babe and the Cloak of Manliness," in *Approaches to Shakespeare,* Norman Rabkin, editor (New York: McGraw-Hill, 1964), pp. 66–89.

Brown, John Russell, *Shakespeare's Plays in Performance* (Baltimore: Penguin Books, 1966).

Brustein, Robert, *The Theatre of Revolt* (Boston: Little, Brown, 1962).

Canfield, Curtis, *The Craft of Play Directing* (New York: Holt, Rinehart and Winston, 1963).

Clay, James and Krempel, Daniel, *The Theatrical Image* (New York: McGraw-Hill, 1967).

Cole, Toby and Chinoy, Helen Krich, *Directing the Play* (New York: Bobbs-Merrill, 1953).

Curry, Walter Clyde, "The Demonic Metaphysics of *Macbeth*" (Chapel Hill, N. C.: 1933).

Dean, Alexander and Carra, Laurence, *Fundamentals of Play Directing* (New York: Holt, Rinehart and Winston, 1965).

De Quincey, Thomas, "On the Knocking at the Gate in *Macbeth,*" *De Quincey's Literary Criticism,* H. Darbishire, ed. (London: H. Frowde, 1909).

Dietrich, John, *Play Direction* (New York: Prentice-Hall, 1953).

Downer, Alan S., "The Life of Our Design," *The Hudson Review,* II:2 (Summer 1949), pp. 242–263.

Esslin, Martin, *Brecht, The Man and His Work* (New York: Doubleday, 1960).

————, *The Theatre of the Absurd* (New York: Doubleday, 1961).

Flatter, Richard, *Shakespeare's Producing Hand* (London: William Heinemann Ltd., 1948).

Fernald, John, *Sense of Direction* (London: Secker and Warburg, 1968).

Furness, Horace Howard, Jr., *Macbeth: A New Variorum Edition of Shakespeare* (Philadelphia: J. B. Lippincott, 1873).

Gallaway, Marian, *The Director in the Theatre* (New York: Macmillan, 1963).

Gassner, John, *Producing the Play,* rev. ed. (New York: Holt, Rinehart and Winston, 1953).

Gibson, William, *The Seesaw Log* (New York: Alfred A. Knopf, 1959).

Harrison, G. B., ed., *Shakespeare, The Complete Works* (New York: Harcourt, Brace and World, 1952).

Heilman, Robert B., *Magic in the Web* (Lexington, Ky: University of Lexington Press, 1956).

Henshaw, N. W., "Graphic Sources for a Modern Approach to the Acting of Restoration Comedy," *Educational Theatre Journal,* vol. 20, pp. 157–170.

Hodge, Francis, *Play Directing* (Englewood Cliffs, N. J.: Prentice-Hall, 1971).

Ionesco, Eugène, *Notes and Counter Notes,* trans. by Donald Watson (London: John Calder, 1962).

Johnston, Alva, "Profiles: Aider and Abettor," *The New Yorker,* October 30, 1948, pp. 28–43.

Knight, G. Wilson, *Principles of Shakespearean Production* (London: Penquin Books, 1949).

Kott, Jan, *Shakespeare Our Contemporary,* trans. by Boleslaw Taborski (New York: Anchor Books, 1966).

Kitto, H. D. F., *Greek Tragedy* (New York: Doubleday, 1954).

Leeper, Janet, *Edward Gordon Craig Designs for the Theatre* (London: Penguin Books, Ltd., 1948).

Masefield, John, *A Macbeth Production* (London: William Heinemann, 1945).

The Norton Facsimile of The First Folio of Shakespeare, prepared by Charlton Hinman (New York: W. W. Norton, 1968).

Satin, Joseph, *Shakespeare and His Sources* (Boston: Houghton Mifflin, 1966).

Shakespeare, William, *The Tragedy of Macbeth,* R. A. Foakes, ed. (New York: Bobbs-Merrill, 1968).

Shaw, George Bernard, *The Quintessence of Ibsenism* (Cambridge: University Press, 1910).

Sievers, W. David, *Directing for the Theater* (Dubuque, Ia.: William C. Brown, 1965).

Sprague, Arthur Colby, *Shakespeare and the Actors* (Cambridge, Mass.: Harvard University Press, 1945).

Spurgeon, Caroline, *Shakespeare's Imagery* (Boston: Beacon Press, 1958).

Stanislavski, Constantin, *An Actor Prepares,* trans. by Elizabeth Reynolds Hapgood (New York: Theatre Arts Books, 1946).

St. Denis, Michel, *Theatre: The Rediscovery of Style* (New York: Theater Arts Books, 1965).

Steiner, George, *The Death of Tragedy* (New York: Alfred A. Knopf, 1961).

Strindberg, August, *The Confession of a Fool,* trans. based on Ellie Schleussner's version, rev. 1st ed. by Evert Sprinchorn (New York: Doubleday, 1967).

Strindberg, August, *The Son of a Servant,* trans. by Evert Sprinchorn (New York: Doubleday, 1966).

Styan, J. L., *Shakespeare's Stagecraft* (Cambridge: University Press, 1957).

Tynan, Kenneth, *Curtains* (New York: Atheneum, 1961).

Waxman, Samuel M., *Antoine and the Théâtre Libre* (Cambridge, Mass.: Harvard University Press, 1927).

Watkins, Ronald, *On Producing Shakespeare* (New York: The Citadel Press, 1963).

Young, Stark, *Immortal Shadows* (New York: Charles Scribner's Sons, 1948).

————, *The Theatre* (New York: Hill and Wang, 1958).

INDEX

Index

Index

Troilus and Cressida, 96, 148, 149
Trojan Women, The, 101, 148
Tryouts:
    materials for, 186
    procedures, 184-190
        callbacks, 186-187
        improvisations, 187
        proper atmosphere, 190
        screening, 185
Twelfth Night, 29, 93, 97, 138, 142, 181, 224-225
Tynan, Kenneth, 108

Uncle Vanya, 132

Valency, Maurice, 106-107
Victimes du Devoir, 31
Visibility, 133, 221 (*see also* Composition)
Visit, The, 106

Vocabulary problems, 105
Volpone, 29, 162

Wagner, Richard, 72
Waiting for Godot, 28
Ward, Edward, 115
Weavers, The, 156
Webster, John, 100
Well-made play, 7
West Side Story, 97
Who's Afraid of Virginia Woolf?, 28
Wild Duck, The, 161-162
Wilde, Oscar, 180, 243
Williams, Tennessee, 22, 23, 31, 44, 64, 96, 99, 221

Young, Stark, 108, 149

Zola, Emile, 7
Zoo Story, 22

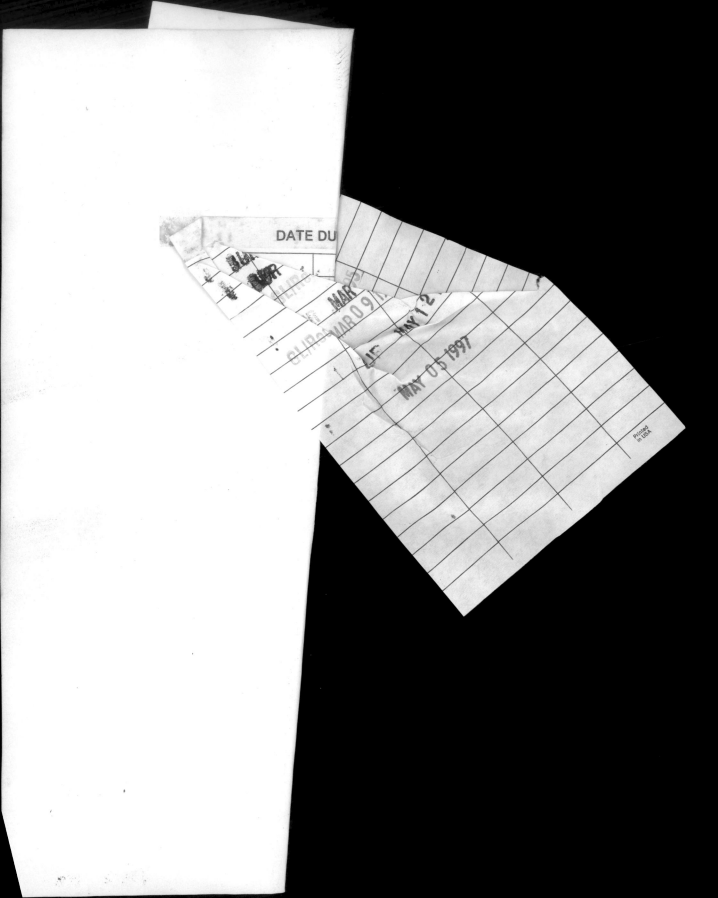

DATE DUE

MAR 0 9

CLIP MAR 0 9

MAY 1 2

MAY 0 5 1997

Printed
in USA